Speak
BUSINESS SPANISH
Like an
EXECUTIVE

Legal & Law Edition

Speak BUSINESS SPANISH Like an EXECUTIVE

Avoiding the Common Mistakes that Hold Latinos Back

Legal & Law Edition

Louis E.V. Nevaer

Copyright © 2012 by Hispanic Economics, Inc.

Manufactured in the United States of America. All rights reserved. No part of this book may be reproduced in any form or by any means, electronic or mechanical, including photocopying, recording, or by information storage and retrieval systems—except by a reviewer who may quote brief passages in a review to be printed in a magazine, newspaper or on the Web—without permission in writing from the publisher.

Although the author and publisher have made every good faith effort to ensure the accuracy and completeness of information contained in this book, we assume no responsibility for errors, inaccuracies, omissions or inconsistencies herein. This book is presented solely for educational and entertainment purposes. The advice offered is provided for educational purposes and it is not offered as legal, accounting, or other professional services advice. The opinions expressed are solely those of the author and do not necessarily reflect the opinions of the publisher, its employees or affiliates.

This book is published by Hispanic Economics, Inc., and expresses solely the personal opinions, conclusions and recommendations of the author. No liability is assumed for damages resulting from the use of information contained herein.

First printing 2012

Publication date: April, 2012.

ATTENTION CORPORATIONS, UNIVERSITIES, COLLEGES, AND PROFESSIONAL AND CHARITABLE ORGANIZATIONS: Quantity discounts are available on bulk purchases of this book for educational and gift purposes, or as premiums in fundraising efforts. Inquiries should be sent to *info@hispaniceconomics.com*.

Hispanic Economics, Inc.
P.O. Box 140681
Coral Gables, FL 33114-0681
info@hispaniceconomics.com
HispanicEconomics.com

ISBN 978-0-9791176-7-1

Cover and Interior Design by John Clifton
john@johnclifton.net

This book is for George C. Beckwith

A scholar, a gentleman and a friend

Table of Contents

Preface 1

Introduction 5

Part I —Words and Phrases that Translate into Career Success 9

Alphabetical Listing 11

Part II —Legal and Law 189

Words, Phrases and Terms 191

Part III —More than Words 301

Rewarding Patience 303

    Gift #1 303

    Gift #2 305

Beyond Language 307

    The Hispanic Diaspora in the United States 307

    The Four Recommendations for Success 311

    Accents 311

    Dress 312

    Mind Your Health 313

    Beware the Bigots 315

A Final Word 318

Websites 319

Notes 320

About the Author 321

Preface

"A rose by any other name would smell as sweet," Shakespeare points out in a famous soliloquy.

True, but words, and how they are used, retain their power to say as much about the speaker as what the speaker says about a subject.

Words do have power, and words do convey a sense of who you are and speak of your intelligence, education, and authority. Use a wrong word, and people will think differently of you. Use a word correctly, and the esteem in which they hold you increases. Use a phrase with confidence and authority, and a sense of trust is established.

In the United States, Hispanic professionals who identify themselves as Latinos have to master a difficult balance: Displaying a command of business English while being expected to, on a moment's notice, convey the same message in business Spanish.

There's no point in trying to deny the obvious: The United States of America is now a bilingual consumer economy.

"Oprima 2 para español" is part of the nation's business language.

You may hate it, or you may love it. It makes no difference: It is here to stay.

Call it a "rose," or call it a "rosa" if you prefer. It smells as sweet. Call it "success," or call it "éxito" if you prefer. It feels as good.

In the quarter century that I have been working in the Hispanic and Latin American business world, I have often seen how many bright and earnest U.S. Latinos fail. And they fail to succeed not because they are incompetent or ill-prepared. They fail because they cannot speak proper business Spanish. Others may not say anything directly to them, but they make judgments: "If this person doesn't know the difference between 'success' and 'éxito,' what else doesn't this person know?"

At the same time, if you are unsure of how to say "budget" in Spanish, or "worldwide web," or even a simple expression, such as "to whom it may concern," it comes across in your lack of self-confidence and the unsure manner of your presentation—in the hesitation, the sweaty palm, the nervous enunciation and uncomfortable body language.

Fortunately, there is a cure for this malady: *Empowerment through knowledge.* The words and phrases in this book will teach you business Spanish and thus empower you to use business Spanish properly. As you learn the words and phrases in this book, and as you apply them in your career, your self-confidence will increase and you will convey to one and all that you speak with authority and have the skill set necessary to move forward and onward, advancing your career. The words and phrases in this book are used by successful businessmen and businesswomen every day throughout the Spanish-speaking world. They form the language that makes them successful in their careers.

This is the vocabulary of success in business.

Learn these words and phrases. Practice using these words and phrases. In short order they will become part of your vocabulary, and others will see that you are fluent in business Spanish and can speak with the assurance that conveys leadership and success. Trust me when I tell you that if you read through this book and learn these words and phrases, you will be able to take your career to the next level and reach your full career potential.

Even with that promise, I recognize that it's tedious to read through a glossary of words and phrases. So let us make a deal. If you read through this, you will be rewarded with two examples of precisely how difficult it is to navigate Spanish in an English-speaking country. The first is an "Aha!" example that focuses on one of the largest and most successful newspapers that consistently gets Spanish wrong. It will demonstrate how difficult it is for those living in the United States to understand—and use—proper Spanish. The other is even more satisfying: It is an example of how virtually everyone in the Spanish-speaking world is oblivious to an *anglicismo* that enjoys widespread misuse, even among people who live and work in Latin America and Spain. This second example will afford you the opportunity to correct someone, in a very gentle way, not only to impress them but also to point out how easily one can fall into the trap of thinking that a specific usage is correct simply because it appears to be correct.

This book is primarily intented for U.S.-born Latinos who are English-dominant. It is also a useful refresher for non-Hispanic Americans who learned Spanish in school, or who want to refresh their business Spanish vocabulary and usage.

The Rolling Stones once wrote a song about the inability to get some satisfaction. If you commit these words and phrases to heart, you will position yourself to move forward and get some satisfaction as you move ahead in your career and life.

Adelante, adelante, adelante.

Louis E.V. Nevaer
Mérida, Yucatán

Author's Note:

If you think of any word or phrase you'd like to see included in future editions of this book, please contact me: LatinoSpanishVocabulary@gmail.com

Introduction

By Rose Guilbault

One of the great challenges Latinos face in advancing their careers is the tendency to lose fluency in Spanish. It's only natural: We live and work in the United States, surrounded by English constantly.

When I was growing up there was also the pressure to "acculturate" and to "integrate" into the mainstream of English-dominant American life. "If you want to succeed, you will have to master English," was the message that was drilled over and over again. Then there was the rejoinder: "Every other immigrant group got ahead by becoming fluent in English!"

That was then, and this is now. The truth is that the reason every other immigrant group got ahead by becoming fluent in English is that they migrated in numbers so small, they did not—and could not—change the "linguistic" balance in the United States.

Spanish changed that! There's no doubt that Spanish is spoken so widely throughout the United States that we have reached the linguistic "tipping point."

To get ahead, it's imperative to be fluent in both business English and business Spanish.

That's easier said than done. I remember being in a business meeting in Mexico, and I simply could not recall the word for "budget" in Spanish. I knew it, but the word "presupuesto" just escaped me. It was embarrassing, and I managed, but it made me understand the importance of having the right vocabulary and phraseology when it comes to business Spanish.

That is what makes this remarkable book indispensable. It brings together the words and phrases that are necessary in business Spanish as it is conducted in the United States today.

Whether you call yourself Hispanic or Latino, if you are living and working in the United States, you need to be fluent in business Spanish. Consider a few statistics:

- *You are more competitive.* Whether it is Starbucks or IBM, candidates who are fluent in Spanish have the advantage. "Fluent" jumps out on a résumé, and makes recruiters take notice. CareerBuilders reports that 88% of employers are enthusiastic about multilingual candidates.
- *You get faster promotions.* The higher you go up the corporate ladder, the more managers and executives you find who are multilingual. Korn/Ferry International noted that 31% of executives speak a language other than English, and being fluent in business Spanish is the #1 language of choice.
- *You earn more money.* Employees who are bilingual make more money. The Census Bureau reports that Americans who are fluent in another language average 4-6% more, depending the industry in which they work. This is true whether you are in the medical profession, or work for an airline. In some industries, such as banking and law, there is a premium paid if you master business Spanish—and financial or legal terms.
- *You have more career choices.* The world may not be your oyster, but you certainly will be more valuable to employers throughout the United States. It also makes you "international" material, meaning you can

advance more rapidly at companies that have operations in Latin America, or have strong business with Latin America.

It is simply a win-win situation, and this little book, which is written in a very approachable manner, with confidence, clarity and wit, is the first step in becoming fluent in business Spanish—or in brushing up on your business Spanish vocabulary.

I'm delighted Louis wrote this book, and I'm as delighted that it is available to English-dominant Latinos in the United States.

San Francisco, California

Part I
—Words and Phrases that Translate into Career Success

Abstract / Síntesis or Resumen

How many times have you read a report or professional article and a brief summary of the piece is presented under the heading ABSTRACT before the actual text begins? It happens often. If you think the Spanish-language equivalent is "abstracto," think again. In Spanish, "abstracto" is closely associated with painting—as in an abstract painting versus a figurative one. Unless you want people to think you are obsessed with art history, the two words that can be used are "síntesis" or "resumen." *Síntesis* offers a synthesis of the entire article, and *resumen* is a compressed presentation of the major points. For most business situations, a brief *síntesis* of a report, article, or PowerPoint presentation will do just fine.

Action or Event / *Hechos*

"Actions speak louder than words" is a common saying in English, business or otherwise. The act of *taking an action*, and when an action becomes *a fact*, is true only once *an event* takes place. These ideas, of actions, acting, events, ideas-becoming-facts, are translated into Spanish by a single word: *hecho*. Refrain from using *acciones* or *eventos* when speaking in a professional setting. In most business Spanish contexts, *hechos* are *done deeds*. They are events that move business forward. *Hechos* are also *accomplishments*. I want you to tell me about your *hechos*, not what you say you are going to do. What have you done? What have you accomplished? What pops out in your résumé as an achievement? Tell me, of which deed are you the most proud? To speak of *hechos* is to speak of things accomplished (*llevado a cabo*), and preferably successfully. Politicians challenge other policitians by demanding to know what *hechos*—concrete acts—they have made happen. "Under my administration, funds were approved and the new highway linking the capital to the Port of Whatever was constructed, and that's an *hecho* no one can deny!" she might reply during a debate.

If you are a man or woman of action, you should have quite a few *hechos* under your belt. It's not uncommon for no-nonsense reporters to address *los hechos del día*, the events of the day. And critics decry things are are *mal hecho* (poorly done), *poco hecho* (done rarely), *el hecho es que* (the fact is that), *de hecho* (in fact or actually), and *el hecho consumado* (a fait accompli). When things go wrong, someone might sigh and say *lo hecho está* (what is done is done) and then blame you by saying *tú lo hiciste, así que a lo hecho* (you did it, so you'll suffer the consequences).

It can also be used to signal maturity, becoming a man or a woman in full. If you can describe your son as *un hombre hecho y derecho*, then you've paid him a compliment by pointing out that he's a fully grown man, with all that implies. If you brag that your daughter *está hecha una ejecutiva*, then you're boasting that she's become quite an executive. Speech being what it is, it's not uncommon to hear a pompous executive refer to the *hechos de los Apóstoles* (Facts of the

Apostles) when speaking of heavy legal matters. Whenever I digress, I am occasionally reminded to get back to the matter at hand by being told *volvamos al hecho.*

Adequate / *Apropiado*

Here is an example of Latinos being unconsciously influenced by the English all around them. One sees the word "adequate" and instantly thinks of "adecudado," right? In business English, "adequate" is almost exclusively used to mean "sufficient." Consider this innocuous query: "Is there an adequate number of hotel rooms at this venue for the event?" What you mean to ask is if there are *sufficient* rooms available. In business Spanish, the word to convey this meaning is *apropiado.* If you were to use the word *adecuado* to ask about the number of rooms, the implication is that, perhaps, the hotel is under renovation and some of the rooms may not be in an appropriate state for guests to use. "Adequate" is almost always "apropiado."

Advance / *Salir Adelante*

If things go well, they advance. One's career can advance, or a project can advance. In fact, the whole of humanity can advance, although one would be hard pressed to find examples of that in recent years. No matter what kind of advances you are speaking about, however, the word "advance" almost certainly conveys the notion of moving forward, forging ahead, and progressing with one's plans. How is this expressed in Spanish? If I'm asking the question, then the answer isn't *avanzar.* Yes, *avanzar* is a word in Spanish, and it does mean to advance—but in a literal way. Traffic is said to move, which is to say *el tráfico avanza.* It also means to progress, and so can be used to describe technological changes in the workplace (*la tecnología avanza rapidamente*).

In short, we are in a realm of nuances. It is one thing to lament that this week is passing by quickly (*la semana avanza muy deprisa*) and another to comment on how a corporate initiative is moving along. Be mindful, however, that in business Spanish the more elegant way of expressing the idea of advancing is to say *salir adelante*. Basically, when someone speaks in English of advancing, that person is expressing satisfaction that something or someone is coming out ahead. Coming out ahead is, in fact, what *salir adelante* means. If you use this phrase, rather than *avanzar*, you're well on your way to coming out ahead in your career.

Aggressive / *Emprendedor* or *Enérgico*

In business English, when we say we need an aggressive director to take over the department, we mean we need assertive and decisive leadership. "Aggressive" is seen a positive attribute. But in Spanish, things are different. "Agresivo" is used to describe someone who is prone to violence, uses disrespectful language, and willfully provokes others. *Agresivo* is used to describe a bully at best, or an unstable and violent person at worst. This is hardly the kind of person anyone needs in their workplace.

In business Spanish, an aggressive director who can turn around the department is best described as "un director emprendedor," or "un director enérgico," either of which means an energetic and decisive director who can turn things around. Of course, given that talent is distributed without regard to gender, what the department may need is "una directora emprendedora," or "una directora enérgica."

Anniversary / *Conmemoración*

Well, happy birthday. How did that happen? I thought you promised yourself no more birthdays this time last year. If it's any consolation, bear in mind this time-tested prediction: You will die within a year of your last birthday. Think about it, Latino. And with that happy thought, let's examine the word "anniversary." In most senses, the word can be translated as *aniversario*. In Spanish, *aniversario* means exactly the same as it does in English, the day when something is remembered each year, whether it's a birthday or a wedding, the founding of the company or the introduction of a successful product. If it happens annually, there's an anniversary associated with it.

In business, however, often there is a solemn nature to events (as is the case in politics). It might be anniversary of the death of the founder of the company, and the company might take time to reflect on that fact. In business English a memo (or e-mail) might go out about the company's plans on the anniversary of the founder's passing, but in Spanish, since *aniversario* has a celebratory connotation, it would appear peculiar to "celebrate" anyone's death. This is the reason the word *conmemoración*—commemoration—is used. When the nation stops to commemorate those who have given their lives for their country on Memorial Day and those lost on September 11, 2001, be careful to distinguish between celebrating an anniversary (*aniversario*) and holding a commemoration (*conmemoración*).

Antecedent / *Antecedente*

This is one of those peculiar words that are seldom used in business English but appear more frequently in business Spanish. In English, *antecedent* means prior or preceding, such as *an antecedent event*. It is also used to describe the history and events that characterize one's earlier life, as in "Much is known about Barack Obama's birth and antecedents, as Donald Trump can readily confirm." In business English, the word *background* is used instead of antecedent when referring to someone's personal history. Not so in business Spanish! *Antecedente* does mean someone's background. It is said that you *tienes buenos antecedentes* if your background checks out. It means your résumé checks out.

Antecedentes, however, is also used to describe *bringing someone up to speed*. Quick! You have ten minutes to bring your boss up to speed on the background of the people who are coming over for a meeting and the topic to be discussed. Now that you are filling her in on the background of who's who and what's what, in business Spanish it is said that you are *poniendo a tu gerente en antecedentes*. When she asks for additional details on the project, she might say, *¿Cuáles son los antecedentes del proyecto?* And when you tell her nothing but the happy details of this win-win situation, a smile comes to her face, her enthusiasm for the meeting rises, and the first thing she says after entering the conference room is, "*Visto los antecedentes, es un placer reunirme con ustedes esta tarde.*" (In view of what's been accomplished already, it's a pleasure to meet with you this afternoon.) See? With the proper *antecedentes* in order, it can be a win-win all around.

Application / *Solicitud*

This is undoubtedly among the most misunderstood words by Latinos when speaking business Spanish. For those living in the Hispanic diaspora where people say things like, "They have to submit their completed applications before they can be considered for the position," it's only natural to think that the word in Spanish for "application" is "aplicación." But in Spanish, *aplicación* is literal: You can apply paint to the wall or polish to your nails, but you cannot apply for employment. (*Aplicación*, by the way, also means *a computer program*. For example, Microsoft Word is the *aplicación* most commonly used for business writing.) The word in Spanish for *application* is *solicitud*. Why? Because when you apply for a job, you are soliciting for a position. In British English the same logic applies: One has to submit a *solicitation* for employment in order to be considered for that position. Make yourself well understood by others by reminding them that they are required to "llenar una solicitud para empleo" if they want to apply for employment.

Appreciable / *Considerable*

In the everyday back-and-forth of business, often there are questions about the amount of this or that. To answer such questions, one needs to know if there are many—an appreciable number of—consumer complaints about this or that, or if there is an appreciable increase in the pressure building up in a fuel tank. Don't make the mistake of thinking *appreciable* in business English is, in Spanish, the equivalent of *apreciable*. In Spanish, *apreciable* refers to something that merits appreciation, like your mother for all the wonderful things she has done for you all your life. In business Spanish, on the other hand, the proper word for appreciable is *considerable*. Is the number of consumer complaints *considerable*? Is the pressure building up in the fuel tank *considerable*? Find out, before the consumer relations office managers blow their lids, or the fuel tank simply blows up.

Argue / *Discusión, Disputa,* or *Porfía*

Gandhi argued that nonviolence would always triumph over aggression. His arguments have inspired generations of activists and pacifists, no doubt. And in business, some people argue that perhaps there should be this or that policy implemented to take advantage of this or that growing market. In business English one argues to advance a position by offering a convincing argument. Not in Spanish! Don't make the mistake of thinking that *argumento* is the Spanish-language equivalent of *argument*. In Spanish *argumento* is to make a case, such as an attorney who offers a narrative on the sequence of events that led to a crime; or a historian, for example, who is an exponent of a specific series of facts that led to the evolution of ideas that are found in the Declaration of Independence.

In the workplace, if you want to present an argument for a specific course of action, or argue your case, and you are doing so in Spanish, the words to use are different. You can offer a *discusión* on the topic at hand to advance your opinion on the matter, or you can present a differing position as a *disputa,* or you can characterize a disagreement between two people who have different opinions as a *porfía*.

"As" / *"Como"*

If there's one thing that Spanish speakers find annoying, it's hearing peculiar diction. In English, it can be maddening to hear the expression "you know" used repeatedly by someone in the same sentence. You know. You know what I mean, you know? It's often the case that Latinos in the United States will adopt the English-language use of the word "as" and use it when speaking Spanish. In English, it's perfectly correct to say, "The manager named Mr. Smith as supervisor for the project," or "The city council named Ms. Smith as superintendent for the district." But if either sentence was translated into Spanish, it would be superfluous to translate "as" into "como." "El gerente nombró al Sr. Smith como supervisor del proyecto" is perfectly understandable, but it's not proper. The sentence should read, "El gerente nombró al Sr. Smith supervisor del proyecto." Of course, this holds true in English as well. The sentence is better phrased this way: "The manager named Mr. Smith supervisor for the project."

Ask For / *Pedir*

This is one of those instances when it's a matter of elegance and style. A mistake far too many Latinos make is to translate word-for-word certain phrases from English into Spanish. Many times you are understood, but your phrasing may be awkward and unclear and leaves the Spanish-speaking listener wondering whether you don't know you're mistaken or if you are being sardonic. "I'll go to the department manager and ask for permission to use the conference room." That's a simple statement. If you translate this in Spanish as "Iré al gerente del departamento y le preguntaré por permiso para uso de la sala de conferencias," can you identify the mistake? Translating "ask for" as "preguntar por" is not proper Spanish. In Spanish it is *se pide* for permission—or anything else for that matter! The verb to use is *pedir*. A more elegant way of making that statement would be "Iré al gerente del departamento pare pedirle permiso para uso de la sala de conferencias." Remember, when you are asking for anything, it's always *pedir*.

Assume / *Suponer* or *Creer*

It's often the case that in business, as in life, one can make assumptions. "I assume the presentation went well, since I have heard no complaints," one manager said to a colleague. "Yes," was the reply, "you assume correctly." But what if you were asked to translate this into Spanish? If you were to begin the sentence by saying, "Asumo que la presentación . . ." then it is I who would assume that you are guilty of an *anglicismo*—confusing an English-language word for a Spanish-language one. In Spanish, the word *asumir* means to take charge of or responsibility for something. I assume the responsibilities of managing this department. She assumes the obligations of the former director. They assume the functions of an office that has since been closed. We assume the obligation for the new marketing campaign. But if you are going to *make* assumptions, there are two perfect choices from which to choose: *suponer* or *creer*. *Suponer* means to suppose. *Supongo que todo salió bien en la presentación*, I suppose all went well in the presentation is pretty much the same as assuming it did go well. *Creer* means to believe. *Creo que todo salió bien en la presentación*, I believe all went well in the presentation is also much the same as assuming it went well since you didn't hear otherwise. Suppose or believe what you will, but *asumir* is seldom the equivalent of assuming in English, unless one is assuming a specific sets of responsibilities or obligations.

At the End of the Day / *A Fines de Cuenta*

In colloquial expressions, it's possible to make yourself understood by using phrases that most people will understand. What does, after all, the expression *at the end of the day* really mean? It's another way of saying, "When all is said and done," or more curtly, "bottom line," or even more crudely, "Cut to the chase." All these expressions in business English suggest impatience. *Yeah, yeah, yeah, I've heard it all before, just tell me where we stand.* If it weren't unpleasant enough to have to deal with people who speak this way, it's not in anyone's interest—certainly not in yours if you want to advance your career—to convey such American impatience when speaking business Spanish. *There are some things that are best lost in translation.*

To that end, here is a gracious Spanish expression that conveys the sentiment implied in these English-language phrases that, in essence, mean *I don't have time to hear you out, so just tell me what the deal is*: *a fines de cuenta*. Get in the habit of using this expression, and you will come across as a cultured businessperson.

Indeed, if you are interpreting for a monolingual colleague who doesn't speak Spanish, you'll have the power to make him or her come across as a well-mannered professional, reality notwithstanding. Should you find yourself in a situation in which an English-speaking colleague says, "Yeah, yeah, yeah, let's cut to the chase, what's the bottom line?" and you have to translate this into Spanish for a client, you can do so by saying, "A fines de cuentas, cuál es su opinón?" Think of the diplomat you have become instantly! Who knew there was such power in language?

@ (At sign) / @ *(Arroba)*

In what may very well belong in Ripley's Believe It or Not, there is a word in Spanish for the "at" sign used primarily in e-mails: *Arroba*. Intriguing, especially if you roll the "r" off your tongue in a theatrical manner! *Arroba*. At sign. @. What's your e-mail? Practice saying it using the word arroba. "My e-mail? You can use 'LatinoSpanishVocabulary,' all one word, *arroba* gmail.com." In fact, using the word *arroba* is *fácil*, isn't it? So use it!

ATM / *Cajero Automático*

Yes, I know, life's like that sometimes. One acronym in English requires a phrase in Spanish. But don't fret, since it works both ways: In English we are always talking about too much of this or too much of that, but in Spanish there is a single word to denote "too much," *demasiado*. Doesn't it make Spanish sound more authoritative when you say *demasiado*? And it can be used in all kinds of situations. Is it, for instance, *demasiado* to ask Latinos to desist translating ATM by saying the letters in Spanish: *Ah, Teh, Eh-meh*? Instead, say the first two words of this acronym instead: *automated teller* machine is *cajero automático*! In the Spanish-speaking world, ATM machines are identified as "cajeros automáticos." (Please note that in some South American countries and regions of Spain, the term "cajas automáticas" is used.)

Remember that if you simply say the letters A, T, and M in Spanish this will only remind Spanish speakers of their kids watching *Plaza Sesamo* (*Sesame Street*) in front of the television set, and not about a place where they can get cash dispensed from a machine. If you want to know why ATMs are called "cajeros automáticos," blame the Mexicans. That's what ATMs were called when they first came into use in the early 1980s. Where was this, you ask? At Mexico City's branches of Banamex along the Paseo de la Reforma, of course! The residents of the Mexican capital were the first guinea pigs when banking executives wanted to see if consumers could be coaxed into using a machine instead of a person (known as a teller, or customer service representative) for rudimentary banking transactions. When that social experiment proved successful, it was only a matter of months before ATM machines (think of redundancy in that phrase "Automated Teller Machine machines") began to be introduced throughout the United States. You can credit or blame the Mexicans for your nearest *cajero automático*, depending on whether you love or hate those contraptions.

(To) Avail / *Acudir*

When was the last time someone availed themselves to you at your job about something? I'll bet it's never happened. Avail. Who uses that word in business English? "I avail myself upon you to help me with the PowerPoint?" What can one reply to such a request? Apart from a smirk or a roll of the eyes, I mean. ("Thanks for availing yourself to me, but before I help you with your PowerPoint, do you mind stepping into the time machine and joining us linguistically in the twenty-first century?") In business Spanish, however, the verb *acudir*, which means *to go* or *to come* (how's that for confusing?) is ubiquitous. *Acudir* also means *to succor* and *to support*. It's a word, in essence, that describes *need. To come. To go. To succor. To support.* What is one to make of *acudir* in a business context? Plenty. Because it is a needy word, it is often used to signal status, and the act of being deferential. If you

23

need to *acudir a alguien*, then you need to turn to (avail yourself of) someone. You can tell junior members of your team that should they need help, they can come to you. In Spanish, this is expressed as *si necesitan ayuda, pueden acudir a mí.*

When someone does try to avail themselves to you, what happens when you can't remember having offered to help them? Your offer doesn't come to mind. This kind of "coming to mind"—or not—is expressed a *no me acude a la mente*. Then that junior staff member will justify his failure to get the job done by complaining that *nadie acudió a mi llamada para asistencia*, meaning that no one heeded his call for assistance. It is going to make for a long afternoon when everyone shows up for the weekly meeting, which in Spanish is *acuden a la reunión semanal*. (*Acudir*, as used here, means to show up, or go to.) If you are going to conduct business in Spanish, get ready to avail yourself of *acudir*.

Available / *Disponible* or *A sus Ordenes*

If you are speaking about people, *disponible* is the Spanish-language equivalent of *available*. This is true only in this one, narrow sense. "My staff is available and at your disposition," one gracious manager will tell another one who has arrived from another office to help on a project. In Spanish you could describe the staff (*equipo*) as being *disponible* for whatever is needed and they are placed *a sus ordenes* (at your orders). But if you are talking about other things that are available, such as the available features of *this* laptop versus the available features of *that* laptop, or the available list of approved colors from which to select for the conference room that is getting a makeover, then *disponible* is not correct. What we have in these cases are *opciones*—options—on features of a specific laptop model, or colors to paint the conference room from which to choose. If by *available* we refer to *options*, then use *opciones*. In most business situations, however, *available* is *disponible*.

Average / *Promedio* or *Media*

If I had a dollar every time I have seen Spanish-speaking executives raise their eyebrows, shake their heads quietly or sport a mischievous grin when a Latino says *averaje*, I'd give Bill and Melinda Gates a run for their billions. I hate to break it to you, but there is no such word as *averaje* in the Spanish language. If this comes as a surprise to Latinos living in the Hispanic diaspora in the United States, don't be tough on yourselves. It's quite understandable that this *anglicismo* is so widespread. First of all, it does sound like a real word, doesn't it? *Averaje*. Is it something that you can store in your *garaje*? Or is it a kind of *maquillaje* that your *abuelita* used to adore? Or perhaps it has something to do with the city's sewer department's new program to make sure debris doesn't clog up the city's *drenaje*.

From *abencerraje* to *yaicuaje*, Spanish had scores of words ending in "-aje" as it is. But taking the English-language word "average" and changing the "g" into a "j" does not a Spanish word make. In Spanish there are two perfectly good words for expressing the idea of average: *Promedio* and *media*. "On average" can be expressed as "como promedio," or "de media." If you want to say that on average there are 200 transactions on a normal day, you can say, *En un día normal hay 200 operaciones como promedio.* "Above average" and "below average" can be expressed, respectively, as "por encima del promedio" or "por encima de la media," and "debajo del promedio" or "debajo de la media." If you are speaking about an average client, then you are speaking about "el cliente medio." And if you are averaging things out, such as trying to average out your working hours to eight a day, then you can say this in business Spanish by saying that you are trying to "trabajar un promedio de ocho horas al día."

B

Balance / *Saldo*

Here is a notorious error that's often made by Spanish speakers who reside in English-speaking countries, from Australia to the United States, and from Canada to the United Kingdom. It's perfectly understandable. One sees a word in English: *balance*. One sees a word in Spanish: *balance*. And one assumes they mean the same thing, much like "piano" in English is the same as "piano" in Spanish. But unlike piano—an instrument with which to make beautiful music in either language—when it comes to *balance*, that's a different story. In Spanish, *balance* is what you have to keep if you don't want to fall while walking a tightrope. It is also what mercurial jewelers use to weigh things to the last gram. But if you are talking about the balance on your bank statements, or the balance of payments of those dismal, debt-ridden over-developed nations somewhere far away, then you are talking about *saldo*. One can speak of *credit balance* or *debit balance* (*saldo acreedor* or *saldo deudor*), or the *average bank balance* (*saldo medio*), or an *overdraft* (*saldo negativo*). It's also possible to speak of the positive outcome, on balance, of an initiative (*la iniciativa tuvo un saldo positivo*), or you can even speak of the leftovers of certain items—a *saldo* can be a remnant. *Saldos* therefore can be merchandise items that are on sale, which is why if something is *de saldo*, it is bargain priced. But whatever it is, it is always a *saldo*, and never a *balance*. That is, of course, unless you ordered 100 scales, and the company shipped 1,000, in which case there are 900 *balances de saldo* at your shop, and at a great bargain prices—which will make the jewelers in town, or those surfing eBay, very happy indeed.

Before, During and After / *Antes, Durante y Después*

As is often the case in business, there are always things to do *before*, *during* and *after* normal business hours. If this phrase were to be used in a business setting, how would it be translated into business Spanish? Here's what I mean. Let us say that the company has scheduled events before, during and after the conference in Dallas next week. If, as many are inclined to do, you think you can write something along the lines of "Contamos con actividades antes, durante y después de la conferencia," stop! Please don't butcher the Spanish language! It turns out that in Spanish, *antes* and *después* need to be followed by the word *de*, but this is not the case for *durante*. As a result, in the example offered, the sentence must read, "Contamos con actividades tanto antes y después de la conferencia, y durante la misma." In English this would read, "We have activities before and after the conference, as well as during it." Yes, it's a minor detail, but this sort of attention will set you apart from the rest, and that's the purpose of this book.

Benefit of the Doubt / *La Presunción de Inocencia*

It's instructive to see how cross-cultural influences are becoming more common in our global village. It took

Arnold Schwarzenegger to say "Hasta la vista, baby" in the "Terminator" movie before it became a mainstream phrase in the United States. And it's taken popular crime procedural shows exported to Latin America to get that familiar phrase, "benefit of the doubt," to become current in the Spanish-speaking world. The phrase, "benefit of the doubt," is now officially recognized as acceptable by the *Diccionario de la Real Academia Española*, as "beneficio de la duda." Nevertheless, while the phrase is acceptable for everyday use, if you are in the legal profession, remain mindful that when speaking of legal matters, the correct phrase to use in Spanish is *la presunción de inocencia*.

Bestseller / *Éxito Editorial* or *Superventas*

Nothing would make me happier than if this book became a bestseller. But that will never happen—at least in the Spanish language. Yes, it's common to hear more and more English words drift into Spanish from the entertainment world, but that doesn't mean it's correct. You can impress people by resisting the urge to call a bestseller "un bestseller." Call it an *éxito editorial* or a terrific *superventas*. Everyone will be impressed with the discipline with which you resist another needless *anglicismo* that's commonly used by Latinos. Better yet, buy several hundred copies of this book for your friends, family and colleagues for Christmas ... and who knows, this book just might become *un éxito editorial*. Did you hear that, Strunk & White?

Biannual and Biennial / *Bianual* and *Bienal*

An event, such as a conference, that takes place twice a year is a biannual event. In Spanish, one could say that a conference which takes place twice a year is a *conferencia bianual*, or it could be described as a conference that occurs *semestral* (every six months). If an event takes place every other year, on the other hand, it is a biennial event. In Spanish that would make it an *evento bienal*.

Bigotry / *Intolerancia* or *Fanatismo*

It's a sad commentary that the FBI reported that, in 2009, of the 1,050 hate crime offenses "committed based on the perceived ethnicity or national origin of the victim," 62.3% were "motivated by anti-Hispanic bias." It's a harsh reality of life for Hispanics in the U.S., one that is exacerbated by the poisonous nature of the public discourse concerning immigration, immigration reform and the draconian laws enacted by state legislatures. If overcoming bigotry is something that comes with being Latino in the U.S., then what's the word for bigotry in Spanish? Don't tell me a bigot is a *bigote*—and I have heard Latinos say this—because you should know that a *bigote* is a moustache and it has nothing to do with bigots or bigotry. *Bigotry* is *intolerancia* or *fanatismo*, and a *bigot* is *un fanático*. There are many kinds of bigotry directed against Latinos, and some are more subtle than others. It's one thing for Herman Cain, a Republican, to make jokes about electrocuting Latin Americans along the border with an electrified fence. It's another when Willie Brown, a Democrat, while mayor of San Francisco, to have discriminated against a Latino organization that organized a tribute to the victims of the September 11, 2001 attacks in San Francisco city hall by refusing to have an opening reception. (Every group that organizes exhibitions in city hall is entitled to a reception.) Cain's brazen bigotry is on the evening news, while Brown's subtle bigotry is marked by a privilege denied. This kind of *intolerancia* is all the more incomprehensible when one considers that, since the mid-19th century, Mexico welcomed runaway slaves, facilitated the Underground Railroad, and outlawed all forms of bondage. "Sometimes someone would come along and try to get us to run up north and be free. We used to laugh at that. There was no reason to run up north. All we had to do was walk, but walk south and we'd be free as soon as we crossed the Rio Grande," Felix Hayward, a black man held in bondage in Texas, told interviewers as part of "The Slave Narratives of Texas." Mexican president Vicente Guerrero, who was half black, like Barack Obama, had banned by decree all forms of slavery in Mexico on September 15, 1829, six years after Mexico declared independence from Spain. In all these discussions about illegal aliens and Hispanics, take heart, Latino, and I want you to be able to remind people that there was a time when illegal aliens from the U.S. crossed into Mexico, escaping slavery and seeking freedom. Herman Cain and Willie Brown would do well to recognize Mexico's role as a refuge for fugitive slaves. It might help end their *intolerancia* against Latinos.

Bimonthly and Biweekly / *Bimensual* and *Bimestral*

Bimonthly and biweekly are easily confused, in English as well as in Spanish. If a magazine is published every other month (six times a year), it is a bimonthly. In Spanish, the word is *bimestral*. A magazine that is published twice a month, on the other hand, is published biweekly. In Spanish, it is published *bimensual* or *quincenal*. *Bimensual* means twice a month and *quincenal*, derived from "15 days," also means twice a month. It might be worth remembering that throughout the Spanish-speaking world, employees are paid twice a month, on the 15th and on the last business day of the month, which is why employees anxiously await the arrival of the *quincena*, or pay day.

Blog / *Blog* or *Ciberbitácora*

There are times when technological changes are so quick and furious that language has a difficult time catching up. One of the more riveting examples is the spread of the word "blog" around the world. Faster than a piece of junk e-mail, the blog, or weblog, denotes a personal online diary or page on the Internet. The purpose of blogs is to allow an individual to post his or her opinions on a personal page online, often in an easy-to-read format, and usually inviting readers to comment, and thus create an online conversation. In Spanish, the word *blog* has proliferated quickly in every day usage. We speak of *los comentarios en este blog*, or of this or that posted by a *blogista*. There is no consensus on a Spanish-language equivalent for this term, although the word *ciberbitácora* has been proposed. Why? The reason is that the literal meaning of *blog* is a *cuaderno de bitácora*, which would be *ciberbitácora*. This word, however, is almost unknown to most Spanish speakers, and would leave most people with a puzzled look. In consequence, it is perfectly acceptable to use *blog* when speaking Spanish.

Bother / *Molestar*

May I bother you for a copy of the itinerary? Quick! How do you say *bother* in Spanish? Yes, that's right! It's *molestar*! This is one of those peculiar situations, Latino, when you have to speak with confidence and authority. Why? Because *molestar* in Spanish sounds terribly close to *molest* in English. No one wants to go anywhere near that word in English, and, truth be told, just thinking about it is enough to have that terrible phrase "hostile work environment" dash through my mind. It is quite bothersome that monolingual colleagues and co-workers will raise an eyebrow should they hear you using *molestar* when speaking Spanish, and may have misgivings about what the of conversation in which you are engaged. This means you have to be sensitive to the possibility of misinterpretations. The solution is to be prepared to explain this linguistic peculiarity, and all will be fine in your workplace, at least as far as this word is concerned. Do note that in business English, "bother" is also used to convey the idea of problems. ("This report is such a bother, considering the department's workload.") It can also be used to convey a sense of caring about something. ("It was thoughtful of him to bother to send a note of thanks for the work I did helping out at the conference.") In these cases, you may want to consider using other words instead of *molestar*. If a report is a bother, it can be said to have *dificultades* or present *molestias*. If someone is kind enough to bother to think of someone else, then the word *preocuparse* is in order.

Bottom Line / *A Fines de Cuentas* or *En Pocas Palabras*

What's the bottom line? It depends on what you mean. If you mean at the end of the day, where do we stand ("What is the bottom line if we move forward on this deal?"), then it's *a fines de cuentas*. If, on the other hand, you mean that you want to get to the conclusion of a conversation that is going on far too long ("What's the bottom line on your talk with Joe?"), then it's *en pocas palabras*. Whichever meaning you are using, be mindful that there are two distinct Spanish-language equivalent phrases for "bottom line." They may seem like a mouthful, but each conveys the idea expressed by the English phrase. There's a world of difference between saying "If we continue with these bottom line results, the department will face layoffs" and "Bottom line: Everyone must adhere to the company dress code." In the first instance, *a fines de cuentas* is the more appropriate translation for "bottom line," and the latter, it's best to use *en pocas palabras*. So, *en pocas palabras*, that's the short on the bottom line.

Branches / *Sucursales*

Rama is Spanish for a branch, such as sprig of a plant, a limb of a tree, or a bough. But it is never another location of a business, such as a branch of Bank of Whatever or some other commercial establishment. The word for this kind of branch is *sucursal*. "Can you provide a list of your branches in Chicago?" is a request for the number of *sucursales* the company has in Chicago. This word is primarily used today to refer to banking and finances, where subsidiary and filial offices are called branches. *Ramas*, on the other hand, is exclusively used to refer to the branches of a plant or tree, or used in colloquial expressions that you may encounter from time to time. If you want to describe someone who is always jumping from one industry or interest to another, without rhyme or reason, you might want to describe that person as someone who "anda de rama en rama," a figure of speech suggesting she is jumping from branch to branch. If someone tells you about their family history, he might say that, "en la rama paterna de mi familia," which means "on my father's side of the family." The only other business usage for *rama* might be in printing, where enclosing types are referred to as *ramas* (*en rama* means raw material, *seda en rama* means raw silk); or when referring to the rack used in the textile industry to bring cloth to its proper length. Otherwise, a company's branches are always its *surcusales*.

Budget / *Presupuesto*

This is one of the more vexing words for Latinos. Is it that, by virtue of living in the Hispanic diaspora in the United States surrounded by English, some words tend to fade from memory faster than others? The word *budget* is one that continues to be a linguistic stumbling block for many Latino professionals. This is unfortunate, since so many snap judgments are made by others when a simple word like *budget* is not translated properly. In Spanish, a budget is a *presupuesto*. The meaning of a *presupuesto* is a calculation of the anticipated income and expenses of any economic endeavor or activity. This could be the monetary inflows and outflows for a department, a company, a household, a government, a military, or the lemonade stand down the street managed by seven-year-old children. Whatever it is, if it has a budget, it has a *presupuesto*, which literally means the monies "pre-supposed" to encompass the economic activity in question. Say this word a hundred times until you know it by heart, since careers have risen or fallen on this one word! I'm not joking. Learn it, or you will regret it as the years go by—and the promotions pass by you!

Business Class / *Clase Ejecutiva* or *Clase Preferente*

Whenever I'm in Mexico City or Buenos Aires, colleagues often asked if I traveled *como gente decente*, meaning *like a decent person*. It's a inside joke, of course, but what they are asking is whether I flew in Business Class, either because of the fare paid on the ticket, or because of a courtesy upgrade carriers often given to frequent fliers. In English, *Business Class* refers to the premium service afforded customers who pay for the more comfortable seats and complimentary in-flight services. The Spanish language equivalent for this term is either *Clase Ejecutiva* or *Clase Preferente*. The more widely-used expression is *Clase Ejecutiva*, primarily because these are the terms used by Aeromexico and Iberia, which are the leading airlines serving the U.S. from the Spanish-speaking world. *Clase Preferente* is used more often throughout South America.

C

Call You Back / *Devolver la Llamada*

Until I change my name to "Back," you can't call me Back. If you live in the U.S. and you are casually talking to someone and you tell him or her that you're going to have to "llamarte para atrás," which literally "to call back," you will be understood, no doubt. This improper usage, however, is an *anglicismo*, and makes no sense to someone who speaks Spanish and may not be familiar with English. In business Spanish the correct expression is to say you are going *to return a call*, and not call you (or anyone else) back. *Devolver la llamada* or *devolver tu llamada* is proper Spanish. This formulation, of returning a call in a professional context, includes *Te devolveré la llamada* or *Te llamaré de nuevo* (I'll call you anew.) Get into the habit of returning people's phone calls, and refrain from calling them "Back."

Cash Flow / *Flujo de Efectivo*

What's the cash flow? Whatever it is, it could always be better. Unless of course your business concerns illicit activities, such as drug trafficking or money laundering, and then the problem is having too much cash on hand. For most businesses, however, having too much cash is seldom the case, since most businesses are honest enterprises. In business English, cash flow is a measure of an operation's liquidity. This idea is translated in Spanish as *flujo de efectivo*. The *cash flow* is the *flujo de efectivo*, and it is defined as a measure of cash liquidity. Do note, however, that in some places the phrase *flujo de caja* is used on occasion, such as Spain and in South America. In the Spanish spoken in the United States and Mexico, however, *flujo de efectivo* is preferred.

Cash on Delivery (C.O.D.) / *Entrega Contra Reembolso*

It's seldom used in most places, but COD sales—cash on delivery—remains a part of business life, especially for consumers who have little or no credit, or live in rural communities. This would include, of course, many new immigrants from Latin America who are Spanish-dominant. Although the word *reembolso* is often used to mean refund, it also means COD reimbursement, and that's the idea behind COD: an item is delivered once cash reimbursement is made. The correct translation in business Spanish for COD is: *entrega contra reembolso*. If this applies to your business, learn it and use it.

Change Your Mind / *Cambiar de Idea* or *Cambiar de Opinión*

There is always the danger of translating an expression word-for-word and thinking that you're arrived at conveying the same idea. That is often a mistake. Would you like to see an example of how wrong? In Spanish, if you say that someone is "una persona sinvergüenza," you are conveying the idea that that person has some nerve, or is fresh and brazen. But—as has been known to happen—a Latino engages in a literal translation of that phrase from English, a completely different meaning is conveyed. *Una persona sinvergüenza* comes out as *a person without shame*! That said, in the business world, *to change your mind* is not to *cambiar de mente*— unless you've had a brain transplant! "I changed my mind," is, in English, a figurative expression, not a literal one. In Spanish, the sentiment is expressed by saying *cambiar de idea* (to change your idea about something) or *cambiar de opinión* (to change your opinion about something), but you can never exchange your current brain for another. Not unless your primary care physician happens to be Dr. Frankenstein.

Casual / *Informal*

Here is another one of those words that confuses Latinos for perfectly understandable reasons. "Casual" in business English is a common word to denote informal, and in Spanish *casual* is also a word. In Spanish, however, *casual* does not mean the same thing as it does in business English. When something happens by random chance, through (indifferent) fortune, accidentally, because of serendipity or by mere coincidence, it is said to have occurred *casualmente*. In English, on the other hand, in the business world, the word "casual" means "informal." For example, in business English in the United States, *casual*, or *informal*, attire is acceptable on Fridays. Be mindful, however, that casual in English also means something that occurs by chance (casual e-mails from a distant friend), leniency (casual attitude to smoking marijuana), lacking intimacy (a casual acquaintance and nothing more) or nonchalance (a casual review of a report, a casual disregard for safety rules, a casual sexual encounter at the company's holiday party in the office supply room). Oh, dear, not another *escándalo*.

Casualty / *Víctima*

Take an English word and think of something that first comes to mind in Spanish and ... you will often end up in trouble. *Casualty* ... could that be *casualidad*? No. Casualty, which is often seen in business and "Breaking News" reporting when a calamity occurs, refers to a person who is injured or dies as a consequence of an unforeseen event. When an airliner crashes, aviation authorities speak of the number of casualties. When there is a train derailment, officials report on the number of casualties in the wreckage. Subsequent reports usually detail the number of fatalities among the casualties. In Spanish, the word is *víctima*. How many *víctimas* are we speaking about? (If one is speaking of casualties in an armed conflict, the combatants killed can also be described as *bajas*. Consider this example, *En el enfrentamiento reciente, el ejército sufrió 12 bajas.*) And what of *casualidad*? Yes, it's a word, alright, but it's more closely analogous to something that occurs *coincidentally*. The meaning of *casualidad* is something that is the result of circumstances that can neither be prevented nor avoided. Remember, however, that in the more common business English usages, the word *casualty* refers to *víctima*.

(A) Challenge and (To) Challenge / *Reto* or *Desafío*

I challenge you to find a better solution. When was the last time you were challenged at work? Hopefully it happens often! Everyone should have a challenging job! That is, of course, until you tell me that "chalengeo" is a word in Spanish! Then you are linguistically-challenged, which is not a good thing. Say "chalengeo" to me and I just might challenge you to a duel to defend the honor of the Spanish language. That would be dramatic, wouldn't it? *A challenge* is a *reto*. It is something that must be met. "The challenge is to increase productivity without any increases in staff," a division manager might announce in a e-mail to the entire office. "We met the challenges our competitors threw at us by successfully defending our market share in Florida," another manager might boast after last quarter's results are announced. "The company is committed to the challenge of raising money for this worthy cause," the company president might state as the firm renews its commitment to sign up as many employees as it can for the charitable 5K race this coming weekend. Whatever it is, if it's a challenge to be met, it is a *reto* to be achieved. But what if a challenge is used as a verb, *to challenge*? In business Spanish, *to challenge* is to present someone with a *desafío*. *Challenge*, as a general description of the undertakings on the horizon, is *desafío*. If your competition launches a new product, and this is characterized as challenging your firm, the phrase in Spanish is *lanzaron un desafío*. Then your manager calls a meeting to let everyone know that the company accepts this challenge, which is translated as *aceptamos el desafío*. Why? Well, everyone knows that deep down your department enjoys being challenged, which is translated as *disfrutamos con las tareas difíciles*. This is great news for you, since you stand out when you have a task that will challenge you. This is expressed as *necesito una tarea que represente un desafío para mí*. In fact, for the department, this task represents a real challenge, which is translated as *esta tarea constituye un auténtico desafío*. On occasion, *challenge* is used to describe a *deliberate confrontation*, in which case, more precise wording is appropriate in business Spanish. If someone challenges your right to decide who gets to park his or her car where in the employee parking lot, in Spanish this is said that someone *puso en duda tú derecho a decidir quien puede estacionar donde*. (*Challenge* becomes *to put in doubt*). Meanwhile at the board meeting, the chief executive is confronting a leadership challenge from several dissatisfied board members. In Spanish, the phrase for this is that there's *un asalto al liderato*. (Challenge becomes *an attack* or *storming* of the leadership.) You can accept the challenge, or *aceptas el reto*, and stand your ground on determining who can park where. The chief executive can vow not to retrench as she faces this challenge, or as she *enfrenta este desafío*. You vow to challenge the challenger by issuing your own challenge, which in Spanish becomes *desafiar a alguien*. Why? Because you are confident you will rise to the occasion this challenge represents, which is *ponerse a la altura de las circunstancias*. Will you prevail? I'm betting on you. And then it happens! The audacity! The person who challenged you, now turns around and challenges me with a condescending, *"What do you know?"* In Spanish, this question posed as a challenge is *¿Tú, qué sabes?* Will challenges never cease? Not in the world of business, Latino, so be ready to rise to the occasion.

Chat / *Conversar, Platicar* or *Charlar*

An online chat, in Spanish, can be translated as *un chat*, and the people who are engaged in *un chat* can be said to be *chateando*. *Chat*, in Spanish, is now an acceptable word to describe two or more individuals engaged in a conversation using electronic messages sent through the Internet, including text messaging. But what about people who are on the telephone, sitting at a table over lunch, speaking to each other over their cubicles, in an elevator or as they walk down the street? These, and every other form of conversation that does not involve sending electronic messages, are not *chats*. These people are *conversando, platicando* or *charlando*. There is nothing as intimate as a gentle conversation with another person over a cup of coffee, tea or drink. There is nothing as human as a quiet conversation over dinner, or with a long-time friend. Depending on where you happen to be and how you wish to express it, remain mindful that a telephone or face-to-face chat between two or more persons is always a *conversación, plática* or *charla*.

(To) Check / *Examinar* or *Revisar*

Unless you are asked to tell someone that their *check* in the mail, never ever use the word *cheque* in business Spanish! One of the more egregious errors Latinos make is to think that because *check* is both a noun and verb in English, the same is true in Spanish. Unfortunately, that is not the case. Yes, your *cheque* can be in the mail, but it will do no good to *chequear* your mailbox for it, since *chequear* has a much more narrow use in Spanish. You can use *chequear* to mean to examine or verify (such as a program before it is launched, or report before it is distributed), and to describe a medical check-up, but that's about it. For more widespread uses, there are other words in Spanish that are more appropriate, such as *comprobar*, *controlar*, *examinar*, *revisar* or *verficar*. As a general rule, use *chequear* only when you are discussing something under review for verification or examination. At all other times, become accustomed to using one of these other verbs when checking things out.

Check in / *Reportar* or *Documentar* or *Facturar*

What time are we scheduled to check in for the flight? Quick! Say that in Spanish. Ha! I knew you'd mess it up. Why? Because you live in the United States where, surrounded by English all day long, you just ... well, you just can't help yourself but be influenced by all that English! No, you don't *chequear* yourself at the airport, I'm afraid. The correct word in Spanish is *documentar* or *facturar* when checking in at the airport. If you are checking in elsewhere—a conference, a hotel room, a job site—the word is *reportar*. The reason different words are used is the natural evolution of how various industries emerged. In situations when you are asked to sign in, whether it is at the front desk of a hotel, or a foreman's sign-in sheet on the factory floor, what you are being asked to do is *to report your presence*. "I'm reporting my presence, in accordance with my reservation," you imply at the front desk, and thus your reservation is fulfilled, and won't be cancelled. "I'm reporting for work," you imply when you check in at the office, or job site. In each of these cases, when a reservation, attendance or presence is being reported, then the word is *reportar* and you are *reportándose*. In the case when greater controls are required, by law or insurance companies or corporate compliance with regulations, then you are *documenting* your presence. If you didn't know that every time you check in for a flight, your data are added to that flight's manifest, you do now. (Airplanes have been known to crash, and all kinds of legalities come into play when such unfortunate events occur.) As a result, when you check in for transportation—car rentals, bus rides, train stations, airports—you are *documenting* your presence for the passage contracted. If you are checking in baggage, then the baggage is also being documented (with those identification strips with the bar codes on them). In Spanish this is expressed by saying that you have to *documentarse* at the check in counter, and you are asked if you have any baggage to *documentar* for the flight. In some cases the word *facturar* is used, simply because receipts are issued, either as a boarding pass or a checked baggage claim ticket, or both. Whether it is *reportarse*, or *documentarse* or *facturarse*, it is never, ever "chequear adentro," Latino!

Chocolate

This is a word that needs no translation. Why is it here? Because in the course of business there will come a time when gifts are appropriate. Chocolate, you may not know, originated in the New World, and it is one of the Hispanic world's most enduring and delectable gifts to humanity. Be proud of this heritage, and know that no matter what the Swiss, French or Belgians might want you to think, chocolate does not come from Europe. As a bold affirmation of cultural identity, I encourage you to give the corporate gift of chocolate—and chocolates from Latin America. And it is without reservation that I recommend one specific brand to anyone who asks. Presuming you are asking, here it is: Ki' Xocolatl. *Ki'* means *delicious*, and *xocolatl* is the word for *chocolate* in the Nahuatl and Maya languages. If your local gourmet shop doesn't carry it, it's available from Amazon.com. It would be difficult to miss the mark with this as a corporate gift.

Clerical / *De Oficina*

Oh, no, not this word! Is there something more beguiling than to see a word that is an adjective for one thing applied to another? In business English, *clerical* is that which is appropriate to or pertains to an office, or to the work of a clerk. It is seldom used to describe that which pertains to the clergy. In Spanish, on the other hand, *clerical* is exclusively used to describe things pertaining to the clergy, ecclesiastical authorities or churches. That's quite a difference. The misuse of *clerical* by Latinos is very widespread, and sometimes results in unintended put downs. Once during a meeting in Madrid, Latinos from Los Angeles were making the case for a customer service back-office operation, when, during a break, one of the Spaniards at the meeting commented that the word clerical was so misused, she had visions of Julie Andrews at her convent with the other nuns singing and dancing as they typed reports and filed away papers in cabinets. She envisioned a scene from "The Sound of Music" that ended up on the cutting room floor. That's funny, because I had visions of Franciscan monks emptying filing cabinets and shredding documents related to unlawful wire transfers dating back to World War II. So what should you say instead? If something is clerical in the sense that it pertains to the office, it is *de oficina*. If you want to say, "The work involved is clerical," it can be properly said, "El trabajo en cuestión es de oficina."

Click / *Clic* or *Pulsar*

"With the click of a mouse, it is done!" Think about how that would sound to people a generation ago. What in the world would you have to do to a mouse to make it go "click"—and why not a hamster, or a gerbil? Better question still, *Are the folks at People for the Ethical Treatment of Animals aware of what you are doing to our fellow mammal?* But of course today we know that "click" simulates the sound the mouse-like contraption that guides the cursor on your computer monitor or laptop makes. In Spanish, "clic" is acceptable as an abbreviation for the sound metal makes when snapping, such as the metal clasp on your child's lunchbox. Over the past decade, however, use of that word has been expanded to include the clicking sounds made by computer keyboards and the mouse. (In Spanish, the plural of "clic" is "clics," by the way.) As a result, it's acceptable to translate the first sentence in this paragraph as, "Con el clic del ratón, es todo!" But Latino beware, there is no such thing as "cliquear" as a verb in Spanish! The correct verb to use to describe the action of clicking is *pulsar*. When it comes to *la pulsación informática*, it is preferable to say *pulsar*, or in case you freeze up and don't remember this word, you could get away with saying *hacer clic*.

Close the deal / *Cerrar el Trato*

At the end of negotiations, what do you have to do to close the deal? A lot depends on where you are in the Spanish-speaking world. The more commonly-used expression is *cerrar el trato*, which literally means to close the treaty. This sentiment can also be expressed as *cerrar el acuerdo* (close the accord), although as a general rule, you *reach* an accord (*llegar a un acuerdo*) before the deal is actually closed. It's also possible to describe the process as a *cierre de la transacción*, meaning the closing of the transaction, but this has a more passive sentiment to it. The closest Spanish-language expression to the notion conveyed by the phrase *to close the deal* is to *cerrar el trato*. Once that is done, it means the terms have been agreed to and all that is pending is the necessary paperwork to conclude formally the agreement on the deal.

Coach / *Entrenador* or *Director Técnico*

It's very tempting to use a word like *coach* when speaking Spanish. There are so many other English words that are familiar to sports fans throughout the Spanish-speaking world that one presumes that everyone knows what a coach means. Yes, it's true that few people will misunderstand you if you say coach. But why use an English word when speaking Spanish if the purpose of business Spanish is to communicate clearly and completely in the language of preference of your audience? In sports, the word for *coach* in Spanish is *entrenador*. In a more general business sense, someone who coaches employees, such as the Information Technology geek who will train the staff on the new computer program, is a *director técnico*. On or off the field, in or out of the office, there are Spanish-language equivalents for *coach*: *entrenador* or *director técnico*. Got that? Now, hit the showers!

Colleague / *Colega, Colaborador* or *Compañero*

"I'd like to introduce you to Mr. Vidal, a colleague and a friend." There's no doubt in my mind you can translate the word *friend*. How would you translate *colleague*? What's the business Spanish word for *colleague*? There are several choices, each one as acceptable as the other.

In business Spanish one can use *colega, colaborador* or *compañero*. There are regional preferences, but any of these words is acceptable when describing a colleague or a co-worker.

Commitment / *Compromiso*

If you make a commitment, then you are incurring an obligation to comply with something. In life there are many commitments, aren't there? These range from the commitments you have to your family, to those you incur by being part of a community, to the commitment you have to yourself to nurture yourself. If you happen to live in the United States and are speaking Spanish it would not be surprising that, once in a while, you will make the linguistic mistake of forgetting how to say *commitment* in Spanish. Why? The reason is that the word is counter-intuitive to English-dominant Latinos. In Spanish, *commitment* is *compromiso*. Don't make the mistake of thinking that *compromiso* is Spanish for compromise! (See, Compromise.) But remember that in business Spanish usage, *compromiso* refers to a commitment, an obligation, and loyalty. If you make a commitment to have those reports on your manager's desk first thing Monday morning, the act of making a commitment to do something is to *comprometerse con algo*. A colleague who lacks commitment can be described as someone who *no se compromete lo suficiente*. If you have to leave work early because of a family commitment, then can say you have *un compromiso familiar*. On occasion, you might use *obligación*. (If there's no commitment to join the executive committee, you can better say it in Spanish by noting that there isn't *ninguna obligación de afiliarse al comité ejecutivo*.) In most instances, however, *commitment* will always be *compromiso*.

Competence / *Competencia*

Is our competition competent? I mention this because if our competition has a savvy Latino like you, then we are in trouble. Why do I ask that? I ask because most Hispanics in the U.S. don't realize that in Spanish, the word for competition and competence are the same: *competencia*. As a result, it's very important to understand the context in which you are using these words. It may sound difficult, but it really isn't. In English, after all, the word *read* means two things, depending on how it's pronounced. "Please *read* the instructions," is a different meaning from, "She *read* the ransom note." And to make matters worse, the ransom note was written in *red* lipstick. If you want the hostage safely released, or just to succeed in business, what is important is *competence*. Are you competent? Is she competent? Is he competent? In each of these cases, because we are speaking of being in possession of the required qualifications, skills, knowledge or capacity; or we are referring to sufficient quantity of the necessary attributes, the word in business Spanish is *competencia*. This, quite naturally, leads to mentioning what every Latino knows about the American workplace: there is a double-standard and Hispanics are scrutinized more closely than non-Hispanics. An example that comes to mind immediately is the frustration of having to deal with less-than-competent people. Consider a struggling publishing company I'll call *Laughable Books*. Management cleaned house under the misguided notion that it could reinvent itself by replacing senior (and expensive) editors, who had established that publisher as innovative and relevant, with young uber-hip editors (at far lower salaries). A common mistake management often makes is in thinking it can replace senior talent with young blood, and in so doing they not only save on salaries but also make their firms "youthful" and more "forward" thinking. The self-defeating nature of this strategy became clear to me while working on a project at *Laughable Books*. An uber-hipster editor, whom I can call Haynes, probably because that was her name, was assigned to work with me. In no time, I began to doubt her competence. One Author Query to my mentioning events that took place in the 7th century B.C.E., 221 B.C.E. and the late 6th century C.E., stated, "the dates jump all over the place." I thought that listing events chronologically, from the oldest date to the most recent one, was logical. Another Author Query asked me to provide Homer's surname. When I shared these details with editors in New York, much amusement, amid a sad sense of disbelief, followed. The ignorance and incompetence that Haynes displayed spoke to me of the biases against Hispanics, simply because during this time I knew of two very accomplished and competent Latino editors who were struggling to find employment. Yet, here I was stuck with a fool who, in my opinon, only had her position because she was non-Hispanic, and enjoying the entitlement that comes with belonging to the mainstream of non-Hispanic America. Had Haynes been a Latina who thought that going from the 7th century B.C.E. to 221 B.C.E. to the 6th century C.E. was "jumping all over the place," I doubt she would have held her position longer than you can ask, "I didn't know Homer Simpon was a Greek philosopher?" Not unlike women half a century ago, today Latinos have to work twice as hard to get half the credit as non-Hispanics. But I bet you knew that. Oh, yes, I almost forgot. *Of Antiquity.* Isn't that Homer's last name? *Homer of Antiquity.* There you are, post-modern hipster non-accuracy delivered to the loser-hipsters!

Complimentary / *Cortesía*

If something is complimentary, then it is offered as a courtesy. This goes for a complimentary upgrade, or a complimentary cocktail or a complimentary car ride back to the airport. If you are being extended any courtesy, it is always a *cortesía*. There are a good number of Latinos in the United States who, by virtue of living in the Hispanic diaspora, believe it's perfectly acceptable to use the word *complimentario*, but that's not case. The problem, of course, with using *complimentario* is that there's no such word in Spanish. You might be perfectly understood by other Latinos, but that's because they, too, are probably English-dominant. (There is a word that looks very similar in Spanish: *complementario*. But *complementario* is *complementary*, meaning that which serves to complete.) I wasn't going to include this word in this book, but I relented, since I thought that a sensible Latino such as you deserved a *complimentary* word as a *courtesy*. There's no need to thank me. But you're welcome.

Compliments / *Halagos*

It's a shame that manners have been devalued to such a degree that they are fast disappearing from the American workplace. Without wanting to become nostalgic, there was a time, perhaps because we had more time, when it was common to treat each other with greater consideration. That courtesy and manners are absent from most interactions is a reflection on the state of our society. That's the bad news, which means there is also some good news. Here it is: If manners are rare, it's easy to distinguish yourself by being polite. In business, the paying of compliments is an easy habit to adopt, one that will set you apart from all the others standing between you and that proverbial corner office.

This isn't to advocate being solicitious in a false way, but if by compliments we refer to acts of expressing praise, admiration or commendation, then it's possible to distinguish yourself through your civility, regard for others and courtesies. In business Spanish the word for *compliments* is *halagos*. More than flattery, to offer *halagos* is, at its most basic, to recognize the contributions of others, and the work they perform. In business, compliments are linked to the development of leadership skills. At some point, I recall being mentored into getting into the habit of managing by putting into practice the following: The 6 most important words: "I admit I made a mistake." The 5 most important words: "You did a good job." The 4 most important words: "What is your opinion?" The 3 most important words: "If you please." The 2 most important words: "Thank you." The 1 most important word: "We." The least important word: "I." If you remind yourself of these guidelines, offering praise will become part of who you are, and you will enjoy success more readily.

Compromise / *Negociar* or *Solucionar*

How many times have I heard a Latino say *compromiso* when translating *compromise* from English into Spanish? The answer is frightening: More times than I've see the "Breaking News" nonsense on CNN, and that's all day long! It may appear to be incorrect, but *compromiso* is Spanish for *commitment*. In business English, on the other hand, compromise means a settlement of differences or disagreements by mutual concessions, or to reach an agreement by adjusting conflicting or opposing demands or claims. It also means an intermediate solution between different things, such as an open floor plan which is a compromise between having cubicles or walled offices. The other meaning, rarely used in our age of fluid values, is the notion of endangering one's reputation, as is the case when one's actions compromises one's integrity. (Quaint notion!) In all these cases, be aware that the proper business Spanish words to use are either *negociar* or *solucionar*. If you are compromising, then you are *negociando* (negotiating) or *solucionando* (finding a solution) differences through the process of mutual concession or reciprocal modification of demands or claims. Thus, the business English expression of delight that is "to reach a compromise" is translated into Spanish as "alcanzar una solución intermedia." In each phrase, the idea that the parties involved negotiated an acceptable solution to their differences is conveyed correctly. In cases when it is important to convey the idea that one entered into a compromise, then one can use the Spanish word *comprometer*. If one *reaches a compromise*, then one has *llegado a un acuerdo mutuo*. If, on the other hand, it is important to convey the notion that there are certain things that are not negotiable and cannot be subject to compromise, use the verb *transigir*, which means *to give away*. "We cannot compromise on this point," in business English becomes, in Spanish, "No podemos transigir en este punto." (If in English the word *cede* or *yield* is used, then the Spanish word to use is *ceder*. "We cannot yield on this point," in business English is translated as, "No podemos ceder en este punto.") In most business situations, however, *negociar* or *solucionar* will be adequate to describe the process of compromising.

Concern / *Negocio* or *Preocupar*

What concerns you? Your career? Your family? Your sense of self-worth? Whatever is of concern to you, there are different ways of expressing it in business

Spanish. If by *concern* you mean something that is related to a business, an interest, a transaction or an affair, then the correct word in Spanish is *negocio*. A business *concern* is a *negocio*. If, on the other hand, by concern you mean a matter that engages one's attention, interest, welfare or care, then the word in Spanish is *preocupar*. If something gives you cause for concern, you can say that in Spanish by noting that something *me da motivos de preocupación*. If you want to show concern for a thing, you can *mostrar preocupación*. If you want to reassure a colleague that the matter is under control and there is no need for concern, do so by saying *no hay motivo de preocupación*. This is straightforward enough, but be aware that Spanish is spoken so widely that you may encounter variations. If an executive expresses the idea that something might be a public concern—is that why a television news team is knocking on the door?—then he or she might say that the matter is *de interés público*. Similarly, if someone wants to tell you politely to mind your own business since the matter is not your concern, he or she might say that the issue *no es de tu incumbencia*. There are other nuances involved, of course, since concern in English means to worry or to be anxious, as is the case when someone shows concern for another's problem. In this case, the word is always *preocuparse*. Then, there's something to be said for being *unconcerned*—even callous—as the situation merits. In fact, in life one finds that one will end up with all kinds of concerns, some of which are peculiar. Did I ever tell you about the time I visited an elder relative at the hospital who was concerned about the indignity of bladder incontinence? He found it humiliating to find himself wearing adult diapers. It was an incessant source of his complaints, bordering on whining. What was the alternative? Wearing *infant* diapers? Besides, what can one say about the nature of life? Most of us will end our days the way we began them: helpless and needing the assistance of others for our most basic needs. After I tired of hearing out his concerns and complaints about this subject, what was there left to say? "Well," I offered as a consolation, "perhaps if you had cultivated urolangia as a fetish in your youth, you wouldn't be having such a difficult time of it now, would you?" Choose your words carefully. After all, I won't be there to correct you should you mistake *negocio* and *preocupar*. Then again, it's really no concern of mine.

Conclusive / *Concluyente*

It would be a mistake to look at *conclusive* and think the equivalent is *conclusivo*. In business Spanish, the word *conclusivo* refers to something that settles something in a definite manner, or to conclude an event. We can say that the *conclusivo* presentation was David's from Finance, meaning that his was the *concluding* presentation at that dreadful all-day meeting. On the other hand, the proper Spanish-language word for *conclusive*, as it is more often used in business, is *concluyente*. The reason is that in Spanish, *concluyente* means something is irrefutable, without recourse or final. If the report found the subcontractor to be negligent in a conclusive manner, then in Spanish you can say of the subcontractor that *la determinación del informe fue concluyente*.

Confidence / *Confianza*

In business English to express your confidence in something is to express full trust and certitude in that thing. This is very different from the word *confidencia* in Spanish! It may look like a no-brainer, but remember that in Spanish *confidencia* refers to secret information. This could be the proprietary information of an organization, or even a confidential list of individuals who will be laid off. On the other hand, if you want to express your full trust and confidence, then the word to use is *confianza*. This word expresses hope and belief, certitude and assurance. *Tengo confianza que usará esta palabra correctamente, verdad?*

Confront / *Confrontar*

In English, the word confront has the connotation of defiance, hostility and contradiction. It can be said that two executives confronted each other in the boardroom with opposing visions for the organization. It can be noted that a power struggle came to a head with a confrontation between two division managers. It can also be noted, with sadness, that someone was confronted with evidence of his or her wrong-doing. In every business context, the word confront shows some belligerence. Be mindful that this is not the case in Spanish. While *confrontar* means "to confront," it also has more gentle meaning, including compare (*comparar* and *cotejar*). It's quite possible to say, *Los gerentes van a confrontar ambas propuestas*, meaning, *The managers are going to compare both proposals*. There's no hostility implied, and the meaning is that the two managers will simply compare the merits of each proposal.

Consistent / *Consecuente*

Ah, yes, another linguistic trap far too many Spanish-speakers in the United States are unable to avoid! Surrounded by English, where things in the business world often run best if they are *consistent* in their performance—airlines, express package deliveries, meals at a restaurant—many Latinos believe that the word *consistente* is the equivalent in Spanish for *consistent*. Unfortunately, in Spanish the word *consistente* refers to *consistencia*, as in the firmness, density or solidity of something, such as a loaf of bread, cement mix, or the loyalty of a friend. If the silicone is not of the proper *consistencia*, it will clog the caulking gun. But if you are trying to convey the importance of being consistent in the service, quality or performance of something, the word in Spanish to use is *consecuente*. That's the best way to praise the department that is *consecuente* in delivering superior results, quarter after quarter.

Contract / *Contrato*

Indeed, contracts are the agreements and accords by which business moves forward. In business, a contract is understood to be an agreement, enforceable by law, between two or more parties for doing, or not doing, things specified within the agreement. Contracts cover specified goods and services, and the expression *under contract* denotes a party which is bound by an agreement or accord. The Spanish-language word for contract is *contrato*. Please note that there is no "c" between the "a" and the "t" in the Spanish word. That's the most common mistake made by Hispanics speaking Spanish in the U.S. With this as an explanation, there will probably be a few phrases that you encounter in the normal course of business with which you should be familiar. *To enter into a contract* is to *firmar un contrato*. *To be under a contract* is to *estar contratado* or *estar contratada*. *To break a contract* is *to faltar de cumplir el contrato*. Do note that if *contract* is used as a verb—"We have contracted debts"—then the corresponding Spanish-language verb is *contraer*. *To contract debts* is to *contraer deudas*. In some rare situations, it has been known to happen, I'm afraid, contracts are taken out on people. *To take out a contract on your boss* is to *contratar un asesino para matar a tu jefe*. Let us try to stay away from these kinds of situations, since they are generally frowned upon by law enforcement.

Convenient / *Cómodo*

In business English, the word *convenient* is used to describe something that serviceable, suitable for a specific purpose or agreeable to the task at hand, meaning, it is useful. *The 4 p.m. departure is a* convenient *flight, if you want to leave Washington and arrive in New York in time for your dinner engagement.* That's a pleasant thing to hear, especially after a day of meetings in the nation's capital. An inconvenient flight would get me to LaGuardia an hour later, making for an unpleasant and rushed evening. In Spanish the word to use is *cómodo*, since this the word that is appropriate for business usage. Yes, it is tempting to think that *conveniente* is the Spanish-language equivalent of convenient, but it isn't. Why? Because in Spanish *conveniente*, which is derived from *convenir*, is more appropriate to describe something that is opportune or expeditious. In most business usages, however, *cómodo* is the more appropriate word to use to make yourself well understood.

Conviction / *Condena*

Alas, it is a sad commentary on the state of the world that in business, the word "conviction," more often than not, refers to executives who are found guilty of crimes, and not individuals who are standing up for their beliefs. George Washington was a man of strong convictions, which is why he pledged his worldly possessions and life to secure America's independence from England. Enron Chairman Ken Lay, on the other hand, was convicted by a jury. Unless you are speaking of someone's strongly-held beliefs, refrain from using *convicción*, and instead use *condena* to convey the idea of being found guilty by a jury. There are, of course, rare individuals who are *convicted* because they were moved to act by their *convictions*—such as the infamous Dr. Jack Kevorkian. In Spanish, he would be described as a person whose *convicciones* ultimately resulted in his being *condenado* by a jury.

Copies / *Ejemplares*

How many copies of the report are needed for the meeting? How many copies of this book were ordered for distribution to the Latinos in your department? How many copies of the magazine profiling your industry do you have on hand? Whenever you are speaking of copies of these things, you are speaking about *ejemplares*. Don't make the mistake of thinking that "copies" translates to "copias." Remember, *copias* is more closely linked to the infinitive "to copy," which is *copiar* in Spanish, and implies to transcribe or to imitate. When it is a question of the number of books (*dos ejemplares del libro*); or an issue of a magazine or a quarterly report (*ejemplares de la revista* or *ejemplares del reporte*); or a complimentary copy of a vanity publication (*ejemplar de cortesía*), then it is always *ejemplar*. By virtue of being a copy of an issue, *ejemplar* also lends itself to describe various forms of publications, such as a back issue of a magazine (*ejemplar atrasado*), or a specimen copy of the report before it goes to the printer (*ejemplar de muestra*). Be mindful that *ejemplar* also means *exemplary*. She was a model manager can be translated as, *Ella fue un gerente ejemplar.*

Copyright / *Derechos de Autor*

Copyright is the legal designation that identifies an intellectual property as protected. The owner has the exclusive right to exploit commercially and to produce, publish and control otherwise an original literary, artistic or musical work. In Spanish this protection is express by the phrase *derechos de autor*. "©" is the internationally-recognized symbol to denote copyright protection, and it consists of the letter "C" inside a circle. In Spanish that symbol is used, usually with the phrase, "Todos los derechos reservados."

Crime and Criminal / *Delito* and *Delincuente*

In the Hispanic diaspora in the United States, burdened by a salacious emphasis on "Breaking News," there is a torrent of crime reports about criminals. It seems that anyone can be accused of a crime and being a criminal, from Andy Warhol who was vilified when one of his Superstars committed suicide, to Martha Stewart who made an unfortunate series of decisions concerning certain stock trades. Latino beware! In Spanish the words *crimen* and *criminal* are used exclusively to denote major offenses, and have a specific moral and legal meaning. A crime against humanity is a *crimen*, and someone convicted of murder is a *criminal*. In every day legal usage, however, be mindful that in a more pedestrian sense—someone who steals a bicycle or holds up a bank—is someone who has committed a *delito* and is a *delincuente*. Think of all the nonsense "cases" brought before Judge Marilyn Milian, that charming Cuban Latina who presides over "The People's Court," on television. Just about every ding-dong case brought before her concerns minor *delitos* by petty *delincuentes*, true?

Cut to the Chase (*See,* At the End of the Day)

Cuts or Cutbacks / *Recortes*

There are times when every industry faces some sort of retrenchment. It's a natural part of the business cycle itself, and on many occasions it may just be the best course of action. There came a time when Howard Schultz, founder of Starbucks, realized that his coffee chain hand grown too quickly and too unruly. As a result, the quality of the products and service offered customers was inconsistent and declining. It was not the kind of experience he had envisioned and worked to create for Starbucks patrons. He decided to take on a greater hands-on approach, closed hundreds of Starbucks locations, and worked to reinvent the entire experience of going to a Starbucks. There were cuts and cutbacks as Starbucks was reengineered. Quick! How would translate either "cuts" or "cutbacks" in Spanish? "Cortés" is not right! In Spanish, "cortés" means courteous and polite. (Note that *cortes*, without the accent over the "e" means courts, as in a judicial court or a legislative body.) It's possible to be genteel in delivering the bad news of impending cutbacks, but the correct word to use is *recortes*. This is the word that describes both cuts and cutbacks. It is always *recortes*.

Dash (*See,* Hyphen)

Dates / *Fechas*

The United States declared its independence from England on July 4, 1776. Everyone knows that, or should. But notice how the date is written: Month, Day, Year. In the Spanish-speaking world—and virtually throughout all of Europe—dates are written from smallest to largest unit: Day, Month, Year. In Spanish, the date in question is written *4 de julio de 1776*. In the business world this becomes an issue when the month is represented by a number. Whereas in the United States, the date of the nation's declaration of independence can be written as 7/4/1776, throughout the Spanish-speaking world it is written as 4/7/1776. See the confusion that arises? When exactly did you make that bank mortgage payment, July 4, or April 7? That meeting was scheduled for the 7th of April or the 4th of July? When did your contract expire …? And so it goes. To avoid this confusion, which has become more common as trade throughout the hemisphere has increased, it's now more common to use Roman numerals for the month. Independence Day, you ask? Why, it's on 4/VII/1776, of course! And it goes without saying that everyone in the United States is familiar with the basic Roman numerals. If they weren't, the Super Bowl wouldn't be represented by Roman numerals, would it? Oh, and by the way, Super Bowl in Spanish is *Super Tazón*.

Days of the Week / *Días de la Semana*

Please refrain from accusing me of being facetious if I have to remind Latinos of the days of the week in Spanish. I'm not. The days of the week in Spanish, beginning with Sunday and ending with Saturday, are: *domingo, lunes, martes, miércoles, jueves, viernes,* and *sábado*. Notice that they are written in lower case letters. The days of the week are *always* written in lower case letters, unless a day of the week is the first word in a sentence. (*Viernes santo es un día de obligación*, meaning, Holy Friday is a Day of Obligation.) Also notice that when enumerating the days of the week, the convention is to begin with Sunday and end with Saturday; in the United States one usually begins with Monday and ends with Sunday. Why? It's a peculiar difference in cultural practices. In the Hispanic (and Judeo-Christian) worldview, the Bible teaches that God created the world in six days, resting on the seventh day, the Sabbath (Saturday). That makes Sunday the first day of the week. (That's why wall calendars begin with Sunday and end with Saturday.) In the U.S. business (Anglo-Saxon) tradition, on the other hand, the first day of business is Monday, making Monday the first day of the week. One more thing: the days of the week are the same whether singular and plural. *El lunes*, means Monday. *Los lunes*, means Mondays.

Definite / *Claro* or *Cierto*

If something is definite, it is said to be exact, certain, precise, determined or clearly defined. In Spanish, two words to convey this meaning are *claro* and *cierto*. To add greater emphasis, it can be said that something is *categórico*, meaning it is certain in a categorical sense. Be mindful of not confusing *definite* with *definido*, since in Spanish the word *definido* is more analogous to defined, which is used to explain or describe (such as the meaning of a word), or to establish the limits or fixed boundaries of a thing (such as the extent of a property, or the authority of a jurisdiction). In business Spanish, use either *claro* or *cierto* to mean *definite*, and about that, I'm most definite.

Demand / *Exigir*

It's easy to make the mistake of thinking that "to demand" in English is the same as "demandar" in Spanish. Unfortunately, this is not the case. In English, demand refers to *asking of, calling for* or *requiring*. One can demand hard work, or call for a more creative solution to a problem. One can also describe something as demanding work, which is the same thing as saying the task requires a concentrated effort. In all these examples, the word in Spanish is *exigir*. *Este trabajo exige mucha dedicación* (This task demands much dedication), or *Exijo una respuesta definitiva hoy* (I demand a definitive answer today) are not uncommon requests in the workplace. Furthermore, there are times when things don't go as smoothly as one would like, in which case you can *exigir un pago* (demand payment), or *exigir cooperación* (beg for more cooperation from someone). The mistake that many Latinos make is to believe that they can substitute *demandar* for *exigir* and be understood. Why won't this work? It won't work because in Spanish, *demandar* means to file a lawsuit, to petition someone or to enter a (legal) action. (Other formal words for "lawsuit" in Spanish are *pleito* and *litigio*.) It's important to stay clear of using *demandar*, since it will complicate your being understood when speaking Spanish, much the same way that confusing *embarrassed* with *embarazada* require an explanation. (*Embarrassed* implies a form of being ashamed, and *embarazada* is pregnant.) Make no mistake, if someone is making a demand of you, they are being *exigente*. If there's any consolation, remember that, over the course of your career, you will find that the best managers and mentors are those who are demanding and exacting, which is to say, those who are *exigent*: "I demand you …" Consider this truth with philosophy: Are you really in a position to demand anything? Why not? If anyone can make a demand, it might as well be you, right? To demand is nothing more than a forceful way of asking for something. "I demand an answer from your department by close of business," or "I demand that the contractor stick to the terms of the service agreement" are not uncommon demands. Also, be mindful that in Spanish *exigir* can also be used to describe a requirement that needs to be fulfilled. "Este reporte exige que lo leas con concentración," is Spanish for "This report demands that you read it with concentration." Why? Perhaps the report is full of technical terms, or perhaps it is written in a boring style. "Esta máquina exige mucho cuidado," simply means that this machine requires much care. It apparently is that fragile. For the most part, however, if it is something you can demand, then it is something that you can *exigir*.

Depending on / *Según* or *De Acuerdo Con*

Next problematic translation among Latinos, you ask? Ah, yes! When *depending on* becomes *dependiendo de* … all sorts of misunderstandings take place. *La conferencia terminará* dependiendo del *número de preguntas al final.* It is correct to point out that the conference's ending time will depend on the number of questions at the end of the presentation. In Spanish, however, only someone else who is surrounded by English all the time will make the connection between *dependiendo de* and *depending on*. The correct terms in Spanish are *según* or *de acuerdo con*. In this case, it's best to say that *La conferencia terminará según el número de preguntas al final.* It's best to stick to concise expressions that are universally understood by Spanish speakers the world over.

Deprivation / *Privación*

With the world going green faster than Kermit the Frog, how do you describe endeavors that are sustainable and also serve a humanitarian purpose? Think of companies that provide clean drinking water in a sustainable way; or flooring that improves the lives of rural communities that are gainfully employed harvesting nearby bamboo that grows in abundance; or training initiatives that allow inner-city youth in the Midwest to have the opportunity to become gainfully employed. In each of these cases, business is speaking about doing good, making a return on investment and contributing in a positive way to individuals that are less privileged than others. It's not uncommon to speak of individuals who have suffered hardships. Most Latinos in the U.S., by the simple virtue of living in the Hispanic diaspora, have first-hand experiences of obstacles and hardship. Most have stories of the challenge of overcoming obstacles. To speak of deprivations, however, is not the same thing as *deprivación*. Look all you want, but there is no such word in Spanish. So how do you say *deprivation* in Spanish? It's *privación*. To *pasar privaciones* is to suffer hardship, and we speak of *la privación que uno superó*, meaning the deprivations one overcame. Keep this in mind, since this book is nothing if it isn't about overcoming the linguistic challenges that many Latinos face as they work diligently to advance their careers in the bilingual consumer economy in the U.S.

Deteriorated / *Desmejorado*

What can we say about our colleague who is ill, and has now taken a turn for the worse? In English we can describe his (or her) condition as having deteriorated. Keep in mind, however, in Spanish only inanimate objects—a building, a road, or an economy—can deteriorate. Human beings, like all other forms of life, on the other hand, become *desmejorados* if their condition worsens. Thus, it would be wrong to report that the colleague in question's condition has become *deteriorado*, but it could be said that he (or she) is now *desmejorado* (or *desmejorada*).

Developer / *Contratista*

One of the most important sectors in the nation's economy is the construction industry. It is housing, in fact, which contributed to the economic crisis of 2008, and many blame banks and over-zealous developers for the problem. In Spanish, bankers are *banqueros*, but what do you call developers? It would be wrong to use the word—as is so often the case—"desarrollador." Why? Because in Spanish *desarrollador* is used exclusively to identify a *software developer*. That's it, really. A developer responsible for construction, on the other hand, is a *contratista* or *promotor inmobiliario* since he or she builds something based on a contract or is responsible for the urbanization of a parcel of land.

Development / *Acontecimiento* or *Contraer* or *Hecho* or *Producir* or *Surgir*

Developments in vernacular usage in a given language happen all the time. This is one reason it's hard to keep up with multiple uses. In business English, for example, the word "development" has so many nuanced meanings that it's difficult to keep the Spanish-language equivalent words clear in one's head. This is why it's necessary to differentiate between uses. "Recent developments in the previous quarter have led us to ..." Well, no matter what these developments may lead management to believe, in Spanish the proper words to use are *acontecimiento, hecho* or *suceso*. You could say, "Los acontecimientos recientes," or "Los hechos recientes," or "Los sucesos recientes," and then go on to enumerate them. If you are speaking about emotions that developed—tensions developed (or arose) between the parties once the terms of the deal were leaked to the media—then this is a situation in which you would describe such tensions as having been *producido* or *surgido* between both parties. Keep this difference in mind: Developments that are actions or events are *acontecimientos, hechos* or *sucesos*. Developments that describe the interactions between people—feelings and emotions—are described as sentiments that are *producidos* or *surgieron* as a result of differences of opinions, ideas or thoughts. Finally, if you are concerned about a sneeze that *develops* into a cold that quickly spreads to other employees throughout the office, then you are speaking about a sneeze in which we run the risk that we will *contraeremos* an illness. The verb in this case is *contraer*.

Different / *Distinto*

In everyday language, we know that *different* is *diferente*. But is that the case in business Spanish? Chances are that the better choice in most business situations—whether you are speaking English or Spanish for that matter—is the word *distinto*. The reason is that in business, when one speaks of differences one usually means of distinctions between things, or various choices. As a result, using *distinto* is the more professional choice, since it offers more options. "There are *different ways* of approaching the problem," also means that there are *various ways* of solving the problem. In business Spanish, by saying, "*Hay distintas maneras ...*" you cover both *different* ways and *various* ways. The same applies to other business expressions. If it's important to make yourself "perfectly clear," in Spanish that phrase is "claro y distinto." Of course, you are free to use *diferente*, but be mindful that *distinto* is the preferred choice.

Directions / *Instrucciones*

Once again, we encounter a situation similar to the one that plagues the word "application." A Latino sees "directions," and instantly thinks of "direcciones." This is a linguistic trap that must be avoided at all costs. In Spanish, *dirección* means several things, the most common of which is a physical location. It can be a street address—if you were to write the president, the address is 1600 Pennsylvania Avenue, Washington, DC 20500—or an electronic address, such as an e-mail. *Dirección* also means the motion in which something moves, such as flow of traffic (one-way versus two-way streets), or trains (south versus north, west versus east, for instance). The word also means management. The *dirección* of an organization is usually found in its *directorio*, or directory. But if you are speaking of directions in the sense of a statement that conveys information, offers knowledge, or provides a set of steps to accomplish something, then you mean *instrucciones*. Manuals that instruct the reader on how to operate a piece of equipment, install software, run a department, set up the conference room for a meeting, or prepare the perfect cup of tea all fall under the concept of *instrucciones*. If it has to do with increasing knowledge through education or providing step-by-step guidance, the word to use is *instrucciones*.

Disappointed / *Decepcionado* or *Desilusionado*

In business, as in life, there are many disappointments. Who knew that this or that would not be as enthusiastically received as someone thought it would be? Remember when the Coca-Cola Company introduced "New Coke"? Alas! The public was not convinced that New Coke was a superior product compared to regular Coke. Consumers demanded that the "old" Coca-Cola be brought back. How do you describe this disappointment in Spanish? There are two adjectives for this. One is *decepcionado* and the other is *desilusionado*. It's only human to be *decepcionado* that New Coke found a hostile reception, and one can be *desilusionado* over all the effort spent in that failed marketing campaign. Be mindful that when speaking of a person, you could also use the words *frustrado* or *defraudado*. Without a doubt, the manager in charge of the New Coke campaign was *frustrado* (or *frustrada*) by the lack of sales. And you can be certain the man behind New Coke—Roberto Goizueta, who was born in Cuba and was the CEO of the Coca-Cola Company—felt *defraudado* by the fickle public. Take heart, Latino, since New Coke was one of the few professional failures Roberto Goizueta encountered in his distinguished career. Under his leadership, the Coca-Cola Company experienced tremendous growth, and launched one of the most successful products in the history of consumer beverages the world has ever known: Diet Coke!

(To) Discern / *Vislumbrar*

Discern is not a common word used in the course of business English, but the reason it is included here is that the Spanish-language equivalent, *vislumbrar*, is used quite often. *Vislumbrar*, which means to discern, to have a feeling for, to be barely visible or something that becomes clearer over time, is a way of expressing *a gut feeling*. In business, if you know something imperfectly; are required to base your opinion on conjecture or speculation; or have a glimmering idea as to the nature of something, it is said that you are basing your decision or formed your opinion on *discernment*. The notion that there is an acuteness of judgment and understanding is a fair assessment of what is often meant in business English when someone speaks of a gut reaction; a gut instinct; or has a feeling about something. In business Spanish, all these expressions can be translated using the word *vislumbrar*.

Diskette / *Disquete*

A measure of how quickly technology changes can be seen in this paradox. Something is invented, and it comes into widespread use—such as a portable diskette for your computer—and by the time there is a consensus in Spanish as to what to call the new invention, technology has moved on. Who uses diskettes, anyway? Indeed, there are very few computers sold today that have a portal for diskettes. Nevertheless, the proper word in Spanish is *disquete*, just in case your *abuelita* wants help copying her bootleg photos of a Luis Miguel concert, looking dashing as he sings the oldies from decades gone by.

Disorder / *Enfermedad* or *Trastorno*

While we are on the subject of illnesses—were we?—if you are discussing a disorder, whether physical or emotional, be mindful that in Spanish, the equivalent word is not *desorden*. In Spanish *desorden* is used to describe a lack of order, usually in the domestic sphere, or civil disorder in the public realm. A parent will reprimand a child if his or her room is *desordenado* (a mess), and the authorities might summon the police if *desórdenes*, meaning civil disturbances, have been reported throughout the city. If the matter at hand is neither colleagues who can't keep their work areas tidy, or civil unrest, there are other words to use. A person suffering from a *disorder*—a peculiar euphemism for ailment—can be said to have an *enfermedad* (illness) or *trastorno* (an emotional or personality disorder).

(To) Displease or Upset / *Disgustado* or *Desagradar*

In life there are many displeasures, aren't there? Precisely how were you displeased or upset recently? And to what degree? Well, if it weren't bad enough to be displeased, now I'm asking to you rate the kind and level of displeasure you feel. That's upsetting right there! Unfortunately, in Spanish there are nuances to the kinds and degrees of displeasure one feels, which might speak volumes about Hispanic culture, but let's not go down that path. To displease is *disgustar*—careful, since this word has absolutely nothing to do with disgust! (Perhaps it should.) Another word for displease is *desagradar*. To be displeased with how the market is doing, or not doing, is to be *disgustado* with how stocks are faring. Remember, that there's no such word in Spanish as "desplesar," which is not unheard of among Latinos. On the other hand, simply because *disgustar* sounds very much like disgust, don't be afraid to use it if it's appropriate. In Spanish *disgustar* conveys the notion of displeasure, with the suggestion of being upset. If you displease or upset your manager, then you have *disgustado* him or *disgustada* her, meaning that more was expected of you. A more gentle way of expressing that idea is by using *desagradar*, which is more analogous to something that is disagreeable in some way. In most business Spanish uses, however, it's perfectly acceptable to characterize someone as being *disgustado* when you mean they are displeased or upset.

Distinction / *Distinción* or *Destacado* or *Sobresaliente*

This is a straightforward translation: *distinction* in English is *distinción* in Spanish. This is true whether we are speaking of business English and business Spanish, or colloquial use in either language. If the purpose of using this word is to establish something that differentiates, distinguishes as different, notes the condition of variations or discriminates between things as being different or special, then *distinción* is the word to use. Whether it is marking distinctions (*establecer una distinción*), or indicating the prerogative of acting without distinction to race or creed in promoting someone (*actuar sin distinción de raza o credo*), the word is always *distinción*. This is not to say that when people in the Spanish-speaking world want to use distinction to mean excellence they will use *distinción*. Be aware, Latino, that if the regional manager showing up to the office tomorrow is a regional manager *of distinction*, the word to use is *destacado*. If someone is distinguished, he or she is *destacado*. (*El Sr. Schmidt es un gerente regional destacado.*) In the same vein, native Spanish speakers will use *sobresaliente* to describe something that is performed or executed *with distinction*. *The team carried out the conference with distinction* is translated as *El equipo llevo a cabo la conferencia de manera sobresaliente.* If something is performed or serves in an excellent manner, then it does so *de manera sobresaliente.* Otherwise, use *distinción.*

Down Payment / *Anticipo* or *Enganche*

On occasion, in the normal course of commerce, the matter of down payments comes up. How much money should be advanced for a good or service to be delivered or performed? I'm not sure, but what I can say is that such monies advanced are tendered in *anticipation* of a good delivered or a service provided. In business Spanish that sentiment is expressed in the word that is used for down payment: *anticipo.* The *anticipo* is the money *advanced*, but be mindful that there is another word, more often used when describing personal transactions, such as buying a car or a home. If you are referring to the down payment on that brand new car, or the down payment the bank requires before it approves a mortgage, then the word often used is *enganche*, which is derived from the word "hook." It's easy to see why: a *down payment* is the *hook* that seals the deal. Either word is correct, but be mindful of the subtle distinction that exists between business Spanish and non-business Spanish usage.

Dramatic / *Drástico* or *Espectacular*

In Spanish, drama is reserved for the performing arts. Only a play can be dramatic, or a film, or the unfolding plot on a favorite *telenovela.* But if you are describing dramatic budget cuts, or a dramatic tour of the company's new facilities in China, there are different words to use in Spanish. If drama is being used to describe something that is drastic in nature (a slashed budget), the word to use is *drástico*. If, on the other hand, you are describing something that is breathtaking or eye-opening (have you been to Dubai lately?), then it is *espectacular*. As a Latino living in the United States you are well aware how American society has changed in unsettling ways over the past generation. Was it the vulgarization of American society through all these debased reality shows? Was it the hysteria that engulfed the nation after 9/11? Was it the proliferation of ratings-crazed drama-queens masquerading as news anchors on cable television news? It makes no difference, since this is where we are: Everything is described as "dramatic," when it should be described as *drastic* (*drástico*) or *spectacular* (*espectacular*).

Drop the Ball / *No Cumplir con una Promesa* or *No Cumplir con un Compromiso*

Dropping the ball is a way of saying that you've let someone down. It's a sports metaphor commonly used in business English, and one that doesn't have a corresponding phrase in business Spanish. In cases of cultural mismatches, a different phrase can be used as a substitute: *no cumplir con una promesa* or *no cumplir con un compromiso*. Either phrase conveys the idea that the person let the team down by failing to perform, or by not meeting expectations. This, of course, is an opportune moment to mention other expressions commonly used in business English that use "ball" as a metaphor for getting things done. If disappointment and failure is described as having *dropped the ball*, then success is nurtured by encouraging someone to *carry the ball*. In business Spanish, this can be described as, *cumplir con una promesa*, *cumplir con un compromiso*, or *cumplir con una responsabilidad*. Each of these phrases encapsulates the encouragement necessary to fulfill one's duties. If someone is told *to be on the ball*, in business Spanish the phrase is to *estar al tanto*. If someone needs to be told *to get on the ball*, presumably he or she has been procrastinating too long, and in business Spanish the word for that is to tell that person that he or she *necesita comenzar*. If you are being made to wait for someone to get back to you with a decision, you can remind that person that *the ball in in your court*. In business Spanish, the phrase is *la decision está en tus manos*. The paradox, of course, is that it's quite possible in business to be successful even if you drop the ball, are seldom on it, or have absolutely no idea where to find it. This realization occurred to me while watching "Morning Joe" on MSNBC. On occasion, I'll turn it on for background noise, while attending other things, occasionally looking up to see if they are saying anything sensible. There is something odd about Joe Scarborough's assembled menagerie. There is Mika Brzezinski admonishing Donnie Deutsch that he's showing more cleavage than she is. Mike Barnicle is raising his feet onto the table to show off his white socks. Willie Geist is photographed in his office with a bottle of bourbon on a shelf. Mark Halperin is calling the president a dick one day, and Donnie Deutsch is on once more trying to get back in Mika's good graces again by giving her a pair of expensive shoes, or he is saying something outrageous such as that what the Occupy Wall Street movement needs is a "Kent State moment." Or you might see Ann Coulter calling Senator John McCain a douchebag. (Did I ever tell you that Ann Coulter and I are classmates from Cornell? Yes, I could have pushed her down a flight of stairs back then when she was over at my fraternity house, but, to the world's regret, I did not. In economic theory, this is called *imperfect knowledge*: Had I known then what I know now. Of course you understand I'm joking about pushing her down the flight of stairs. Speaking of which, *ain't no joke* in business Spanish is *no te tomo el pelo*; *What a joke!* is *¡Qué chiste!*; *a practical joke* is *una broma pesada*; and *a practical joker* is *un bromador pesado*.) Now back to the other joke in question, "Morning Jo(k)e." The guests, otherwise sensible people, are paraded through for a 30-second sound bite in which they can utter a few phrases, but few complete sentences. Who dropped the ball on this? I don't know. I do know that if Latinos had a program this vacuous and disrespectful, it would be cancelled within weeks for being offensive. Or it would be moved to the Comedy Channel. Who's responsible for this mess? This mess is brewed by Starbucks.

I am critical of MSNBC's programming for one reason. MSNBC claims that "America's conversation starts here with 'Morning Joe'" when it comes to public affairs and current events. Yet, on MSNBC program after program throughout the morning and into late night, there is no Hispanic presence or voice. Almost 50 million people are excluded from MSNBC's version of "America's conversation"—and you, Latino, are one of those 50 million whose voice is absent from this conversation. In fact, MSNBC devotes an entire hour each evening to the Smarmy-American community, but not a single minute is devoted to the voice of Hispanics.

More often than not, when I do tune in to MSNBC I find myself putting "Morning Joe" on mute, while I turn on NPR, for a sensible way to start the morning. The problem with Leaning Forward is that that is precisely what Narcissus did as he admired his own reflection in a pool of water, with unfortunate consequences. There it is *en pocas palabras*, Latino. If you fail to carry the ball, or even if you drop it, it's still possible to come out ahead in the game of business.

Dude or "Bro" / *Güey* or *Wey* or *Buey*

Why is this word even listed here? For a good reason: 80% of U.S. Hispanics are of Mexican origin or ancestry. In the same way that English informs the Spanish used in the Hispanic diaspora in the United States, at times Mexican slang finds its way into the Spanish that is often heard among Latinos and Latin American immigrants. *Güey* is a very informal way of calling another man a "dude" or a "dummy." It's a vernacular (working class) way of referring to one's buddies, or just another guy. It is also slang and often used by young men joking around, often as a sense of endearment. *(¡Qué onda, güey!* means "What's up, dude?"). It can also be used to signal mistrust of someone. *(¡A ese güey no lo quiero ver!* means "No way, I don't even want to see that jerk.") The word can also be written or said as *wey*. In this case, it is used to convey some anger or frustration at a situation. *(¡Sí, wey, está carbon, tener que trabajar este fin de semana!* means "Yes, it's messed up, having to work this weekend!") *Buey* is Spanish for ox, and it is a term of endearment used by Mexican working-class immigrants. It's almost impossible not to walk past a construction site, or agricultural fields or the kitchens of restaurants without hearing young Mexican men horsing around calling each other "buey." Its origins go back to the mid-20th century when rural dwellers throughout Mexico began to migrate to the cities and encouraged one another that they had to work as hard as oxen if they hoped to make it in the big city. It was a way for manual laborers to bolser their spirits. It's a colloquialism analogous to "meat head" that was popular in the U.S. in the 1970s, or the way "dude" was bantered around in the 1980s, and how the terms "bud" and "bro" are used among buddies today. It's not an insult, but it's not good form either. In a professional business setting refrain from using this word under any circumstance, but since you are bound to hear it, you might as well be aware of its origins. Remember that however it is used in Spanish, it should never be confused with *way* in English, as in "No way." More importantly, these are words that are never, ever used by individuals in management positions.

Earnings / *Ingresos* or *Ganancias*

Have you heard the expression to be caught "like a deer in the headlights"? It means to be caught by surprise or off guard so suddenly that you cannot think or move. Quick, Latino, how do you say "earnings" in Spanish? I know you're not like a deer in the headlights. Why? Because there are several words that are crossing your mind, and you are wondering about the context in which *earnings* is used, right? *Claro, lo sabía*. It depends on the context. *Earnings* can be either *ingresos* or *ganancias*. If you refer to earnings, as in the gross income that is being generated, then the word is *ingresos*. If, on the other hand, you refer to the earnings as the revenues minus the costs of sales, applicable taxes and general operating expenses over a given time period, then the word is *ganacias*. On occasion someone will use the word *beneficios*, but usually this refers to profits (*utilidades*). In general business usage, however, become familiar with the difference between *ingresos* and *ganancias*. Consider the appropriate context in which each word is used, and you'll be fine.

Efficient / *Eficaz* or *Eficiente*

Is this the most efficient use of tree carcasses? What? I'm just wondering if a tree wasn't cut down in vain if its pulp was used to make paper on which this book is printed. God knows that *Christopher Unborn* by Carlos Fuentes is a crime against forestry. But I digress, Latino, I digress. If the matter at hand is a question of efficient use of resources, the business Spanish word is *eficaz* or *eficiente*. I hope you're not disappointed that there are two words, and that you have to think of which one might be more appropriate as situations arise. If by efficient (*eficiente*) you refer to something that functions or performs in the best or optimal manner with the least waste or effort; that which is competent or reliable; that which is satisfactory and economical to employ or use; or that which has and uses requisite knowledge, skill, know-how and industry, then use *eficiente*. If, on the other hand, you are describing the attributes of a person (*ella desempeña sus responsabilidades en una manera muy eficaz*), or a measure taken (*permitir que los empleados decidan la hora que quieren almorzar es una política eficaz*), or the force of a remedy (*el medicamento es tan eficaz que con sólo una dosis basta*), then the word to use is *eficaz*. This is one of those cases when it is a matter of elegance in usage; use *eficaz* now and then properly, and you will signal a greater command of the Spanish language.

Elaborate / *Detallado* or *Intricado* or *Complejo*

Here is one of those words that prove problematic on many levels. It would appear natural to translate "elaborate" as "elaborado," but the words don't mean the same thing in common business usage. In Spanish, *elaborado* refers to something that is intricate and detailed, and usually done by hand. It's possible to say that a wedding dress is very *elaborado*, or the detailing on the wedding cake is also very *elaborado*, or the process by which the floral arrangements were designed was *elaborado* as well. In each of these cases, the implication is that there was a good amount of handwork performed by a seamstress, a baker or a florist. In business usage, however, when you are asked to elaborate on a presentation, you are really being asked to present more details. Remember, there is a difference between details (more information) and detailing (which often means attention to handiwork). For most business usages, the Spanish-language words to use for elaborate are *detallado, intricado* or *complejo*. A manager might ask for more *detalles* about a presentation, or indicate that a proposal is very *intricado*, or that the process to be used going forward is more *complejo* than it has previously been.

E-mail / *Correo Electrónico*

In English, e-mail is shorthand for "electronic mail." In Spanish there is no abbreviation, but a straightforward translation: *correo electrónico*. In some parts of Latin America informal abbreviations are being used, such as *correl*, but words such as this one are still considered slang. Please refrain from using slang in the workplace. (Slings and arrows work better than slang, or perhaps not.) Be mindful that it's acceptable to speak of *mensajes electrónicos*, or to ask someone for their *dirección electrónica*.

Enforce / *Hacer Cumplir*

It's tempting to invent words once in a while, especially when it sounds like a real one. Take the English word *enforce* and many Latinos instantly think that *enforzar* must be the Spanish-language equivalent. I regret being the bearer of bad news, but *enforzar* does not exist in the Spanish language. In business English, however, a good number of things are asked to be enforced—from the policy on vacation pay, to the company's dress code, to the procedures governing how vendors deliver products. So which is the correct word to use in Spanish? In each of these cases, one is referring to complying with policies, rules or regulations. To ensure compliance is to demand *cumplimiento*. In consequence, in business Spanish, *hacer cumplir*, which literally means "to make comply," is the appropriate choice. *Hacer cumplir las reglas sobre la entrega de mercancia a la bodega*, is the Spanish-language equivalent of reminding someone that he or she must enforce the rules regarding the delivery of merchandise to the warehouse.

Entrepreneurial / *Empresarial*

If this word is counter-intuitive, it's understandable. *Empresa* means *a company* or *a firm*, so it seems natural to think that *empresarial* would be an adjective appropriate for a company. Unfortunately, Latino, an *entrepreneur* is an *empresario* and *entrepreneurial* is *empresarial*. The idea, of course, is that someone who is engaged in an entrepreneurial activity is enterprising, which leads us back to *empresarial*. (Be mindful that *enterprising* is *emprendedor* or *emprendedora* when used to describe someone.) In business Spanish, however, to convey the notion that an endeavor, initiative or person is *entrepreneurial*, the correct word to use is *empresarial*.

Eventual / *A la Larga*

If you are like many Latinos in the United States, you are using the word *eventual* to mean eventual. But in Spanish, eventual means *ocasional*, something that happens every once in a while, or by coincidence. That's a different meaning from the standard usage in business English, where eventual (and eventually) is used to convey the idea of something that will occur at some future point in time, or at some undetermined date. In Spanish the correct phrase to use is *a la larga*. "There will be an eventual increase in the number of staff at the customer service office," conveys the idea that the increase will come about at some indefinite point in the future, or *a la larga*. Bear in mind, however, that *eventually* usually means *finally*. In this usage, which is common in business, eventually is not *eventualmente* in Spanish. It is best translated by the phrase, *tarde o temprano*. "Eventually, all our customer support will be done online," is best translated beginning with, "*Tarde o temprano ...*"

Excited / *Emocionado*

Without a doubt, when there's good news people become excited. A new client! A new market! A new product! Even better: New responsibilities with that new promotion! How exciting! If you, however, think that *excited* in English can be translated into *excitado* in Spanish—STOP! The proper word to use when you want to express *excitement* in Spanish is *emocionado*. All the foregoing examples of good news are reason to be *emocionado*. Remember this! Why? In Spanish, the word *excitado* can mean *agitated*, but usually means *sexually aroused*. Enough said.

Expect / *Prever*

Let us say your manager sends you a confidential e-mail letting you know to brace for the worse, since more budget cuts are expected. How would you translate the word "expected"? If your answer is "esperar," then you'd be mistaken. Remember, in Spanish *esperar* is closely linked with the notion of hope, as in hopeful. Unless there is some dark streak running through your office and you are only happy when there's bad news, one would not "hope for" bad things! When the word "expect" is used to mean "anticipating" or "waiting for," the correct verb to use is *prever*. In this case one would lament that, *Se preven más recortes al presupuesto del departmento*. (Again, it would be incorrect to translate this as, *Se esperan más recortes al presupuesto del departamento*, unless you were looking forward to the budget cuts.) It's understandable that this word is so often misused by Latinos in the United States. One reason is that the word is often used incorrectly by news reporters. How many times has someone reported that officials expect the number of fatalities to increase once rescue workers reach the site of an accident? If it's reported that se *espera que la cifra de víctimas aumentará*, then the reporter is saying that he or she is hopeful there will be more fatalities. Only a misanthrope would want that! What the reporter should be saying is that *se prevé que la cifra de víctimas aumentará*, which is something that, should it come to pass, will make no one happy.

Expiration / *Vencimiento* or *Caducidad*

If someone is said to have expired, that's the end of their career, isn't it? Fortunately, in most business usages, expiration seldom refers to death. What expiration refers to is the conclusion of a contract, period of guarantee or the end of an offer. The promotion on the 2 for 1 deal expired yesterday, a store manager might tell a tardy customer. The expiration date on this bottle of aspirin is four months from now, someone might point out as you wonder if the box of medicine in the break room is good. These kinds of expirations are common, and the word in Spanish is not *expiración*. The correct word is *vencimiento*. In business Spanish, *vencimiento* refers to the period of time when a (product or service) guarantee, contract or term runs out. It also refers to the time when a maturity, such as a bond or financial investment, comes due. It also indicates the date when a payment falls due. (If you have to make your mortgage payment on the first of the month, and today is March 1, then the *vencimiento del pago* is today.) It's worth noting that *vencimiento* also means victory, since it is used in political rhetoric as a term for being victorious: *El vencimiento de la revolución* ... But unless you're office is run by Che Guevara, chances are that the *vencimientos* that will concern you have to do with the maturity of your Certificate of Deposit (CD), or when the 2 for 1 promotion your company is running expires. In addition, while *expiración* is associated with death, the equivalent of expiry in English, there is another business meaning to *expiration*. These are the "sell-by dates" often found on the packaging of products, and are of great importance in the food and pharmaceutical industries. It's a natural, and understandable, mistake many Latinos in the United States make when they want to translate *Expiration Date* they end up saying *Fecha de Expiración*, when it should be *Fecha de Caducidad*. Unless you know something no one else knows ... it's impossible to know someone's *death date* beforehand.

The only exception that I can think of concerns people on Death Row whose execution date has been published, and there is no hope of the Supreme Court intervening, or a pardon being granted. But how often is that? In business Spanish, *expiration date* will almost always be *fecha de caducidad*.

Fabrication / *Falsificación*

Here is another word that is used in business with greater frequency, unfortunately. In business English, fabrication is used to denote something that is false. The figures were fabricated in this report, or the product was manufactured (fabricated) in violation of existing patents, meaning it is counterfeit. Yikes! Sounds like pirating to me, doesn't it? It would be wrong to translate this as *fabricar*. In Spanish, *fabricar* is used to describe something that is manufactured or assembled, and is a value-neutral word, meaning that there is no suggestion that something that is *fabricado* is in any way improper or unlawful. The correct word to use for fabrication is *falsificación*. In business usage, fabrication is almost always used to speak of something that is false, and not in its other meaning of the word, which something that is *manufactured*. Alas, such is the way of the world!

Facilities / *Instalaciones*

After months of delay, your employer announces that the new facilities are ready and everyone will be moving early next month. Hooray! After setbacks and delays, it is done. But how do you tell your mother the good news? Well, if you think facilities can be translated into Spanish as *facilidades* ... oh, no, you are going to confuse your poor *mamacita*. In Spanish *facilidades* means ease, of various kinds. One can have a gift for something (*tener la facilidades para los idiomas*, meaning a gift for languages) or one can enjoy preferential *facilidades de crédito*, meaning easy payment terms, at the bank. But if you are talking about a new building, offices, factory or corporate campus, you are speaking about the *instalaciones*. Of course you can refer to the new swank offices as being in a new building, which is *edificio*. But for facilities—which encompass all manner of workplaces—use *instalaciones*.

Fallacy / *Engaño* or *Mentira*

It's a fallacy that Latinos are not management material. But it still is an erroneous and false idea among upper management throughout corporate America, I'm afraid. Notice how I defined fallacy in the sentence above: Erroneous and false idea. That's a *fallacy*. In Spanish, on the other hand, *falacia* means something altogether different. *Falacia* does, indeed, mean an untruth, but there is the connotation that there is something sinister under foot. A *falacia* implies the deliberate attempt to deceive or defraud someone through duplicity. That's probably more than you want to imply when you use the word "fallacy" in a business setting. This is the reason a fallacy can best be translated into Spanish as *un engaño* (a deceit or falsehood) or *una mentira* (a lie). And that's the truth.

Fast Food versus Junk Food / *Comida Rápida* versus *Comida Chatarra*

What is the difference between fast food and junk food? Who can say for sure, but usually fast food is purchased at a restaurant, and junk food can be bought at a convenience store. That's not to say that fast food isn't junk food as well, or that convenience stores don't sell junk food that is served up fast, either from the deli counter or the self-serve island. But it makes no difference, since, as a Supreme Court justice once said about another matter, you know it when you see it. That said, the standard nomenclature when speaking Spanish is that *fast food* is *comida rápida*, a straightforward translation of the English-language phrase. Junk food, however, is a bit more problematic: What does one mean by "junk"? Just empty calories? Or something that actually harms one's health? The linguistic consensus in Spanish is that junk food is just that: junk. The term *comida chatarra*—where "chatarra" refers to scrap metal and the stuff one finds at a junk yard—is now the most widely-accepted term throughout Latin America. Be mindful, however, that in Spain the preferred phrase is *comida basura*, and "basura" means garbage. Bon Appétit!

Feeling / *Impresion*

If you've read this far, I hope you're getting a good feeling about what I am sharing with you, and that your confidence is increasing now that you understand how simple it is to become proficient in business Spanish. That's my goal, after all. If you agree with my characterization, how would you describe, in a business sense, your feelings? Remember that in business, when we speak of feelings, we are speaking about instincts, gut reactions, an assessment of some kind, and not at all about *sentiments*. There's a difference. It's possible to have a good feeling about a client, or have misgivings about a colleague, and not mean any sentimental emotion. In business Spanish the word to use is *impresion*, which has positive connotations. "I have a good feeling about our new colleagues," is best translated as, "Tengo una buena impresion de nuestros colegas nuevos." In business, feelings are always *impresiones*, and not *sentimientos*—unless someone is leaving the company and you will miss their friendship. Then it's fine to get misty-eyed, one more reason to befriend him or her on Facebook. Be mindful that the other meaning of *impresion* is a print run, such as the number of books published in an edition, but in general business use, *impresion* refers to one's feelings about a person, situation or project.

Field / *Campo*

No, I'm not referring to Strawberry Fields, or any other kind of field, such as the ones where cows pasture. (Do cows pasture in fields any more?) Bovine lifestyles aside, if the word *field* is used in any technological sense, the correct Spanish-language word is *campo*. This sentence, "The first *field* on the form is your name," is properly translated as "El primer *campo* en el formulario es su nombre." When it comes to a form, on paper or online, *field* is always *campo*. And this is true, regardless of where Elsie the Cow is spending her time!

Figures / *Cifras*

Go figure! No, not that kind of figure! And I don't mean *your* figure, however shapely or unshapely it may happen to be. If you are speaking of someone's body shape, then you mean *figura*. If you are speaking of someone's standing—she is a leading figure in the community—you also mean *figura*. (*Ella es una figura destacada en la comunidad*.) If you mean a figure in a book or report, you can use *figura* or *ilustración*. But if you are referring to figures as in numbers or statistics, then the word to use is *cifra*. This is the most common translation of *figure* when speaking business Spanish in the United States. Sales figures in Spanish is expressed as "cifras de ventas." Monthly figures in Spanish is expressed as "cifras del mes." One can speak of depositing the sum of a million dollars, which in Spanish would be, *la cifra de un millón de dólares*. One can estimate that the figures have risen as expected, expressing the same thought in Spanish as, *Se estima que las cifras han subido como esperábamos*. If a figure has to do with numbers, then it is about *cifra* and *cifras*.

File / *Expediente*

The world is full of files, isn't it? A generation ago, we all were told that with technological advances in personal computers, online record retrieval and sophisticated electronic record-keeping, paper would go the way of the three-martini lunch and smoking in the conference room. (Alas, the good old days of yore!) In fact, now that I think about it, it was *Business Week* back in June 1975 that had an article titled "The Office of the Future," and that office of the future didn't have paper! Then why are files full of paper sliding across my credenza? I am shaking my head, but it makes no difference. Suffice it to say that *a file* in business Spanish is *un expediente*. The idea of a *file* as *a collection of related papers belonging to a specific matter* is an accurate definition of *expediente*. Be mindful, however, that *expediente* also has another meaning: it is a file opened in connection with an inquiry or investigation. *To open a file* on someone, or *abrir un expediente*, is to begin to compose a dossier. This is usually done in a business context for the purpose of taking disciplinary action or to start proceedings againt an employee. While it is good to have your files in order, having a file opened on you should be reason for caution.

Findings / *Conclusiones* or *Hallazgos*

What were the committee's findings? To which committee are you referring? The one that was looking for Bernie Madoff's billions, or the one charged with determining whether the staff prefers Pepsi over Coke in the break room? *Findings* in the business world are conclusions, discoveries or information that are ascertained. *Findings* are the facts that help management formulate policies and strategies. *Findings* are the solid research that gives managers confidence as they implement the company's plans. In business Spanish, *findings* can be translated as *conclusiones* or *hallazgos*. *Conclusiones* are the facts that one reaches after all considerations have been taken into account. *Hallazgos* are the facts that offer insights, often in unexpected ways. The difference is nuanced. They are the subtleites between saying, "Well, we've come to the conclusion that most employees prefer Coke over Pepsi," and saying, "We have to report the recent discovery of a bank account in the Cayman Islands with $1 billion linked to Bernie Madoff." In the former case, this finding is a *conclusion*. In the latter one, such a finding is one great *hallazgo*.

Finicky / *Especial*

There's only one reason this word is included: in Mexican Spanish *especial* means both *special* and *finicky*.

It's a polite way to describe someone who is finicky about things. "Remember to order one sandwich without lettuce because Mr. Smith will not eat anything that has lettuce," one person might tell the other who is ordering lunch for the meeting. "He's finicky." In Spanish, Mr. Smith would be described as being "especial." It's important to know that the word *especial* may not mean *special*, but rather, *finicky*. I just wanted you to know; I'm finicky that way about words.

First Name / *Nombre*

Last name first and first name last is a common request in English. That means that John Smith is being asked to write his name as Smith, John. This is a natural way of expressing this request because in business English Americans are accustomed to using the "first name" and "last name" formulation, rather than resorting to distinguishing between a *given name* and a *surname*. In Spanish, on the other hand, one's first name is referred to as *nombre*, and one's last name is called *apellido*. To say *primer nombre*—first name—becomes a redundancy, and like most redundancies, they are unnecessary by definition. (Be mindful that if you are asking someone for their first name, it's not uncommon for someone to refer to *nombre de pila*, a reference to the name given at baptism, since *pila* is a baptismal font.) In the course of business, should you come across the expression *su nombre me suena*, it means that your name rings a bell or sounds familiar to the speaker. If your manager is only your manager in *name* only, one way of saying that in Spanish is, *Es nominalmente mi gerente*. The bottom line, however, is that in Spanish it's enough to say *nombre* when one is referring to someone's first name, and *apellido* when speaking of someone's last name.

First of All / *Antes que Nada*

First of all, I want to commend you for reading this far, and I hope you are learning a few things, while enjoying yourself. Second of all, what's the deal with Latinos walking around saying "Primero de todo" as if that made any sense in Spanish? Ah, yes, now I get it! It's an *anglicismo—first of all* becomes *primero de todo*. Sorry, but no it doesn't. The proper business Spanish expression that corresponds to "first of all" is "antes que nada," which literally means, before anything. *Antes que nada le quiero encomiar ...* is how the first sentence in this entry would be translated into business Spanish. (*Encomiar* is Spanish for *to commend*, by the way.) On occasion, you might also want to use the phrase *en primer lugar*, which literally means, *in first place*, but for most business situations I recommend *antes que nada*. The reason is that *en primer lugar* suggests that there are other announcements before getting on with the set agenda, and that may not be the case. You may just want to say, *Antes que nada, quiero reconocer el excelente trabajo del departamento de contabilidad*, by way of saying that first of all you want to recognize the excellent work done by accounting and then proceed to the business at hand. Remember, *antes que nada*. Get in the habit of saying "Antes que nada ..." and never, ever "primero de todo."

(The) First Thing / *Lo Primero*

What's the first thing on the agenda? Adjourning the meeting, I hope! Of course I'm being foolish, since you and I both know that many minutes will drag on before this meeting is adjourned. But now that we are all assembled for the meeting, what is The First Thing on the agenda? If it's speaking Spanish properly, then the phrase *la primera cosa* is nowhere in sight! Too many

Latinos in the U.S. mistakenly believe that a word-for-word translation of the phrase, "the first thing" results in proper business Spanish. That's not the case. The proper phrase is *lo primero*. What's the first thing on the agenda? *Lo primero es* ... and then continue with whatever happens to be the first thing on the agenda. Adjourning the meeting is still what I'm hoping to hear!

Folders / *Carpetas*

Perhaps at some future point the Latino tendency to say *folder* (or in the plural, "fólderes") when they mean *carpeta*, will not send shivers through the spines of fluent Spanish speakers. Until that day arrives, be very careful, since snap judgments are made when a gaffe of this nature is made. Papers are filed or kept in a *carpeta*, not a *folder*. Please refrain from using English words for simple objects around the office. A pencil is a *lápiz*. A pen is a *pluma*. A briefcase is a *maletín*. A stapler is an *engrapadora*. A folder is a *carpeta*. A printer is an *impresora*. A computer is a *computadora*. A cell phone is a *teléfono celular*. But, of course, with so many new gadgets coming into use, there is still an emerging consensus on the proper Spanish-language equivalents. A laptop is really a computer-on-the-go, so the terms used in Spanish are several: *computadora portátil* (most common in Latin America) or *ordenador portátil* (often used in Spain), or even *computo portátil* (occasionally used). Be also aware that iPhone, iPad, Blackberry and so forth are *brands*, not distinct gadgets, and most are combinations of cell phones and laptops, which means they fall in those categories. Feel free to use iPhone or Blackberry, just make sure that you turn them off and put them away in your *maletín* before the meeting begins!

Follow Up / *Seguimiento*

What's one of the most important things in business? It's following up and following through on leads. There's no need for me to point that out. Many times, the contacts made at a conference or convention result in considerable stack of brochures, pamphlets and business cards. Who has the time to go through and compose follow-up hand-written notes? Yes, I'm old school that way and actually send a written note, probably because I have fond memories of receiving letters in the mail as a youngster, and I think it's special when someone receives a hand-written note. Whether by e-mail, or text message, or a note written on Crane's stationery, follow-up is important. Many Latinos make the mistake of believing that there is no Spanish-language equivalent for follow-up, probably because in English it looks like a recent invention by virtue of it being a hyphenated two-word phrase. Following up on business is as old as human commerce. If you say, "El programa de *follow-up* después de la convención está lista," then you'd be making a grave mistake. Yes, it is great that there is a program for following up after the convention, but that's not how to express it in Spanish. The word is *seguimiento*, from *seguir*, meaning to follow. If you have *un programa de seguimiento*, then say so correctly in Spanish!

Forecast / *Pronóstico* or *Previsión*

Forecast? Night followed by day, with dismal weather forecasts in between. Oh, wait, that's my forecast for what the Weather Channel will be reporting tomorrow. When it comes to forecasts, in business we mean predicting, calculating or anticipating a future condtion; or to plan or conjecture beforehand. These are *forecasts* that can be used successfully in business planning and development. During times of greater economic uncertainty and stock market volatility, the ability to develop concise *forecasts* of likely events is all the more crucial. In business Spanish the words *pronóstico* or *previsión* are used. What is the difference between these words, you ask? *Pronóstico* is more closely associated with a prognosis, and as a result it is used primarily when forecasting the weather (*pronóstico meteorológico*), or in medicine (*un pronóstico grave* is a serious condition). A *previsión*, on the other hand, is more closely associated with a judicious or informed forecast of likely events or scenarios. Depending on the context either word can be used. In most cases these words are used interchangeably in business Spanish. A general observation is that *pronóstico* is more often used in Latin America and *previsión* tends to be preferred in Spain.

(To) Format / *Formatear*

How do you describe the action of formatting a computer disk? Well, there is now a new verb to describe this action: *Formatear*. The definition in Spanish is the same as in English: To format a disk or diskette. A disk can be described as being formatted (*formateado*) and the act of formatting is *formateo*. Bear in mind that if you are referring to the format of a meeting, an article or a presentation, such as "What's the format of the meeting?" or "Is this the right format for the annual report?" there is a different word. It is *formato*. "¿Cuál es el formato de la presentación?" or "¿Es este el formato para el informe anual?"

Forms / *Planilla* or *Formulario*

If you're asked to fill out a form for whatever reason—whether it's at the dentist's office, returning an item at a store, or by the HR department—what you are being asked to do is to fill out a *planilla* or *formulario*. While *forma* is a word in Spanish, and it has many meanings, none includes a piece of paper asking for information to be used for bureaucratic or clerical purposes. Stick with either *planilla* or *formulario* when speaking Spanish and you will be universally understood by listeners.

Freeway and Highway / *Autopista*

Another common example of English creeping into the Spanish spoken by Latinos in the United States is evident in everyday words. A client is arriving for a meeting and she wants to know the easiest way to get to your office, since she's renting a car at the airport. Just get on the freeway once you exit, and in no time, you'll be there, since the office is only a few miles from the interstate highway. If you try to say that in Spanish, chances are that you will be using "freeway" and "highway" without even thinking about the directions. The proper word in Spanish for either "freeway" or "highway" is *autopista*.

Frequently / *Frecuentemente* or *A Menudo*

How often do you check your e-mail? If you're like most people it is frequently. In Spanish, of course, the word for *frequently* is *frecuentemente*. Frequent is *frecuente* and frequently is *frecuentemente*. There's nothing wrong with using *frecuentemente* to mean *frequently*. Then again, here we have a case where language becomes a matter of style and elegance. As you advance in your career, you will find that there will be times when how you say things is as important as saying them properly. How frequently do I check my e-mail? *A menudo*, I tend to reply. I sometimes say, *con frecuencia*.

Whichever one you prefer, try to get in the habit of using *a menudo* or *con frecuencia* to describe something that is done with frequency. It's an elegant expression that will set you apart from others.

Full-Time and Part-Time / *Tiempo Completo* and *Tiempo Parcial*

The question of full-time versus part-time employment is one that vexes Latinos, since as a demographic group, they are among the ones who have suffered more during the economic challenges confronting the world since the real estate bust. But how do you translate these phrases? The most commonly-used expressions are *tiempo completo* and *tiempo parcial*. *Afortunadamente trabajo a tiempo completo*, means you fortunately are employed full-time. Be mindful, however, that in some places the phrases *jornada completa*, or *media jornada* are used. In these cases, *jornada* means a working day, and it is derived from the fact that *jornada* means the time in the course of a day, hence a journal in English is what you record as having done or carried out in the course of a day, and a journey is the distance one could travel by land from sunrise to sunset.

(To) Furnish or (To) Provide / *Proporcionar*

No, I'm not referring to furnishing your office, gentle reader. What I am referring to is the annoying habit of Latinos of thinking that *dar* (to give) is an appropriate word to use in a business setting. You can give this or that to whomever, and whenever, you like, but if you're in a business setting, it's best to use business language. When speaking business English, for instance, you refer to the goods furnished by this company and the services provided by that firm. In business Spanish the word to use is *proporcionar*. The concept is to create symmetry, and as such, one party provides another with this or that in exchange (usually) for an agreed-upon payment. "Nuestra empresa proporciona servicios de transporte terrestre," simply means that your firm provides ground transportation services. Take note, however, that in a non-business setting, *proporcionar* is often used to mean *cause*. "Esa vecina sólo proporciona disgustos," meaning that that neighbor only causes trouble. Every neighborhood has one of those, if not several, right?

G

Get it Together / *Organizarse* or *Nos Organizamos*

Getting it together in business is different from getting it together in your personal life. It's one thing to tell a teenager to get it together and clean up her room, or to tell your brother to pull himself together after he learns that one of your parents has been diagnosed with cancer, or to look at yourself in the mirror and tell yourself that you have to keep it together even if it's going to be one of those days. It's another to discuss, in a business setting, about getting things together. In business, one is probably referring to organizing things for a project or an initiative. In Spanish the idea of getting things together is expressed by speaking about becoming organized. *Organizar, organizarse* or the phrase *nos organizamos* succinctly convey this concept. *Nos organizamos para afinar el plan de mercadotecnia* is one way of expressing the idea that you are getting it together to fine-tune the marketing plan. Be advised, however, that it's one thing to get it together, and quite another to keep it together.

Homepage / *Inicio*

Will technology ever stop long enough for us to catch our breath? I doubt it! So it's only natural for language to struggle to keep up with changes. With this caveat out of the way, let's get back to business. How do you say homepage in Spanish? That depends on what you mean. Homepage, in the sense of returning to the first page of a website, is *Inicio*. A few years ago, it was called *Página Principal*, literally, principal page, but the consensus now is to use *Inicio*. This consensus emerged simply because *El País*, one of the leading Spanish-language newspapers in the world, settled on using the world *Inicio* to let visitors to its website know how to return to the "front page" of its online edition. As a result, most websites have adopted *Inicio* to denote the homepage on their websites. When speaking business Spanish, so should you.

Hope (for) / *Expectativas* or *Prever*

Hope springs eternal, poets tell us. In business, however, hoping for something is less poetic, and more pragmatic. Be mindful that translating hope for the word *esperar* is not always a perfect fit. In Spanish the word *esperar* implies something that you wish will come true, but in English, hoping for something, not unlike waiting for something, is a more neutral expectation. This is the reason it's preferable to use *expectativa* or *prever* in many cases. What is the thing being hoped for? If it a value-neutral thing, then *expectativa* might be the better fit. "We are hoping for the delivery of the merchandise this week," is a rather mundane expectation. "Nuestras expectativas son que se entregue la mercancia esta semana," would be a fair way of translating this declaration. It conveys a positive message—*expectativas* are almost always good things—in a professional manner. On the other hand, if you are waiting for a downward revision in last quarter's profits, or are expecting the sales to be worse than anticipated, then use the verb *prever*. "Se prevé que ..." In business, when you are hoping for just about anything, it's best to express this as *expectativas* or as *prever*, depending on the context.

Hyphen / *Guión*

I'll bet that often enough you are linguistically lazy. (Yes, there is such a condition, although it is not recognized by the American Medical Association.) When that happens, instead of saying the two-syllable word, "hyphen," you prefer to say the one-syllable word, "dash." Example? "The tracking number is A, B, C, dash, one, two, three." But in the tracking number "ABC-123" we both know that there's no dash. But there is a hyphen. Which leads me to the question: How do you say "hyphen" in Spanish? The answer is *guión*. Yes, I know, it's a two-syllable word ... and if you would like to believe that "dash" in Spanish might be a one-syllable word, I'm sorry to tell you but you are out of luck. Dash in Spanish is *raya*. Alas. Look at the good news: Now that you know that hyphen is *guión*, you can use it properly. To the query: "By the way, did that package I sent to our client in Kyoto arrive?" now you can reply, "Perhaps the easiest way to find out is to go online and look up the tracking number." Remember that this scenario is unfolding while we're at a conference in Madrid, and the situation calls for speaking Spanish only. Then I answer, "El número del envío es A, B, C, guión 1, 2, 3, 4, 5, 6, 7, 8, 9, 0." See? You didn't say, "¿Qué?" when I said "guión," since you know that *guión* means hyphen! That was easy, wasn't it? Stick to *guión*, since that's the proper word when speaking business Spanish.

I Don't Know / *No Se* or *Ignoro*

Of course there's really no point in telling you that "I don't know" in Spanish is "no se." It's straightforward enough. But what many Latinos in the United States don't know is that, in a business setting, a more professional way of expressing lack of knowledge or information is by using the word *ignorar*. At first it may appear odd that the verb for ignorance is used to characterize not knowing, but unlike in English, in Spanish there is no negative connotation to *ignorar*. The word is innocuous in how it is used: *Ignoro la temperatura en Roma*. This simply means you don't know the temperature in Rome. That's what the Weather Channel is for, right? So don't be afraid to use *ignoro* when you want to say that you don't know last week's sales figures, or whether the overnight package arrived early this morning, or how investors are reacting to the company's press release on earnings issued after the markets closed yesterday evening. *Ignoro las cifras ... Ignoro si el envío ha llegado... Ignoro la reacción de los inversionistas ...* are all appropriate phrases to express not knowing something. But if you don't know, find out! That will be all the more impressive. Then again, what do I know?

Ignore / *No Hacer Caso*

In business English when you are asked to ignore something, what you are being asked to do is to disregard it. "Ignore for a moment that headquarters has not approved such an approach," your manager might ask you in the course of discussing various options on this or that. How would you translate into Spanish? It would be a mistake to use "ignorar," since that implies a lack of knowledge or fact. What your manager is, in fact, asking you to do is to disregard a known fact in a hypothetical situation. The correct phrase to use is Spanish is "no hacer caso," which means, "pay no mind" to something. Ignore it, in other words.

In Addition to / *Además de*

This is one of those cases when it is a matter of form, and not of being misunderstood. The *anglicismo* "en adición a" is very common among Latinos who simply translate the English-language phrase "in addition to" when speaking. There's no danger of being misunderstood, but be mindful that the proper phrase in Spanish is "además de." If you wanted to say that in addition to the problems the department has encountered, the accountant announced his resignation, there are several ways of reporting this in Spanish. "Además de los problemas que el departamento ha tropezado, el contador anunció su dimisión," is perfectly acceptable.

Including / *Incluido* or *Inclusive*

Which are the services this vendor is contractually obligated to provide? Who knows, since I don't have a copy of the Scope of Services from the contract in front of me at the moment. But whichever services are included, it would be a mistake to translate this into Spanish by using the word *incluyendo*. Remember, in English "including" is both a gerund and a participle, while in Spanish, "incluyendo" is only a gerund. What does this mean? That when you want to point out that the Scope of Services contemplates providing this or that to your offices throughout the region, including Boston and Providence, then the right way of saying this in Spanish would be: "El vendedor proporcionará servicios a las ciudades de la región, inclusive Boston y Providence," or "El vendedor proporcionará servicios a las ciudades de la región, incluido Boston y Providence."

Industry / *Giro*

In what industry do you work? Quick! Translate that into business Spanish? I'm sorry, but if you automatically said *industria*, you could have made a better choice. *Industria*, as is the case in business English, usually refers to manufacturing, or certain service industries, such as tourism or entertainment. One can speak of light industry (*industria ligera*) or heavy industry (*industria pesada*). One can speak of the tourist industry (*sector turístico*) or entertainment industry (*sector del espectáculo*), and one can speak of specific industries (*industria naviera* is Spanish for the shipping industry; *industria aeronáutica* is Spanish for the aircraft industry, etc.). One can also speak of industry as hard work (*aplicación* or *labor* or *trabajo útil*). In general use, however, when one asks you about your industry, they want to know the field of work in which you are involved, and the word for that is *giro*. In business Spanish you will also hear the expression *¿A qué te dedicas?* Literally it means, To what do you dedicate yourself? Figuratively it means, What do you do for a living? Then you reply, and the conversation ensues about the *giro* (industry) in which you work. Be mindful, of course, that *giro* means other things: to turn (a helicopter rises because of *el giro del rotor en el eje vertical*); a money order (*giro postal* or *giro telegráfico*), a bank draft (*giros bancarios* are *órdenes de pago*). In general business terms, however, giro refers to the business or industry in which a commercial activity is engaged. What's my *giro*? Do you mean right now? I'm in the business of compiling a glossary of indispensible words and phrases used in business Spanish.

(To) Influence / *Influir*

This is one of those cases when it's a matter of style, and not grammar. Yes, *influenciar* is word in Spanish, which means to influence. Yes, you would be perfectly understood if you were to say, *Fuimos influecidos por la presentación* (We were influenced by the presentation), but this is incorrect. In business Spanish, however, there is another verb, more concise and elegant, that is used in professional settings: *influir*. *Fuimos influidos por la presentación* is more elegant and concise, and the preferred usage. Remember that this is one of the litmus test words; know it, use it, and your influence in the business world will flourish.

Ingenuity / *Ingenio* or *Inventiva*

What is ingenuity? It's one of the characteristics necessary to create new products and services that have the power to change business. Think of William Austin Burt who, in 1829 secured a patent for the "typographer," and is now widely credited with having invented the typewriter. That example of ingenuity certainly changed the way business was conducted for more than a century and a half, didn't it? But how do you say ingenuity in business Spanish? The fact that I'm asking that question, of course, means that the answer is not *ingenuidad*. In Spanish, ingenuity is either *ingenio* or *inventiva*. These words adequately describe the ingenuity that Steven Jobs, for instance, showed in creating so many of the wonderful machines that allow us to live our lives the way we do at the beginning of the 21st century. (Praise or blame him, depending on your perspective is all I can say!) Oh, yes, before I forget: What of *ingenuidad*? In Spanish, *ingenuidad* refers to candor, frankness, ingenuousness and openness. As a general observation, the older one becomes, the more *ingenuidad* one displays. Think of the candor Katherine Hepburn displayed near the end of her life when she spoke of the tawdry affairs of her youth, or of your *abuelito* describing things that, half a century later, really don't matter, so he feels comfortable opening up and speaking from his heart.

International and Domestic / *Internacional* and *Nacional*

It's peculiar to see opposites mixed and matched. If foreign is the opposite of domestic and international is the opposite of national, one would expect to see them paired together in a consistent form. One does—but not always in English! First, consider the logic of consistency. In the U.S. military, for instance, the oath of enlistment is logical, since one takes an oath "to support and defend the Constitution of the United States against all enemies, foreign and domestic." One does not take an oath to defend against all enemies, international and domestic. But outside the military, logic breaks down in the business world of civilians. Consider, say, airports throughout the country. Arrive at any airport in the United States, and there it is: One terminal for international departures and international arrivals, and another terminal for domestic departures and domestic arrivals. *¡Qué confusión!* Why isn't there a terminal for foreign departures and foreign arrivals, or another terminal for national departures and national arrivals? If a flight originates in New York bound for London, then that's an international (or foreign) flight. If another flight originates in New York bound for Los Angeles, then that's a national (or domestic) flight. So much for American logic, Latino! That means you have to be cognizant that when speaking in Spanish, linguistic logic prevails. Airports throughout the Spanish-speaking world have terminals for *vuelos internacionales* and for *vuelos nacionales*. That's it. Throughout the Spanish-speaking world you will never find a terminal anywhere for *vuelos domésticos*. Why? The reason is that in Spanish, *doméstico* is used exclusively to refer to things that pertain to a household. A domestic appliance, such as a refrigerator, is something normally found in a home. That means that, when speaking Spanish, unless you happen to live in a house large enough for a flight to take off in your living room and fly you to your dining room, there are no such things as *vuelos domésticos*. When it comes to air travel, it is always a question of *vuelos internacionales* or *vuelos nacionales*.

Internet / *La Internet*

Is "Internet" masculine or feminine? Is it *la Internet* or *el Internet*? Inquiring Latinos want to know. Well, the answer is actually arbitrary, and it was decided upon by the Spanish Royal Academy. In an effort to be consistent and find a logical answer to this question, it settled on the following rationale: since network (*red*) is feminine (*la red mundial*, meaning the worldwide web), then Internet should also be feminine. It's *la Internet*. All the problems in the world should be this easy to solve!

Introduce / *Introducir* or *Presentar*

Now, if you would please turn off all distractions for a second. This is one of those vexing words that trip up Latinos all the time. "Introduce" in English is a multi-tasking word that has many meanings. One can introduce a disk into the computer to get things going, or one can introduce a friend to a colleague so they make each other's acquaintance. Not so in Spanish! If you are speaking about an instruction manual that indicates you have to introduce a disk into a hard drive, then the word to use is *introducir*. In Spanish, *introducir* means to put one thing inside another. If on the other hand you are referring to introducing one person to another one, then the word to use is *presentar*. "I would like to introduce the new director to you," is best translated as "Me gustaría presentarte el nuevo director." It's a bit more elegant, a throwback to the late 19th and early 20th centuries when people commonly had "presentation" cards with their names, and the act of presenting one person to another had more formality. In Spanish this continues, and as such, be aware of the difference between introducing one object into another, and presenting one person to another.

It's a Deal / *Trato Hecho*

Few things are as rewarding as getting to yes. In fact, there's a book by that name. When you get to yes, it's a deal. How do you say that in Spanish? It's a deal, becomes, *trato hecho*. A deal, *trato*, is derived from treaty, which makes it easy enough to remember. Of course, a deal is also a kind of accord or agreement, and in many business situations certain phrases are more accurately translated using some of these words. If you are brokering a deal, this, in business Spanish, is *negociando un acuerdo*. If you are closing the deal, then in business Spanish, one says you are *cerrando el acuerdo*. What if you return to the office and someone says that it's a raw deal? In Spanish that would be *un trato injusto*. Tell that to your mentor who wants to encourage you by saying not to worry about it, since it's no big deal. In business Spanish, that's *no es para tanto*. That's great, because another colleague tells you that, good or bad, you have to deal with it, or in business Spanish, *aguantarte*. That is, of course, until next time, when you are likely to deal a winning hand. In business Spanish, that would be *repartir la mano ganadora*. It's a deal. *Trato hecho*.

L

Lacks / *Carece*

What do you find lacking about your job? There must be something. No one has the perfect job, and even if it were the perfect job not everything about it a source of pleasure all the time. What do you find lacking in your boss? Does your boss find anything lacking in your performance? Lacking is to want something, to be without, a kind of deficiency. How do you translate this into Spanish? It's an uncommon word, of course, but it's one that's used in business all the time. "We found your company's proposal to be lacking," one might hear after their bid was rejected. "The regional office's performance is consistently found to be lacking," is a statement that foreshadows a shake-up in regional directors. "This candidate's qualifications were found lacking compared with others who applied for the same position," a hiring officer might say. In each of these cases the word *lacking* corresponds to *carecer* in Spanish. A job candidate *carece de experiencia* means that the candidate is lacking in experience. If a proposal *carece de sentido*, it is a non-starter simply because it doesn't make any sense. A department that *carece de personal* is short-staffed. Remember that if it's lacking, it means that it's *careciendo algo*—something that can't be said of your business Spanish, right?

Latin America / *América Latina* or *Latinoamérica* versus *Hispanoamérica*

If you thought I was going to make this easy, then you are mistaken. What is the proper way of saying "Latin America" in Spanish? There are two equally proper ways of translating "Latin America." One is "América Latina" and the other is "Latinoamérica." Either term refers to the nations in the Western Hemisphere where a language derived from Latin is spoken. The languages are Spanish, Portuguese and French. (Nations where English and Dutch are spoken are not part of Latin America.) If you want to refer only to those nations where Spanish is the official language, then the term for that is *Hispanoamérica*. Why is that you ask? The answer is that *hispano* simply means that which is related to the Spanish language. Mexico and Argentina are part of *Hispanoamérica*, but Brazil is not.

Lawsuit / *Pleito* or *Litigio* or *Demanda*

In life, there are many lawsuits. In the United States, there are too many lawsuits. In business Spanish there are several words used for *lawsuit*. They reflect colloquial usage and regional preferences throughout the Spanish-speaking world. In the same way that in English litigation, proceeding, suit or claim are used to mean lawsuit, in Spanish the words *pleito* or *litigio* are used to mean lawsuit. Either of these two words is universally understood throughout the Spanish-speaking world. In Mexico, however, *demanda*—meaning a legal demand—is commonly used. It's important to be aware of this, simply because a disproportionate amount of business transactions that require business Spanish centers on dealing with Mexico. I would suggest that you use either *plieto* or *litigio* when you mean lawsuit, but if you should happen to encounter *demanda*, you now know that the speaker or writer refers to a lawsuit, not a request. Please don't confuse *demanding* with *demandando*. To demand in English is *exigir* in Spanish. (See, (To) Demand for clarification.) *Demandar* in Spanish is *to sue* in English. A *demanda* is a *lawsuit*. And a lawsuit is always a *pleito*, *litigio* or *demanda*.

Lead / *Liderar*

Who is going to lead this initiative? Don't look at me, since my leadership days are over! But someone has to lead? Might that be you? *Lead* in business Spanish is *liderar*. *Leadership* in business Spanish is *liderazgo*, or *dirección*. The difference is that *liderazgo* refers to the quality of leadership, whereas *dirección* refers to the people in charge, or upper management. If it's a question of being a leader, the business Spanish word to use is *líder*. Yes, that's a word, not Spanglish! *Líder*. Funny, isn't it? When it's a matter of leading, leadership and being a leader, the words are *liderar*, *liderazgo* and *líder*. I have to warn you, however, that in many business English expressions that use the word *lead*, other words are used in Spanish. If you lead by example, in Spanish it is *predicar con el ejemplo*. If you are asked to lead the way, then it's *enseñar el camino*. If something will only lead to trouble, then it will *sólo te dará problemas*. If you need to lead someone by the nose, then it's *tener agarrado por las narices*. And of course, you can lead a horse to water but you can't make him drink, in Spanish, it is *puedes darle un consejo a alguien pero no puedes obligarlo a que lo siga*. (Horse analogies are seldom used in business Spanish. Using bulls, on the other hand, is a different manner. If you want to translate *taking the bull by the horns*, in Spanish that's said, *tomar el toro por los cuernos*. If someone is *as strong as a bull*, in Spanish it is *ser tan fuerte como un toro*. If someone tells you *a cock and bull story*, in Spanish that's translated as *un cuento chino*. And of course, if someone is like *a bull at a gate*, then the expression in Spanish it is *de modo muy rápido*.) In common business Spanish situations, however, the question of leading, leadership and being a leader will almost always be *liderar*, *liderazgo* and *líder*.

Leader (*See*, Lead)

Leadership / *Liderazgo*

Quick! If a leader is *líder*, then what's leadership? Yes, it's true that a leader can also be a *jefe* (chief), *guía* (guide) or *supervisor* (supervisor), but when you want to express the notion that a leader is a person who *heads* an initiative or project or department, then you are speaking about a person who *encamina* or *enseña el camino*. In every instance, however, one hopes that the leader is capable of sound leadership. The one word for that is *liderazgo*, and one hopes that the leadership is capable of offering direction (*dirección*) and is, in fact, capable (*capacidad*). These words are interlinked when discussing *liderazgo*, which is why one must be mindful of the growing emphasis on visionary leadership (*liderzago visionario*) and the role that charismatic leadership (*liderzago carismático*) plays in today's business world. The importance, however, is that whether it is inspired or transformative, leadership is one of the key words that Latinos need to understand and use properly in order to advance their careers.

Ledger / *Registro* or *Libro Mayor*

Who uses a ledger these days? It's probably some APP on your iPhone or iPad. But ledgers are still used in business English, a linguistic legacy from a time before computers when there was one principal book for record-keeping. It is a charming word, and one that evokes black-and-white movies and television programs on the TV Land cable channel. Throughout much of the world, however, small businesses do keep ledgers, from family-owned pharmacies off Leicester Square in London to the Gran Vía in Madrid, and from Avenida Santa Fe in Buenos Aires to Avenida Hidalgo in Guadalajara. The correct translation for *ledger* in business Spanish is *registro* or the phrase *libro mayor*. The *registro* or *libro mayor* is the *libro principal* where a company's business records and transactions are kept. It is the authoritative book for official record-keeping. As time goes by, there will be fewer uses of this word in business, but, for now, remain mindful that if you hear someone refer to their company's *registro* or *libro mayor*, they mean the company's *ledger*.

Legacy / *Legado*

When American Airlines declared bankruptcy in late 2011, the news reported that this was the last legacy airline in the United States to file for bankruptcy. Ouch! In everyday speech we're used to *legacy* being used as a gift of property, usually as a bequest upon one's death. How many times has the Alumni Affairs office called you asking for a legacy gift? How many times have you heard someone during the PBS membership drive mention that public television would be delighted to receive a legacy gift from you? Yes, when you finally die, they want to be included in your will. If you're tempted to bequeath your body to your company, don't bother; they already have your soul, and they don't need your cadaver! In business, however, *legacy* refers to something that is handed down from the past or is a predecessor. American Airlines is a *legacy* airline because it is one of the oldest carriers, and it is still around. Many other airlines, from Pan American Airways to Eastern Airlines, have long passed into history, their legacies disappearing from memory. In the workplace, legacy refers to the traditions and culture of an organization that informs how it operates. It can be the legacy of Walt Disney that suffuses the Disney family of companies, and it could be the legacy of Coco Chanel that shapes how that brand is merchandised. Speaking of airlines—were we?—did I ever tell you about the most harrowing flight I ever took? It was Iran Air, from Isfahan to Tehran. Avoid it if you can! But I digress. Oh, yes, in business Spanish the word for *legacy* is *legado*.

Library / *Biblioteca*

If you thought that "library" in Spanish was "librería," don't be hard on yourself. It would make perfect sense. When it comes to language, however, sense is not often the case. That's part of its charm, since language reflects how societies grow and evolve, and how people express themselves as time goes by, for various reasons. In the case of this word, do note that "library" in Spanish is "biblioteca." Also note that both words are derived from "book." The word "library" entered the English language in the late 14th century, and is derived from the Anglo-French word "librairie," meaning a collection of books. That's what "biblioteca" means in Spanish as well: a place that has a collection of books. It's important to note that "librería" is indeed a word in

Spanish. What does it mean? A *librería* is Spanish for a bookstore.

Link / *Enlace*

If you had to give a rundown on the links on your website, how would you express that? Remember, it may be tempting to say that "links" is the same in English as it is in Spanish, but that would be wrong. "Link" is a multi-faceted word in English. It can mean connection (*conexión* or *vínculo*). It can also mean ties between things (*enlaces* or *nexos*). It could mean to bring together (*juntar* or *unir*). It could also mean to connect together (*encadenar* or *enlazar* or *ensartar*). In almost all business usages, however, the word *enlace* (noun) and *enlazar* (verb) will suffice. In fact, this is now the preferred use, since it is the word that is almost exclusively used for computers, computer programming and the Internet. As the business world becomes more technological in nature, it's important to know that *enlaces* are the links that are accelerating the pace of globalization throughout the world.

Locate / *Ubicar* or *Localizar*

What's the location for that conference? If it's a question of finding the address or location of something the word to use is *ubicar*. This word implies a physical location. When I say the old Pan Am Building in New York, can you quite place it? (Hint: Metropolitan Life bought the building and put the word "MetLife" on it. Can you believe the hubris of that firm?) If you think to yourself, "Ah, yes, the old Pan Am building is adjacent to Grand Central Station," then, by locating its position, we can say that *ubicaste el edificio*. The same can be said of a person. If someone asks, *¿Cómo te ubico?* or *¿Cómo* *te localizo?* they are asking how they can contact or get a hold of you. If it's a question of getting one's bearing or identifying a physical location, it's best to use *ubicar*. It can also be used figuratively. *No me ubico* means that you haven't quite settled in and are still getting your bearings. *No lo ubico* means you can't quite place the person in question. ("Remember the time at the conference Mr. Johnson embarrassed himself?" one person might ask. If you can't quite place Mr. Johnson, you might reply, *"No lo ubico."*) *Ubicar* implies precise location, and by inference precise placement. In everyday use it indicates where things are placed. (Remember to tell the deliverymen that they are to *ubicar el sofá en la sala*, meaning to place the sofa in the living room). *Ubicar* is the word to use to indicate that you know the lay of the land; where offices, convention centers, airports, public facilities and so on are located. It is used to place people, and to find things in specific locations. If can be found, it can be *ubicado*. *Localizar*, on the other hand, means *to locate*, of course, but it also is used *to indicate a kind of confinement*. If the doctor tells you that your child's infection *se localiza en la garganta*, she means the infection is localized in the throat, and hasn't spread. As a verb, *localizar* also means to track down: *¡Localiza al gerente de inmediato!* (Track down the manager immediately!) The manager? Isn't he arguing with the insurance agent about MetLife's policy not to pay insurance claims if an infection is localized in the throat? How do I know? I'm still recovering from the fall I took when I tripped over that lame monument to Juan Terry Trippe, founder of Pan American Airways, on the ground floor of the MetLife Building, and I had the very same argument with the same insurance agent! What are the chances?

Look / *Imagen*

There's no doubt that a product's appearance has a great deal to do with how the public perceives it. The more attractive the look is to the targeted demographic, the greater the sales. The same can be said about a store, for that matter. A store that caters to the hipsters of West Hollywood has a distinctly different look from one that caters to conservative clients in New York. Shopping at Post 42 on La Brea in Los Angeles is a far different experience from shopping at Brooks Brothers on Madison Avenue in New York. If you had to describe the importance of the looks of each establishment, what word would you use in Spanish? Don't say that *look* in English is acceptable when speaking Spanish! The correct word to use in business Spanish is *imagen*. *La imagen de cada tienda es muy distinta* means, The look of each store is very different. One can also use *aspecto*, but *aspecto* is more suggestive of appearance than it is to an identifiable look consumers can instantly recognize. That's the reason all Gap stores have a signature look, and so do McDonald's restaurants. It confers a competitive advantage if customers can identify your product, store or signature style instantly by its *look*, or its *imagen*, depending on the language you are speaking. If you're wondering what kind of consumer I am, who shops both at Post 42 and Brooks Brothers, let's just say that it's all somehow related to anthropological research I'm doing, and we can leave it at that.

Lunch / *Almuerzo*

The enemy of business Spanish is *Spanglish*. I'm sure you knew that. It may be true that the Royal Spanish Academy recognizes the Spanish spoken in North America as a distinct regional form of Spanish, but this does not give Latinos license to make up things as they go along. *Lunch* is not *lonche*. And it might be true that some people in Mexico use the word *lonchar* to mean "to have lunch," but that is slang, and is incorrect. (Pity Mexico, so far from God, but so close to the *anglicismos* of the Hispanic diaspora in the United States!) Moreover, be advised that this is one of those words that, because it is used in social settings and is part of everyday speech in the workplace, is a marker of sophistication. Others judge you by the words you use, the colloquialisms you favor, and whatever slang creeps into your casual conversation. When it comes time to have lunch, then it's time to *almorzar*. Throughout Latin America *almuerzo* means lunch, although *comida del mediodía* in used in many parts of Spain.

Making the Case / *Exponer un Argumento* or *Dar un Argumento*

Let us say you are asked to make the case on why this or that should be done. Let us further say that you have no problem with this, because you have an entire list of reasons to bolster your position and make a convincing case. Making the case is really about advancing your position through reasoned argument, isn't it? But if you tell me that "making the case" is "hacer *el* caso," bear in mind that while "hacer caso" is a phrase in Spanish (meaning *to pay attention*), "hacer *el* caso" isn't. Got that? *Hacer caso* is *to pay attention to someone*, and *hacer el caso* means not much of anything. In business Spanish, furthermore, to make the case is to *exponer un argumento* or *dar un argumento*. There is a subtle difference that you may want to consider. *Exponer un argumento* is to make the case by offering a series of reasons to back your position. *Dar un caso* is to make the case in more general terms without going into elaborate details. No matter how you want to make the case, make sure that you do so with confidence and conviction.

Mandatory / *Obligatorio*

It's not uncommon for Latinos to describe things that are *mandatario*. The problem with this, however, is that in Spanish a *mandatario* is either a person who represents a government, usually a head of state; or a mandate given to someone entrusted to fulfill that specific order. These uses are seldom used in business Spanish. The correct Spanish-language word for mandatory in a business setting is always *obligatorio*, which means something that is required. If it's mandatory that everyone attend the Monday morning meeting a 8 a.m. sharp, then it is *obligatorio*. If there is a new mandatory dress code, then this is the attire that is *obligatorio* for the staff. Unless you work for a despot who is in the habit of issuing decrees and mandates, nothing is *mandatario*, but it could very well be *obligatorio*. One more thing: Although you might believe that your boss is a despot, remember that until the United Nations so recognizes your boss as a head of state who is a despot, then your boss is not an actual despot. Pity no one explained this to Leona Hemsley while she was alive.

Manners / *Modales* or *Educación*

There was a time when courtesies were extended as part of doing business. I remember my grandmother, for instance, being put off by Fidel Castro not because he was a Communist, but because he didn't know how to hold a glass of wine properly when she attended a dinner party held in his honor by some misguided friends in Mérida, where the future dictator found refuge while planning his return to Cuba. On the other hand, his exiled mess, the Shah of Iran, who was relegated to a vast compound in Cuernavaca, Mexico, she said, had the most exquisite manners. Isn't it odd that way? Here you have to ruthless dictators, despicable men who, without a qualm, would execute their enemies and plunder their nations, one with the manners that would make Emily Post proud, and the other as if he were an extra who had escaped from the set of National Lampoon's "Animal House." In business Spanish the question of manners is an important one. Manners can mean actual manners—*modales*—by which I mean how one uses tableware, holds open elevator doors, or greets others when entering a room. I once saw a business deal collapse simply because an American executive in Mexico City was the first to sit down at a conference room, and he slid his business card across the polished table to the Mexican colleague with whom he was negotiating. The Mexican executive later expressed to me his reluctance to do business with someone who would not wait until everyone had entered the room to be seated, or who had the audacity to slide a business card across a table rather than physically handing his card after shaking hands.

Manners also mean *educación*, in a figurative sense. In business Spanish one speaks of another's *educación* as a metaphor for upbringing. It has to be pointed out that in the Spanish-speaking world there is that lingering question of *class*, similar to the social code expressed in the Northeast by the put-down, NQOC (not quite our class). This kind of snobbery lingers, I'm afraid, and be aware that if a conversation in Spanish turns to the subject of someone's *educación*, it's not that person's Alma Mater that is being discussed, but rather his or her upbringing and background. The expression *falta de educación* refers exclusively to one's lack of manners, poor upbringing or outright rude conduct. Make of it what you will, but be cognizant of the implications of such a conversation.

Marketing / *Mercadeo* or *Mercadotecnia*

Did I mention the argument that JFK, Jr. had with his wife, Carolyn Bessette Kennedy? It had something to do with JFK, Jr.'s enthusiasm for collecting the work of Britto Romero and Enrique Salazar, for neither of which she cared. One's work was too evocative of cartoons, and the other's portraits of the Virgin of Guadalupe were too contemporary. The point, of course, is that JFK, Jr. was unable to convince her of the merits of these artists' work, and Carolyn was hung up on the marketing, or lack thereof, that went into the commodification of works of art. In the previous sentence I used the work marketing, which has to do with the concept of buying and selling. If you were to tell this anecdote in Spanish, which word would you use for *marketing*? Don't even think of answering "el marketing," because you know better than that. Marketing is a word in English, but not in Spanish. The more common word used is *mercadeo*, which itself is derived from *mercado*, or market. *Mercadeo* describes the entire process of understanding a market, developing goods and services to bring to market, developing a campaign to promote the sale of these

121

goods and services to customers, and resolving both advertising and distribution to get the good or service to the marketplace. That rather well sums up what marketing is all about. The entire process is also described as the *técnica de mercado* or *mercadotecnia*. If you come across these terms, you now know what they mean. Be advised that marketing, of course, is a multi-faceted process. One can speak of a *departmento de mercadeo* (Marketing Department) or a *campaña de mercadeo* (Marketing Campaign). A *Director de Mercadeo* (or *Directora de Mercadeo*) is the Marketing Director, and they normally develop *una estrategia de mercadeo*, or a marketing strategy, which in turn often reflects *análisis de mercados*, or market research. No matter what it is, it requires a sound marketing program, one that will convince consumers of the merits of the good or service a firm is providing. *Mercadeo* is the process by which this is accomplished, so it behooves you to become familiar with these terms and expressions in order to make yourself well-understood when speaking business Spanish. If only Carolyn had understood it as well as John did. Then again, JFK, Jr. learned a great deal from the terrific staff at his magazine, *George*.

Months of the Year / *Meses del Año*

In the same way that I brought up the days of the week, I'm bringing the months of the year to your attention. It's for the same reason: the months of the year in Spanish are never capitalized unless a month is used as the first word in a sentence. And as long as we are on the subject, here are the months, properly spelled: *enero, febrero, marzo, abril, mayo, junio, julio, agosto, septiembre, octubre, noviembre* and *diciembre*.

Multi-task / *Multitarea*

There are some words that shouldn't exist in any language. Multi-task is one of them. The idea that, in business as in life, it is possible to accomplish several tasks with divided attention is to diminish the value of each task. If the proliferation of multi-tasking was not bad enough—did you miss the exit while composing a poorly-written text message on the way to the office this morning?—the grating "Spanglish" abomination *multi-tasquear* that is often heard coming out of the mouths of Latinos in the U.S. is enough to make you want to step on the gas and end it all. No, I'm afraid there is no such word as *multi-tasquear*. One reason is that, as it is used in business, a *task* is an assignment, which in Spanish is *tarea*. The implication is that a *task* is something of merit, and therefore worth doing. If you must translate multi-task into Spanish, do so sparingly, and use the proper word: *multitarea*. Before you get in the habit of engaging in this dreadful activity, consider for a moment that multi-tasks and multi-tasking are where life's paradoxes become self-evident. How? Well, because it seems that the only times when multi-tasks are successfully accomplished are in nefarious situations. Consider Gavin Newsom, former mayor of San Francisco, who busied himself with the multi-tasks of committing adultery and betraying his best friend simultaneously—by having an affair with his best friend's wife. This is hardly the kind of multi-tasking accomplishment about which your parents can boast. In politics, however, things are different: Put that "achievement" on your résumé, as Gavin Newsom did, and you might end up as the Lt. Governor of the State of Californication!

Networking / *Contactos Profesionales*

Yes, a network is *una red*, and the network is *la red*. That doesn't mean a noun can be converted into a verb when switching from English to Spanish. In consequence, *networking* is not now, has never been and will never be *redeando*! If you are discussing the use of social networks—*redes sociales*—such as Facebook, Twitter, LinkedIn, and so forth, then you are using the word *networking* to describe the act of *establishing professional or social contacts*. In Spanish, the phrase used is *establecimiento de contactos sociales o profesionales*. These contacts are useful in overcoming obstacles, such as *glass ceilings*, which in Spanish are *impedimentos profesionales*. When you succeed in overcoming these obstacles you will be able to move up the *corporate ladder*, which in English is a euphemism for career advancement. In Spanish, the phrase to use for corporate ladder is *avanzar su carrera*. Once you are well on your way, you will be able to be a mentor to younger professionals. This in Spanish is to be *un mentor*, *guía* or *consejero*. This will make you a *role model*, which in Spanish is *un buen modelo* or *un buen ejemplo*. With so much at stake, get out there and start networking—which you now know is the act of *estableciendo contactos profesionales*.

Office / *Oficina* or *Bufete* or *Consultorio* or *Despacho*

"I'll see you at my office," is a common expression. "Fine, I'll be there." How do you say office in Spanish? Do you think I'm joking? Isn't *oficina* Spanish for *office*? Yes, that's right. Everyone knows that. In business Spanish, however, there's a long tradition of being more specific about the nature of one's office. *Oficina* means *office*, but it also means a workshop and the lower apartments in a building, what corresponds to the cellar in English. Of more immediate concern, Spanish still maintains the tradition of using specific names for different professions. A doctor doesn't have an office; a doctor has a *consultorio*. Why? That's where he or she gives medical consultations. Attorneys and Public Notaries work out of a *bufete*, since that word suggests an office designed for writing documents and storing archives. Public officials, executives and scholars work out of *despachos*, since that word implies offices from where orders or instructions are issued (dispatched). There's nothing wrong with using *oficina*, but be mindful that you will encounter *consultorio*, *bufete* and *despacho* in the course of conducting business in Spanish, and you need to know the differences between them.

On Sale / *De Oferta* or *Rebaja*

Let us say the store you work for wants to get rid of some merchandise to make way for the new collection. Let us further say that the unwanted merchandise will be put on sale. If you were to say that the unwanted items were "en especial," you'd be mistaken. Throughout the United States many Latinos use the phrase "en especial" to indicate something's on sale. In Spanish, however, there are two ways of expressing that idea. You could say the merchandise is *de oferta*, meaning it's on sale. You could also say there are *rebajas* on the merchandise, meaning there are mark-downs on its price. Make yourself well understood! If it's priced to go, it's *de oferta*, meaning the *rebajas* on the price are irresistible, just like your business Spanish!

Online / *En Línea*

When speaking Spanish steer clear of using *online* when you mean *online*. If you are online, by which you mean you are connected to the Internet, which in Spanish is, *la conexión a la Red Mundial*, then you are *en línea*. The use of *online* when speaking Spanish is an *anglicismo* that is frowned upon, since *en línea* is now in widespread use throughout the Spanish-speaking world. This is one of those situations when a word or a phrase says a great deal about the speaker. Yes, should you say *online*, everyone will probably understand you, but if you say *en línea*, then you are conveying that you are careful enough to stay away from the unnecessary use of English words when speaking business Spanish. This harks back to the elegant arguments advanced by Mexican President José López Portillo in the late 1970s which galvanized the whole of *Hispanoamérica* to become proactive in defending the integrity of Spanish.

Order / *Encargar* or *Pedir*

In Spanish, *ordenar* means to arrange, to put in order and to organize. A child can *ordenar* his room by cleaning it up, or it's possible to *ordenar* one's files on the computer in order to find things more easily. The conference room can be *ordenado* to be put in order, and it's even possible to *ordenar los archivos*—organize the files—as a way of making more room in the filing cabinets. *Ordenar* is also used to give out instructions: *El gerente me ordeno a preparar la presentación*, meaning that the manager ordered you to prepare the presentation. (In a religious sense, *ordenar* means to be ordained and to receive holy orders.) But it's not possible to *ordenar* lunch for the meeting or to *ordenar* computer equipment to be delivered next week for the new hire. Neither of these two uses, gentle reader, conveys the idea of putting things in order. In Spanish there are two verbs that are used to request things: *encargar* or *pedir*. One can *pedir* lunch for the midday conference and one can *encargar* the new computer for delivery next week. Be mindful that when it is a question or ordering things that are purchased, the verbs to use are either *encargar* or *pedir*.

Outsourcing / *Contratación Externa*

There are few things as controversial as outsourcing, which is viewed politically as the export of jobs from the U.S. to other countries. If you were asked to explain this to someone in Latin America, how would you translate *outsourcing*? It's not immediately apparent, is it? It's such a new concept in the world of business that there is no complete agreement among Spanish-speakers on what should be the Spanish-language equivalent. The prevailing consensus is that the phrase *contratación externa* conveys that notion. It's not completely satisfying, since outsourcing usually (but not always) implies *outsourcing overseas*. It's possible to outsource domestically. A firm in California outsources to a firm in Illinois, or even within a state: one company outsources a specific function to another down the street. For now, however, *contratación externa* means outsourcing, although in some places the term *tercerización* is used. If you encounter this word, you know the speaker is referring to outsourcing, but my recommendation is to stick to *contratación externa*.

Overcome / *Superar*

In business there are many obstacles to overcome if you want to be successful. These are challenges, of course, and it is in meeting these challenges where success lies. That said, what's the Spanish-language word for overcoming an obstacle or a challenge? The word is *superar*. The idea of overcoming is demonstrating the ability to rise above a situation. If you are asked to pull together as a team to overcome a challenge, in Spanish that would be asking the team to *aunar los esfuerzos para superar el desafío*. One of the more important things to overcome is the natural tendency to lack discipline. As a demographic, Hispanic youth in the U.S. fails to overcome the challenges they face that prevents them from succeeding in school. This is one of the greatest challenges the Latino community in the U.S. encounters. Years ago I sat in during a high school geometry class in Miami. The teacher was discussing the definition of a point in geometry. A point indicates position but doesn't occupy any space, she told the class. I looked around the students, and it was clear that the ones who were disinterested were predominantly Latinos and African-Americans. Others in the room were deep in thought: What does that mean? What does it mean that something indicates a position but does not take up any physical space? What a concept! Some leaned forward, others were deep in thought. What will it take to get Latino youth to become engaged in education to such a degree that they overcome whatever obstacles they encounter in their lives and stay in school? What will it take for Latino youth to *superar* the obstacles that compel them to drop out of school?

Parking / *Estacionamiento*

Is there parking available at the convention center? I hope so, because I'd like to drive over to the show, then leave immediately after I make the rounds. This is a familiar sentiment, isn't it? Getting out of Dodge as quickly as possible is what unwelcome folks were advised to do on the old TV Western "Gunsmoke." If you had to explain the origin of the expression "get out of Dodge" to someone from Latin America, it wouldn't be that difficult since American Westerns were popular shows throughout the region for decades. But what if you were asked to translate *parking*? What would you say? *Parqueo* is slang, an *anglicismo* that gives many in the Spanish-speaking world goose bumps every time they hear it or see it in print. *Parqueo* isn't Spanish; it's Spanglish. Of course you're going to object and tell me that you've seen it written all over San Juan, Puerto Rico and on the both sides of the U.S.-Mexico border. It is still not proper Spanish. In Spanish the word for parking is *estacionamiento*. This is the most widely-used word, although in certain areas one encounters *aparcamiento*, which is also an acceptable word for parking. For now, however, please learn that *parking* is *estacionamiento*.

Password / *Contraseña*

How many times have Latinos stumbled upon this word? Let me not count the times, since this book is a brief exposition on business Spanish. Suffice it to say that if the word *contraseña* did not instantly jump to mind, it is best you become familiar with this word right now. *Password* is *contraseña*. Of course, Spanish being spoken in so many regions of the world, one would naturally expect to find, well, *regional* differences. In the same way that car is *carro* in some places, and *auto* in others, *contraseña* is also called a *código de seguridad* (security code) or *clave personal* (personal key), but these last two are used primarily in financial transactions, such as when you are trying to access information from a bank or financial institution, usually over the phone. When it comes to computer passwords, or other questions surrounding IT (Information Technology)—or throughout military institutions—the preferred word is *contraseña*.

Pay Cash / *Pagar al Contado*

A common strategy for enticing consumers (and businesses) to buy something is to offer them a discount for paying cash. This is the case the world over, especially at a time when banks are increasing merchant fees for accepting credit cards. The phrase to *pay cash* is *pagar al contado*. Note a curious observation: While a company lets its clients know that there are incentives for paying cash (*pagar al contado*), buyers describe what they are doing as *pagando en efectivo*. *Como me ofreces un descuento si pago al contado, te voy a pagar en efectivo*, means, "Since you're offering me a discount if I pay cash, I'm going to pay in cash." Become familiar with these phrases, and it will make it so much easier to communicate with Spanish-dominant customers and clients.

(To) Pay Out / *Desembolsar*

In most industries, employees are seldom advanced a per diem to use for expenses incurred while on business. As a result, employees are expected to pay out monies, which will subsequently be reimbursed by accounting. (One hopes!) But if you were asked to explain this policy to someone from an office in Latin America, how would you translate this in Spanish? Fortunately, there is a single word in Spanish for this expression: *desembolsar*. The word *desembolsar* means to pay out, to disburse and to expend. In a business setting, it refers to the monies that are paid by an employee in connection with official duties performed on behalf of an employer, and which will be reimbursed. Be mindful, however, that in business English the phrase "pay out" is also used to refer to the compensation that someone receives usually upon leaving a company through a severance package, the selling of equity in the firm, or a combination of both. In Spanish this kind of payout is simply referred to as a payment, or *un pago*. Until that happens to you and you can happily retire from the workforce, keep in mind that an expenditure that is *reembolsable* is eligible for *reimbursement*.

Payroll / *Nómina*

What's the proper translation for *payroll*? I hate to break it to you, but it isn't *payroll*. There's no such thing as "el payroll" when speaking Spanish. If you are speaking about the list of employees on staff, who are paid for their work, and who may or may not have to sign a pay slip (known in Spanish as an "hoja de salario"), then word for all these things is *nómina*. Each company has a *nómina* of the individuals who are paid employees or staff of the establishment. The word is derived from the list of *nombres*, or names, of a company's workers.

People Person / *Personable*

The best customer service representative is someone who is a "people person." Why does the curmudgeon inside me want to say that those "people persons" have something wrong with them? In business Spanish a "people person" is simply someone who is "personable," or someone who is personable and agreeable. That leaves me out, I suppose. Besides, I wonder, what would be the opposite of a people person? An inanimate object person? We already have term for that: Geeks. (In Spanish a *computer geek* is an *experto en computadoras*; in Spanish geeks are experts in their respective fields.) As a general observation, do note that being a gracious and agreeable person will help you get ahead in your career.

PIN / *NIP*

A Personal Identification Number, such as the one required to access ATM machines, is known as a PIN. That is, needless to say, if you're speaking English, since in Spanish "PIN" is not a word. It may be an acronym for something somewhere, but if you want to translate PIN, bear in mind that the Spanish translation is NIP. This, after all, is the acronym for *Número de Identificación Personal*, which is someone's personal identification number. Come to think of it, you really shouldn't be asking anyone for their PIN or NIP, and if anyone asks for your PIN or NIP, please don't disclose it. If, on the other hand, you are reminding someone in Spanish that he needs to memorize his NIP to use his bank card at ATMs, or for some other transaction, then that's fine. Whew! The last thing I want is to get hate mail from the American Bankers Association!

Pinche / The "F" Word

Why is this word even here? It's included for a simple reason: Fully 80% of all U.S. Hispanics are of Mexican ancestry, and *pinche* is a ubiquitous swear word in Mexican Spanish. Almost as commonly used as the "F" word is in American vernacular, *pinche* is heard everywhere Spanish is spoken in the U.S. You may not say it, but you will definitely hear it, and therefore you need to know what it means, and why you should never use it in any business setting.

Play a Role / *Desempeñar un Papel*

Did I tell you? I was asked to let you know that the powers that be want you to play a high profile role in next summer's industry convention. They've been impressed with your job performance; they want you to have a higher profile in the company. That's why they want you to play an important role next year. In fact, they don't want you *to play just a role*, but they want you *to play an important role*. Quick! How would you tell this bit of good news to someone who spoke only Spanish? If you're like most Latinos, you'd mention something about *jugar un papel*, right? That's wrong, I'm afraid. In Spanish, *papel* means paper and a role. But when you use the infinitive to play (*jugar*), the thought that comes instantly to mind is that you are *playing with a piece of paper. Jugar un papel* becomes easily confused with *jugar con un papel*. So, what's the listener supposed

133

to think? That you're making a paper airplane? In business English, *to play a role* means *to carry out a usual or customary function in a firm*. In Spanish, the verb *to carry out* is *desempeñar*. As a result, the proper Spanish-language translation for *to play a role* is *desempeñar un papel*. Of course, there's a role to play, and then there's role-playing. Did I ever tell you about a conference I attended in Brussels on investment products for high net worth individuals? During one of the ill-advised attempts at "bonding," the organizers of the conference held a "talent" night. It should be noted that this was shortly after Tina Turner had made her comeback with the release of her album "Private Dancer." Suffice it to say that a couple of American bankers re-wrote the lyrics to that song. "I'm your private banker, a banker for money, I do what you want me to do. I'm your private banker, a banker for money, any currency will do," they sang. Alas. That's how the world got into the mess that it's in. That was then, and this is now. No role-playing for you, but there are a good number of *papeles para desempeñar*!

Prevail / *Prevalecer*

To prevail has two primary meanings in business English. The first is to prove superior in ability, strength or power, and as a result, to come to predominate. The other is to use persuasion or inducement successfully. In brand management the end result of any strategy is to become more widespread and known throughout the marketplace. To prevail, in essence, is to grow strong. These meanings are conveyed by the business Spanish equivalent: *prevalecer*. Whether the intent is to convey the idea of becoming *successful*, *persuading* or *predominating*, the one word to use is to *prevalecer*. Be mindful that in colloquial expressions, the synomyms noted are often used. *In the prevailing market conditions* can be translated as *en las circunstancias actuales del mercado* as well as *en las circunstancias que prevelen*. If you *hope justice prevails*, that can be expressed *que esperas que se imponga la justice*. If it's noted that *Starbucks prevails in the local market*, someone might note that *Starbucks predomina en la región*. If your manager wants *to prevail upon* senior management, that can be expressed as her wanting to *persuader* or *convencer*. These words convey the same notion, and are common enough, but if you stick to *prevalecer* you will be completely understood by anyone speaking business Spanish.

Preservatives / *Conservadores*

It all depends on the industry in which you work, doesn't it? The use of preservatives is normally confined to the food and beverage industry, since most consumer perishables have to do with these industries. Then it becomes a question of what kind of preservatives are used in the preparation of foods or beverages. But be careful! If you think that the word *preservatives* is translated as *preservativos*, you are in for a *sorpresa*. *Preservativo* is normally used to mean a *condom*. Yes, technically it also means a preservative in a product, but in Mexico, where most U.S. business in the Spanish language is conducted, it is almost exclusively used to mean condom. The business Spanish word to use instead is *conservadores*. (Be mindful that *conservador* also means conservative, as in political ideology; and it means curator, as in a museum curator.) In most business usages, however, *conservadores* means *preservatives*.

Principal / *Director*

The call goes directly to voicemail, since you don't recognize the number immediately. Then when you check your message, you find out that the principal would like to speak to you about your child—and so would the nice lady who is the liaison with juvenile detention. Thank goodness you live in the U.S, where 8-year-olds are sent to jail, and not some other (crazy) country where they don't incarcerate children! (Go figure that one!) But how do you break the news to your mother that you are going to cancel lunch, as you text while you speed down the streets, paying more attention to the GPS than the road? "Voy a ver al principal!" you text furiously, only to get back a text with three question marks. Oh, yes, you fast and furious multi-tasking Latina, who won't be Mother of the Year, in any language. That's right! *Director* (or *directora*) is the proper Spanish-language translation for *principal*. In Spanish, *principal* refers something that is the main thing, the most important thing, the first floor of a building, or the head of a commercial establishment. In Spanish we speak of the main problem with your child ("el problema principal"), which is what the *Director* said when he was waiting for you as you rushed through the main door ("la puerta principal") and he met you on the second floor ("la planta principal"). (Take note, in British usage, the principal floor is the first floor, and in the United States the principal floor is the second floor.) And after you learn what your child has done, it's clear to you he will have a difficult time becoming the *principal* of a Fortune 100 company in the decades ahead, unless things change.

Profits / *Utilidades*

Business is all about making profits, which means at the end of the day, you have more income than expenses. If you spend more than you make, you are not profitable. *Profits* are not *profetas*, smart aleck! A *profeta* in Spanish corresponds to a prophet in English, which is a person who, through divine inspiration or revelation, speaks on behalf of God. In business, profits always refer to the earnings generated by the concern. The word in Spanish is *utilidades*, which means the profits or earnings made by the business. Be mindful that in certain phrases, other words are used: Profit-making is either *rentable* or *lucrativo*; profit-sharing is *utilidades*, and occasionally the phrase *participación en las ganancias*. Profit-taking is *toma de ganancias*. Note that in certain areas of the Spanish-speaking world the words *ganancia* or *beneficio* are also used, but in a more formal business setting, the preferred term is *utilidades*. Why? The reason is that *ganancia* can also mean winnings, as in gambling, and *beneficio* can refer to the general benefit of something. If you want to be clear—and you do want to be clear—use *utilidades* and everyone from the department manager to a Wall Street analyst will know what you mean.

Promising / *Prometedor* or *Prometedora*

There's nothing more satisfying than seeing people come aboard that are promising. They bring an optimism and energy that holds the prospect for a brighter future. How is *promising* translated into business Spanish? *Promise* in Spanish is *promesa*. If you, however, like many Latinos, think you can get away with saying *promesante*, think again. That's not a word! The correct word is *prometedor* or *prometedora*. Of course in business, as in life, there are various degrees of promising. Did I ever tell you about the time I was angered by someone who showed no promise? There was a time when I worked in Midtown Manhattan and the area around Lexington Avenue and the mid-50s was my neighborhood. Once, when I was meeting a writer for lunch at P. J. Clarke's we ran into each other by the FDR Post Office. We chatted as we walked past a homeless man, sitting on the sidewalk. Dominick Dunne pointed him out, shaking his head in disbelief. I'm sure this homeless person was part of the community, but I had never noticed him before. After he was pointed out to me, I kept seeing him in the weeks ahead. On one occasion I engaged the man in conversation, noticing he was barefoot. That stuck with me. A couple of weeks after that, I had the opportunity to give him a pair of shoes and socks. A few weeks later, I saw him again, and he was barefoot once more. I asked him why he was barefoot, and he told me the shoes gave him blisters and the socks had holes. Perhaps the next time someone is kind enough to give you a pair of shoes and socks, I replied, you should put on the socks first, and then the shoes. Alas, this was one of those cases where the likelihood that this person would improve his life were not very promising.

(To) Put Up With / *Soportar*

Did I ever tell you about the time that I had to put up with Chilean generals who were running the telephone company during the regime of Augusto Pinochet? We can save it for another time, but putting up with their requests was rather bizarre. (Point of information: These were career military officials who were placed in positions of authority at Chile's national phone company, didn't believe the military had any business in politics, and they didn't know much about the telecommunications industry. In fact, they were more interested in buying state-of-the-art bicycles than they were in ruling the world.) In business, there are a lot of things one has to put up with (including sentences that end in prepositional phrases). If that isn't bad enough, there are times when one is at a loss for the Spanish-language equivalent for certain words and phrases. "Put up with" is one such phrase. It might be tempting to say that "put up with" should be translated as "aguantar" in Spanish. But *aguantar* is more closely associated with *to suffer*, as in suffering that fool down the hall. In business English, on the other hand, *to put up with* conveys the notion of enduring, bearing or standing ("I can't stand my manager," is translated as "No soporto mi gerente.").

It can be argued that the phrase "put up with" itself is colloquial and unprofessional, but it is so widely used in the American workplace that it needs to be translated into Spanish. As a result, it is important to know that in most business uses, the preferred word in Spanish is *soportar*. Be mindful that while *soportar* is the equivalent for *put up with*, there are other common expressions heard in the workplace that use "put" but must be translated differently. *To be put on the spot* in Spanish is *poner en la mira*. *To put aside for the moment*, is to *poner a un lado por el momento*. *To put a feeler out* is to *tantear el terreno*. *To put all your eggs in one basket* is to *poner toda la carne en el asador*. *To put the record straight* is to *poner las cosas en su sitio*. In each of these cases, there is a Spanish-language expression that is equivalent of the English-language one. *Put up with*, however, is almost tinged with a sense of despair.

It conveys the notion of having to endure, or to bear, or to tolerate a situation or condition that is seen as unfair. *Soportar* in Spanish conveys that sentiment. As

Hispanics living in the Hispanic diaspora in the United States, Latinos have a great deal to tolerate, intolerance being high on the list; Latinos in the U.S. are seldom cut much slack. Consider, for instance, how non-Hispanic America is willing to forgive (or overlook) the human shortcomings of heroes, and concentrate on the good they did. There are statues to George Washington, Martin Luther King, Jr. and even Harvey Milk. Yet, George Washington was slave owner, and held other men and women in bondage. Martin Luther King, Jr. was a serial adulterer, and betrayed his marital vows without a qualm. Harvey Milk was a pedophile, and had sexual relations with young males who had not reached the age of consent. On the other hand, Hispanics of merit, whether they are of Spanish, Mexican or Californio descent, are often vilified by non-Hispanics in the U.S. This includes Father Miguel Hidalgo, José Castro and Junípero Serra, who have had their statues removed from public view, based on the accusation that Spanish colonialism was cruel to the indigenous peoples of the New World. And what? Slavery was a benign institution thrust upon Africans forcefully brought here? And women don't suffer when their husbands are unfaithful? And youngsters aren't traumatized for life as a result of being sexually molested by sexual predators?

This, Latino, is the bias that you have to *soportar* by virtue of choosing to live in the Hispanic diaspora. Don't get mad. Instead, get motivated to act. Why isn't a statue of José Castro raised in front of his home on Market Street in San Francisco, Mr. Mayor? The point, however, is that in business one has to put up with a great deal. In business Spanish when you want to express the sentiment that you have to bear or stand or endure something, then the word for all these tests of your patience is *soportar*. Finally, remember that *soportar* is not the same thing as support! In business

Spanish, *apoyar* means *to support*. But when you are putting up with something then you are *soportando* something. Much like this entry!

Quote / *Cotizar*

Did someone get a quote for the equipment? Quick! Translate that into Spanish. Let me guess. The word "quote" is making you stop and think. The business Spanish word for *quote* is *cotizar*. I know it would have been easier had the question been, "Did someone get a price for the equipment?" There are times, however, when quote—often shorthand for "price quote"—is used in business English. Be mindful that *cotizar* means both *to quote* and *to prize*. In some cases it also means *to be valued*, as in "El conocimiento del español te cotiza mucho," meaning that knowledge of Spanish makes you more valuable. In the world of business *cotizar* can also mean to pay, as in, "Los trabajadores tienen que cotizar al plan de salud," meaning that workers have to contribute to the health plan. The most common usage, however, is to quote prices. Did someone get a deal on the equipment?

Raising the Bar (*See,* Take it to the Next Level)

Realize / *Darse Cuenta*

"I didn't realize that the meeting had been moved back to 11 a.m.," one manager comments to a colleague. How would you say this in Spanish? If you were to begin by saying "No realicé que ..." I would have to stop you right there, before you embarrass yourself any further. In Spanish *realize*, when used to become aware of something, is expressed with the phrase *darse cuenta*. "I realize we're late with this suggestion," is expressed in business Spanish as "Me doy cuenta que ..." To become aware of something is to *darse cuenta*. There are other common expressions in business where the word "realize" is used, of course. One manager can speculate that there is much profit to be realized from this project, which in Spanish is translated as speculating that "se pueden obtener grandes ganancias." One person might lament that because of certain setbacks, it will be difficult to realize his full potential, which is expressed in Spanish as "no podré realizar mis esperanzas." Another person, on the other hand, might be delighted to have realized her dreams, which in Spanish is expressed as "pude hacer real mis sueños." If on the other hand, your expectations were realized, then you could say that in Spanish by noting that "mis expectativas se realizaron" or "mis expectativas se vieron confirmadas." The point is not to stay away from using the word *realizar*, but that you use it properly. I hope you realize—*se da cuenta*—that when it comes to becoming aware of something, it's always *darse cuenta*.

Reboot / *Reiniciar*

On this one, you have a pass. *Rebotar* is a word in Spanish, and it means several things, which lends itself to being easily confused for a word that might mean the same thing as *reboot*. *Rebotar* means to bounce or rebound. A ball bounces off a wall (*la pelota rebotó*). A bullet rebounds off the sidewalk (*la bala rebotó del pavimento*). In colloquial speech it's also used to refer to a sudden change in your mood, such as when someone makes a joke at your expense and you become sour (*no le gustó la broma y se rebotó*). It is also, interestingly, used to describe e-mail that bounces back (*el mensaje rebotó*). These definitions, however, do not include rebooting a computer system. If you are referring to having to shut down, or restart, you computer, cell phone or any other kind of electronic device, then the word you want to use is *reiniciar*, which means to re-initiate. Whatever it is, if it has to be rebooted, then the verb to use is *reiniciar*.

Register / *Registrar* or *Darse de Alta*

This is one of those complicated words, because it is used to mean several things. Be mindful that *registrar* does mean *register*, but what else does *registrar* encompass in its multiple meanings? I'm glad you asked, inquisitive reader. *Registrar*, of course, means *to register* and *to record*. In most cases, students register for a class (*El estudiante se registró para el curso*), and a department can register an increase in work (*El departamento ha registrado un aumento en trabajo*). Remember, however, that, as is the case in English, someone can *matriculate* in school as well (*El estudiante se matriculó para el semestre*). In Spanish, moreover, there is another meaning to *registrar*: to search. A building can be searched, and so can a person. *El jefe va a registrar a todos*, someone might say, to indicate that everyone will be searched. Or it could be a blanket policy: *La seguridad en el aeropuerto registra a todos los pasajeros*, meaning that the TSA screens all passengers at the airport. The other usage for registering in the business world today is to subscribe to something online. This could be as simple as registering for an e-mail account on Gmail, or signing up on Amazon.com or requesting to be included in an e-mail list. For these kinds of registrations, the preferred business Spanish expression is *darse de alta*. It's possible to make yourself understood by other English-dominant Latinos if you say you registered for an e-mail account on Gmail, or as a customer on Amazon.com, or to receive a newsletter online, but the recommended phrase is *darse de alta*, which is worth learning, since you will come across it.

Reimburse / *Reembolsar*

There's nothing more fun after a business trip than compiling all the receipts for accounting, is there? Of course I'm kidding, mind you, but in business Spanish, the word for being reimbursed is *reembolsar*. It's a versatile verb, since it means to be reimbursed for expenses (*gastos*), or to receive a refund (*restitución* or *devolución*) or to be repaid for a debt (*deuda*). In most common business settings, however, it is used to refer to reimburse an employee for expenses incurred on behalf of the company. For international travel, be mindful that the noun (reimbursement) in Spanish is *reembolso*. Why? Because you often see this word on expense reports generated by offices throughout Latin America.

Relevance / *Pertinencia*

This is one of those natural mistakes that are hard to avoid for anyone living in the Hispanic diaspora in the United States. "Where is the relevant report?" one might hear. "What's the relevance of these figures to our projections?" In each of these cases, the word relevance speaks to something that is connected to the matter at hand, or that pertains to the subject being discussed. *Where is the relevant report*, is asking to find the report that is pertinent to the matter at hand. *What's the relevance of these figures*, is asking how these specific figures are pertinent to the projections being considered. Notice that in each case I used the word pertinent to underscore the meaning of relevance. There's a reason for that. In Spanish, *relevancia* means something that is important, of great consequence or of grandeur. It is seldom used in business Spanish, so which Spanish-language word should be used when translating "relevance"? How about *pertinente*? If something is relevant to the matter at hand, then it is has *pertinencia*, doesn't it? "¿Dónde está el informe pertinente?" is an appropriate translation. "¿Cuál es la pertinencia de estas cifras a nuestras proyecciones?" is a fine translation. Always bear in mind that if something is *relevant*, it is *pertinent*, and if it is *pertinent*, then the word is *pertinencia*.

Remittances / *Remesas*

This is a peculiar word to find being used in the United States as frequently as it is. Its wide use arises from the enormous commerce that takes place between the U.S.

and Mexico. Ever since Nafta went into effect, trade across the border has grown substantially, and with it so has the transfer of money back and forth. *Remittance* in Spanish is *remesa*. This refers to the sending of money back and forth across the border, and it's one of the more lucrative financial services for businesses that serve Latin American immigrants. Be aware that *giro* is also used, primarily when speaking of a *wire transfer* (usually through Western Union or a similar service provider). On occasion, one hears *envío de dinero*, literally "the sending of money." But the more inclusive term is *remesas*. Financial institutions and government agencies report on the remittances from here to there and the *remesas* from there to here. You should as well.

Remove / *Borrar* or *Quitar*

How many times have you heard someone say the word *remover* in the workplace? I'll bet it's been more than once. Unless, however, you work in a restaurant or in the mental health industry—one conjures up the other, oddly enough—it's probably been used incorrectly. In Spanish, *remover* means to stir or toss things, such as pots of soup that are stirred or salads which are tossed. (Think of a restaurant.) *Remover* also means to revisit emotionally, both memories and the past. (Think of a psychiatric ward in a hospital.) In short, in Spanish *remover* means to move things repeatedly, to move physically a thing from one place to another, or to stir up emotions and memories. "There she goes again, stirring things up by bringing up the time she was four years old and we handcuffed her to the boa constrictor exhibit at the serpentarium at the zoo," your mother might say of your sister, rolling her eyes. How many times has she brought up that episode at the dinner table? In most business settings, however, if, as many

Latinos are inclined to do, you believe that *remover* means the same thing as *to remove*, then you are mistaken. That would be an *anglicismo* that is best removed from your mind! In business Spanish *to remove* is best translated as *borrar* (as in *to erase*) or *quitar* (as in *to take away*). If it's a question of removing a superfluous clause in a PowerPoint slide, it's *borrar*. If it's a question of removing the slide altogether, it's *quitar*. The context will guide you on whether to use *borrar* or *quitar*, but there is almost never any reason to use *remover*.

Resign / *Demitir* or *Renunciar*

When you reach the point when you have had enough, you can always resign. But what if you don't want to resign, but are merely resigned to being miserable? The world is full of people who hate their jobs, and live lives of quiet desperation. Isn't that what Henry David Thoreau said? So you see, Latino? The more things change, the more you have to resign yourself to their staying the same. How do you translate the various meanings of *resign*? When resign is used to mean to submit or surrender without much resistance, as is the case when one is resigned to the restructuring that was announced with a sigh, then the word in Spanish is *resignarse* or *rendirse*. Either word denotes the idea of relinquishing or ceding. On the other hand, if *resign* is used to indicate the giving up of a position, office or abdication, then the word is either *demitir* or *renunciar*. In business English the word *resign* is often followed by a prepositional phrase beginning with *from*. "Mrs. Smith resigned *from* the position of CEO." This was followed by other news: "Mr. Jones resigned *from* the directorship of the board." In each of these cases the sentences can be properly translated by using either *dimitir* or *renunciar*. It should be noted that *dimitir* is more widely used, especially in journalism, for one reason: it is a shorter word, and therefore fits more easily in headlines. Be mindful that the noun for *dimitir* is *dimisión*. *La Sra. Smith entregó su dimisión ...* is the business Spanish wording for Mrs. Smith's handing in her resignation. Don't follow suit!

Respect / *Respeto* or *Respecto*

It's fair to say that Aretha Franklin doesn't speak Spanish, otherwise she would not have belted out R-E-S-P-E-C-T with such confidence. Why? Come on, you know the answer to that: In Spanish there are two similar words for *respect*: *Respeto* and *respecto*. Each means something different. Be aware of this linguistic trap! Respect, as in regarding others with consideration, attention and even veneration, is *respeto*, without the letter "c." In the business world every single person deserves to be treated with respect, mindful of their human dignity. In the Spanish-speaking world, for a variety of historic reasons, the idea of respect is closely linked to the notion of everyone's inalienable human rights and dignity. That said, here are a few common usages and expressions to learn. "Por respeto," means "out of consideration for." "Con respeto," means "with respect" or "with regard to." "With all due respect" is "con el debido respeto." To be disrespectful is to "faltar al respeto," and self-respect is "respeto a sí mismo." (Note: *Respeto* can also mean fear, so if you are afraid of heights, then you can express it by saying that you "tienes respeto a las alturas.") The word *respecto*, with the letter "c," on the other hand, means with regards to; in relation or proportion; and relativeness. "In respect to market developments ..." becomes in Spanish "Respecto a los acontecimientos en el mercado ..." If you are speaking about one thing being respective to another, then you are speaking of something *"al respecto de ..."* Remember, if it has the letter "c," then it concerns something. That's about enough *con respecto a la palabra* R-E-S-P-E-C-T, *con todo el debido respeto.*

Restricted / *Restringido*

If you can't go somewhere because it's a restricted area, that's a polite way of saying "Keep Out." How would you say that in Spanish? Don't even think of saying "restrictido," because you know very well that there's no such word in Spanish! (The closest thing to *restrictido* that is a word in Spanish is *restrictivo*, which means *restrictive* or *restringent*.) Indeed, the word for *restricted* in Spanish is *restringido*. The primary use is to describe an area that has *limited access*, whether it is a room, or an entire installation, or anything else for that matter. It is a sad testament to the state of affairs in the world nowadays, but there are more *restricted areas* with each passing day. In business usage, rectricted areas are *áreas restringidas*. Be mindful that in certain business situations, the Spanish-language word *restringida* also means *confidential*. A *confidential document* can be described as *un documento confidencial* or *un document restringido*. Such a report, in other words, is not meant for wide distribution, but probably on a need-to-know basis to a select number of recipients. For the most part, however, in most business English usages, you will use *restringido* whenever you want to describe something as being *restricted*.

Retaliate / *Tomar Represalias*

What kind of business book would omit mentioning retaliation? Office politics can be nasty, brutish and short—something out of Thomas Hobbes's book, *Leviathan*. The idea of undermining someone else, or getting back at them, or retaliating for some reason is as ingrained in human nature as anything else, I suppose. One can take a dim view and say such urges, while natural, must be contained. Others can take a more value-neutral stance, and not really care about it one way or the other. In the business world, friendly tit-for-tat retaliation is often seen as healthy competition among rivals, whether it is in the workplace, or between competitors. However the scenario plays out, what can be said with confidence is that it is incorrect to translate *retaliate* into Spanish by using *retaliación*. Yes, it's true that in Spanish the word *retaliación* exists—as do *retaliar* and *retaliador*. But when it comes to business Spanish, it is also a matter of style and elegance in speech, written or spoken. By this I mean that in Spanish no one speaks of *retaliation* in polite company at the workplace. What one speaks of is *reprisals*. To retaliate is *to take reprisals—tomar represalias*. One speaks of an action taken *as a reprisal for something*, which is to take an action *como represalia por un hecho*. One can also justify an unkind act *by way of reprisal—a modo de represalia*. Retaliate all you want, if you are inclined to do so, but call it a reprisal. *Tomar represalias* is the way to go when conducting business, as if inspired by Machiavelli. That's *Maquiavelo* in Spanish, by the way.

Return Policy / *Reglas de Devolución* or *Reglas de Reembolso*

In retailing, there's a natural tendency to translate expressions from English to Spanish word-for-word. Perhaps this is the case because it appears natural, particularly when Latinos in the Hispanic diaspora are surrounded by English all the time. If you were, however, to think that return policy is *póliza de retorno*, then you are mistaken. This *anglicismo* is understandable to most Spanish speakers, but it is terrible form. The correct way to translate "Return Policy" is either "Reglas de Devolución" or "Reglas de Reembolso." Remember that *devolución* is a form of *devolver*, to return. *Reembolso* is a form of *reembolsar*, to be reimbursed. In either case there are strict rules that constitute a company's policy governing the terms under which items can be returned, replaced or exchanged. There are businesses that allow for exchange of similar merchandise, others that give consumers store credit to be applied to subsequent purchases, and others that provide for a full refund. Regardless of which policies are in place, the correct translations in Spanish are "Reglas de Devolución" or "Reglas de Reembolso."

S

Safe / *Salvo*

Every Latino knows that *safe* is *seguro*. If by safe one refers to free from harm, danger, risk or injury; involving little or no risk; or being secure from liability to harm or injury, the word is *seguro*. In describing a person as *safe*, we mean someone who is dependenable or trustworthy: a person who is *seguro*. (A *safe*, as in a repository for valuables, usually a steel or iron box, is a *caja fuerte*, literally a *strong box*.) In ordinary business Spanish, however, *seguro* is used as *sure*. "Are you *sure* the meeting is today at 4 p.m.? becomes in Spanish "¿Estas *seguro* que la reunión es hoy a las 4 p.m.?" "Yes,

I'm sure," becomes, "Sí, estoy seguro." Be advised, however, that in many other business situations, the word *salvo* is used instead of *seguro*. When you are sure the safety of someone or something has been determined, the word to use is *salvo*. To arrive safe and sound in Spanish is to *llegar sano y salvo*. To be safe, is to *estar a salvo*. To secure documents to ensure they are safe is to *poner los documentos a salvo*. If something is safe, it is *a salvo*. Be mindful, too, that *salvo* also means except when used as a preposition. If everyone in the department is expected to attend today's 4 p.m. meeting, except you, your manager might say that *todos tienen que atender la reunión de las 4 p.m., salvo tú*. If there will be a training seminar for everyone, except those who attended last year's conference, this might be expressed by saying that *es obligatorio que todos asistan al taller salvo los que participaron en la conferencia del año pasado*. One person might mention that except for the manager, no one else knew how to operate the equipment, which would translated as *salvo el gerente, nadie sabía como operar el equipo*. In most business Spanish situations, *salvo* is used to mean *safe*. ¿Estas claro?

Satisfied with / *Satisfecho de*

"I'm satisfied with the situation," one manager might mention to you. Quick, translate that into Spanish! Oh, I'm sorry. If you said *"Estoy satisfecho con la situación,"* you're wrong. In Spanish, one can be satisfied *of* something or someone, but not *with* something or someone. The English-language expression *to be satisfied with* is the Spanish-language equivalent of *estar satisfecho de*. What the manager said to you was, "Estoy satisfecho de la situación."

Samples / *Muestras*

A client asks for samples to examine. If you reply that you are authorized only to give one "samplo," then you are not likely to be understood. I hate to break it to you, but despite what you have heard, "samplo" is not a word in Spanish. The word for *sample* is *muestra*. A *muestra* is a physical sample, and a *muestrario* is a sample case. These words are closely linked to *mostrar*, to show, and convey the notion that a sample is representative of the product that is given for a potential buyer to examine, try out, scrutinize for quality and test for attributes. It is presumably left free of charge, and without the obligation to place a purchase order subsequently. Remember, in business Spanish *muestra* is the noun for *sample*. If, however, you are using "sample" as a verb— I'd like to sample our customers on the new store design, or I'd like to sample the new menu items—then the words to use are *sondear* (conduct a public opinion survey) or *probar* (to sample the new menu items, or the in-flight service on the new Chicago-Buenos Aires nonstop flight). When the question is of leaving *physical* samples, however, the word to use is *muestras*.

(To) Save / *Ahorrar* or *Economizar*

Here's a paradox to ponder: If the world has spent so much of the past quarter century becoming aware of the need to save things, from money for retirement to natural resources, then why is there such a feeling of loss? Truth be told, saving things, from one's breath to used office paper is almost always a good thing. Being frugal is always prudent. In most cases, however, in Spanish, the word *salvar* has the connotation of being spared. *Salvar* often means to be saved from danger, or to be rescued. It denotes something that is overcome or escaped. If you escaped eternal damnation you are said to be saved by faith, which is, *se salvó por su fé*. In most business Spanish situations, however, *salvar* is a poor choice. The more appropriate words to use are *ahorrar* or *economizar*. The manager might request that staff take HR's advice about the various programs to save (*ahorrar*) for retirement, or that as part of a program to save money (*economizar*) the office will now use recycled paper. If it's a question of saving resources, it's *ahorrar*. If it's a question of saving out of financial consideration, then it's *economizar*. In either case, in almost every business setting, it is better to use *ahorrar* or *economizar* and almost never *salvar*. Other kinds of *saving*, you ask? Please be mindful that in business Spanish, when it comes to computers, *Save* is *Guardar*. *To save a document* is to *guardar un document*. Why? Because when you save a document on your computer nothing physical is involved; you are only safe-keeping a memory file. In most other business uses, stick to *ahorrar* or *economizar*.

Schedule / *Programa*

Get with the program! On occasion this is heard in the business world, part colloquialism, and part exasperation. Get with the program? What program is that? The implication, of course, is that you have to follow more closely the itinerary or items on a schedule. Ah, there it is! In business Spanish, *schedule* is *programa*. This is true whether schedule is used as a noun ("What's next on the schedule?") or a verb ("We're going to have to schedule in this guy's presentation somewhere.") If it is a schedule, it's a *programa*. If it is scheduled, it is *programado*. Here's a caveat to keep in mind, however. In business English there are occasions when schedule is used in ways that other words may be more appropriate in business Spanish. If the schedule is a list of prices, it's best to say *lista* or *catálogo*. "May I see the schedule of prices?" is seldom used, but it does occur once in a while. In that case, the Spanish-language usage preferred is: "Puedo ver una lista de precios?" or "Puedo ver un catálogo de precios?" The other exceptions are when *schedule* is used in specific phrases to refer to time, being on time or being late. "Things are on schedule," can mean one of two things in English: 1) that everything is accounted for on the schedule, or 2) that nothing is running late. In the first use, one would say that things are on the *programa*, of course. What about the second example? In this case you would say, "Todo está de acuerdo con el horario previsto." This means everything is running on time. If the schedules are jammed pack—"This conference is running on a tight schedule"—the notion you want to convey is that there is little, if any, discretionary time for additional things. You can say this by noting that "Esta conferencia cuenta con unos plazos muy estrictos." As a general observation, schedules for public transporation, airlines, trains or anything that has a *published timetable* is an *horario*. If it is a question of the time between scheduled events, then you are referring to the *plazos* between events. If it is a question of timing—are we arriving on schedule or are we behind?—is a question of *previsión*. ("We are scheduled to arrive at 11 a.m." becomes in Spanish "Está previsto que lleguemos a las 11 horas," or "Estamos programados llegar a las 11 horas.") With the exception of these questions of time-precision, a schedule is a *programa*, and something that is scheduled is *programado*. I'm glad you're now with the program! Now, what's the next item on the schedule?

Scenario / *Suposición* or *Hipótesis*

Remember how I pointed out that in Spanish "drama" was used exclusively for the *dramatic*—as in a performance, movie plot, screenplay or theatrical production? Guess what? Oh, you guessed! Yes, that's right: Scenario in Spanish refers to the *physical* theatrical scenario or stage (theater stage, sound stage). It is where a performance takes place, or is a specific location where something took place, whether it is where the ribbon-cutting ceremony was held, or the crime scene cordoned off by police detectives. In the business world in the United States, however, "scenarios" are often discussed to analyze various options and "What if" situations. "What's the scenario for the deal if we are out-bid?" one executive might ask, by way of discussing various options should that situation come to pass. "If things don't improve in the next quarter, what is the scenario for the distribution of investor dividends?" another might inquire. When speaking Spanish, you are well advised to keep in mind that when contemplating options and possibilities, developing strategies for "What if" situations and developments, there are two words to use: *suposición* or *hipótesis*. The "What if" of the business world is one in which several hypotheses are explored, or suppositions are made. In Spanish one can offer his or her ideas ("*Supongo que una opción sería* ..."), or one can offer a theory on the best course of action ("*Una hipótesis es que si rechazan nuestra propuesta* ..."). The scenarios are virtually endless, all the more reason to be aware of the words that adeptly convey the notion of business world scenarios. (One gentle reminder: in non-business English the word scenario refers to the outline of a plot or narrative in a dramatic work, screenplay or television drama, but this usage is falling into disuse.)

Security Guard / *Vigilante* or *Guardián*

In the film "A Few Good Men," there is a famous scene in which Tom Cruise's character is questioning Jack Nicolson's character in a courtroom. "I ordered him to have Santiago transferred immediately," Nicholson says. "Why?" Cruise asks. "His life might be in danger," is the reply. "Grave danger?" Cruise asks. "Is there any other kind?" Nicholson replies. The point is that "grave danger" is redundant, since any danger is grave. The question of being redundant also applies to the phrase "security guard." Every guard, by definition, is there to offer security. If one translates *security guard* as *guardia de seguridad*, then one is being redundant. In Spanish, a security guard is either a *vigilante* or *guardía*. That's it, pure and simple, with no further comments for the time being.

Setting / *Configuración*

What's the setting on your computer that's making that annoying ringtone go off? It's driving me crazy! *Setting*, when used in the context of technology, is *configuración*. There once was a time when only the IT personnel had to be fluent in such technology terms, but times have changed. Remember that neither *setting* nor—Am I making the sign of the cross again? —*settear* or *settearonar* are words in Spanish! Do bear in mind, moreover, that there are other kinds of settings. If you are *setting up* a company, the word to use is *constituir*. ("I am thinking about setting up a company," in Spanish is expressed, "Estoy pensando constituir una empresa.") If someone is *setting* the table for an official reception at headquarters, then the word is *poner*, since the person who is setting the table *esta poniendo la mesa*. But when it comes to technology, *setting* is always *configuración*.

Slide / *Deslizar*

If you slip, lose your balance and slide across the floor, then the word for that in Spanish is *resbalar*. This kind of sliding is not often the case in the business world—unless you are in the fashion industry and someone, in a misguided moment, no doubt, thought that she could carry off walking in one of Lady Gaga's shoes. For most of us, however, in a business setting we are referring to sliding cards of one kind or another. It could be an ATM or credit card, a company ID badge, or a fare card for public transportation. Whatever it is that we are asked to slide (please refrain from using the word "swipe," since this is slang), the word is *deslizar*. One point to consider is that this word is more often heard than read. That is to say, you are more likely to hear it from customer service representatives on the telephone who are trying to help you than you are likely to read it as part of a set of instructions. Become familiar with the word, and how it sounds.

Software / *Programas Informáticos*

It's not uncommon for technical words and terms to be confusing in any language. In English *software* refers to computer programs. The word in Spanish for that is *informáticos*. In business usage, however, be aware that *informáticos* is used as an adejective, not a noun. This means the correct phrase is *programas informáticos*. When writing, once you've established that you are referring to *programas informáticos*, you can simply use *programas* for the remainder of the text.

Sold Out / *Cupo Completo* or *Agotar*

If there's no room left at the inn—or the flight, hotel or convention center for that matter, how do you express the idea that something is sold out? If you say "*Está sold out*," you are asking for eyes to roll ... and no one wants eyes to roll. The proper translation in Spanish is *cupo completo*, which literally means the (physical) capacity is completely full. In short, there is no more space, room, or availability. An easy way to remember this phrase is that *cupo* refers to quota, which is the maximum capacity of a thing—number of seats on an aircraft, suites at the hotel, or seats in a conference hall. *No hay cupo* means "there's no room." Notice that *cupo completo* is used when something is filling up, whether it is the number of seats on an airplane or the rooms at a hotel. But what if you're running out of something? What if those new-fangled iPhones are selling fast and running out? When you want to convey the idea that the inventory of an item is depleted, then the verb to use is *agotar*. When a store runs out of supplies, or the quantity of something is used up (copies of the annual report, for instance), then the item is described as *agotado*. Of course it goes without saying that this is a great verb to describe becoming exhausted. (*Esta convención me agota*, you might say to let your spouse know that the convention is wearing you down, and you are exhausted at the end of the day. There goes the idea of carrying out a tawdry affair while on business in Seattle!) Remember, if you want to convey the fact that something sold out, then it's *cupo completo* or *agotado*.

Solicitation / *Solicitación*

This is a word that is used more often in business Spanish than in business English. *Solicitation* is a petition or a request, an entreaty or importunity. What does this resemble most in the course of business? It is a *request* for a work bid. An RFP, Request for Proposal, is the standard public solicitation for proposals encouraging companies to submit bids for specific contracts. The scope of services is included in the RFP, and companies, whether it is a sole proprietorship or a multinational firm with offices spanning the globe, are invited to submit proposals in response to this solicitation. In Spanish, *proposal* is *propuesta*, but it is almost always used in reference to a *marriage proposal*. In consequence, in business Spanish, the word used more often for a bid, an RFP or anything that requires submitting a plan or proposal to secure a contract is a *solicitación*. Learn it, since you will encounter it frequently.

Speak Your Mind / *Decir lo Que Piensas*

There are times when the urge to translate a phrase word-for-word seems natural, especially when speaking with other Hispanics who are fluent in English. When you are asked for your honest opinion, or you ask someone for theirs, it seems a no-brainer to translate "speak your mind" into "hablar tu mente." Unfortunately, "hablar tu mente" makes no sense in Spanish. The correct expression is "decir lo que piensas," which literally means "to say what you think." Isn't that what speaking your mind is all about? It's simply about expressing your true thoughts, without self-censorship. The same can be said for other English-language euphemisms, such as "getting things off your chest," or "coming clean" with your opinions. All these expressions can best be said in Spanish with a simple instruction: "Decir lo que piensas."

Spending Time / *Pasar Tiempo*

Another phrase that trips up Latinos in the United States is "spending time." In English, "spending" has several meanings. One could mean public expenditures (public spending), individual discretionary consumption (spending money), economic household consumption (consumer spending) or time allocated for socializing (spending an evening with a friend). Be mindful that in Spanish, "spending" can be translated as *gasto* or *pasar*. The first three examples can be translated as *gastar* (*gasto público*, *dinero para gastos*, or *gasto del público consumidor*, respectively). The fourth, however, is a different kind of spending, since the idea of spending time with friends, family or colleagues is a form of passing time with others. When it comes to time spent with others, it would be wrong to use *gastar*, since in this context the implication is that the time is wasted, or could have been used more wisely. In Spanish, the word is *pasar*, and as such, "spending time" is correctly translated as "pasar tiempo."

Sponsor / *Patrocinar*

There are such negative connotations in English with the word *patron* that it's problematic. There is the loathed *patron-client* relationship that speaks of dependency, colonialism and the mercantilist system that oppressed multitudes of humanity throughout history. There's the notion of *patronizing* someone, by way of treating him or her in a condescending or arrogant manner; dismissing them without a thought; or treating them like a child. There are *patron* saints in

Catholicism, which spooks Protestants into fearing the mysticism of Catholics and Episcopalians (among others Christian denominations). There are, of course, positive connotations for "patron" in business English. Benefactors are great patrons of the arts, or a cause. Reliable customers are said to be good patrons of one's business. When it comes to *sponsor*, as in sponsorship, sponsoring an event, or being a sponsor for something, however, the correct word in business Spanish is *patrocinar*. One can sponsor a summer intern or a high school team, or a community event. Corporate sponsors contribute greatly to the communities they serve, and many organizations rely on their financial sponsorships (*financiar*) for various activities, from sponsoring a community sporting team (*patrocinar el equipo*) to underwriting a social club (*apadrinar un club*). To be in a position to sponsor anything is always a good thing, and so is the word *patrocinar*.

Staff / *Equipo* or *Personal* or *Tripulación*

There are several words in Spanish for staff, much the same way that there are different words for office. In general, *staff* is the *personal* (personnel) that works in a given place. In hospitals, the nursing staff is *personal de enfermería*. In schools, the teaching staff is *personal docente*. Many museums count on a volunteer staff, which is *personal voluntario*. If those volunteers require staff training, that's *formación de personal*. On occasion, the word *equipo* (as in team) or *cuerpo* (as in corps) is preferred. Medical staff can be either *personal médico* or *cuerpo médico*. If your staff works as a team, then they *trabajan como equipo*. First responders have rescue teams, which are *equipos de rescate*. The high school football players comprise the *equipo de fútbol americano*. The lifeguards work as rescue teams, or *equipos de salvamento*. Be mindful that first responders rescue people while lifeguards save people from drowning, hence the difference between *rescate* and *salvamento*. In some circumstances *plantilla* is used, often for factory workers. To be on a factory's payroll is to *estar en plantilla*. Please note that the crew which works on a ship or an airplane is called a *tripulación*. If nothing else, be familiar with these various words for staff, since they are used with regional preferences throughout the Spanish-speaking world.

Stock Market / *Bolsa Bursátil* or *Bolsa de Valores*

The world of investment has become much more volatile in recent years. There is no doubt that the markets are turbulent. Unfortunately, there is a great deal of turbulence in the Spanish spoken in the United States when it comes to finance. Stock market can be translated in one of two ways. One can say *bolsa bursátil* or *bolsa de valores*. There is no preference of one over the other; it's a matter of style. Financial newspapers tend to prefer *bolsa bursátil* and general reporters prefer to use *bolsa de valores*. There is a slight technical difference. If you want to be exact, *bolsa bursátil* is the *stock market* itself and *bolsa de valores* is the *stock exchange*. In the rapid-fire staccato that one finds among the talking heads on CNBC one hears about this stock market and that stock market, with little regard to other expressions that may be lost in translation. What about other "related" markets that are commonly used in business—and in desperate need of proper translation into business Spanish? If you refer to the "market" and assume everyone knows you mean *stock* market and not a supermarket, you can say *la bolsa*. If things are going poorly and we are in a *bear market*, then it is a *mercado a la baja*. If things are going splendidly and prices are rising, a *bull market* is called a *mercado alcista*. If a company is trying to *corner the market* in something, it is trying to *monopolizar la plaza*. The dismal job market these days is the *mercado laboral*. If you are one of the few who is fortunate enough to *be making a killing in the market*, you can be said to be *ganando mucho dinero por comprar acciones*. (Yes, it's a cumbersome expression, but that's the way it is.) Those who are involved in an illicit activity are said to be in the *black market*, which is the *mercado negro*. In a linguistic twist that reflects cultural differences, the expression "Like a bull in a china shop," in Spanish becomes, "Como un elefante en una cristalería." Why? Because everyone knows that bulls are graceful and do not wreck crystal in china shops. This is an Anglo-Saxon myth about Hispanic society, where bulls are a dominant cultural theme. In fact, the popular cable show "Myth Busters" on the Discovery Channel debunked this myth in an episode called "Red Rag to a Bull." And you can take that to the bank, or the stock market!

Success / *Éxito*

There will be times when someone commends you for a successful presentation, report or job well done. How do you convey your pride in your success to you *abuelita*? Quick! What's Spanish for *success*? Don't tell me you don't know, Latino. (Here's a hint: It's similar to the English-language word found over most doors leading out of the building, usually in red.) *Éxito* is Spanish for *success*. (Reminder: *Exit* in Spanish is *Salida*.) But if no one in corporate headquarters wants you to exit the premises just yet, simply because you are that valuable to the company, the reason probably is because you are terrific at your job. *To be a success* is to *ser un éxito* and *to meet with success* is to *tener éxito*. A *success story* is simply *un éxito*. In many non-business areas, of course, there are antiquated forms to convey the same idea. If you hear that someone is a *persona afortunada*, or that the project turned out to be *un asunto afortunado*, the speaker is referring to a successful person or affair. When someone doubted that something would turn out well, but it did, they might say something ended with *un fin bueno* (a good end), or *con buena fortuna* (good fortune) or even *una buena salida* (a good end/exit). These situations will be rare, and far more often you will encounter *éxito*. One thing you should also bear in mind is that in advertising and marketing the word *éxito* is used to mean *a hit*. If you hear that Apple's new device was *un éxito*, it means that people were lined up for hours in front of the Apple Store and the product is selling well. If you hear that the next song to be played is Jennifer López's *nuevo éxito*, then Jenny from the Block is headed for another hit song on Billboard. *A hit*, which means to be *un éxito*, is the highest form of success in the marketplace.

In life, however, there are many kinds of success, aren't there? Hendrik Coetzee, whom I briefly knew, represented the kind of success that comes from following his dream. "Too often when trying something no one has ever done, there are only 3 likely outcomes: Success, quitting, or serious injury and beyond," he wrote in his online blog. "The difference in the three, are often forces outside of your control. But this is the nature of the beast: Risk." I mention him because he anticipated the worst possible outcome: *beyond injury*. Henrik died on December 7, 2010 at the age of 35, miles down the Lukuga River in the heart of Africa, when a crocodile charged him, dragging him under water. To be eaten alive is one of every human being's primordial fears, and Hendrik enjoyed tremendous success in life because he, without being reckless, chose to face danger and took risks. It is how he lived his life that is important, and it is how one lives one's life that spells success. In his brief time, he enjoyed more success than most of us will ever have in lives twice as long. It is peculiar beyond words to be able to say, "Did I ever tell you about a friend who was eaten alive by a crocodile in Africa ..." It is also tragic beyond words. But if you learn the words and phrases in this book, you will succeed in your professional career and make yourself proud by becoming *un gran éxito*.

(To) Suffer / *Sufrir* or *Aguantar* or *Padecer*

In everyday speech, "to suffer" is a transitive verb that means loss or defeat ("We suffered inventory losses because of the floodwaters."). It also means to tolerate ("I had to suffer fools in high school."). In Spanish, the respective words are *sufrir* and *aguantar*. If, however, we are speaking of suffering from a condition or an illness, then the word is *padecer*. A division manager might want to let staff know that a new hire suffers from Multiple Sclerosis and that Human Resources expects everyone to be sensitive. (*El nuevo empleado padece de Esclerosis Múltiple.*) The challenge, of course, is that because there are various choices for "to suffer" when speaking Spanish, one has to think of which context is most appropriate to the situation at hand. Otherwise, a fluent Spanish speaker will have to *aguantar* your poor Spanish!

Support / *Apoyar*

"Without your support, our sales force will not be successful," the memo, sent via e-mail on a droid, stated. OK, so it's an impersonal pep talk, right? But these days one has to take encouragement where one finds it. And while I want to support you as much as possible in forging ahead in your career through a better understanding and command of business Spanish, I have to take a tough stand and remind you that I will be displeased if you have the nerve to tell me that *support* in business English is *soportar* in business Spanish. It is not. In Spanish, *soportar* means to endure, to bear, to put up with or to be forced to tolerate. (See, Put up With.) On the other hand, in business English, *support* means to sustain, to maintain, to lend encouragement and to back. These ideas are conveyed by the word *apoyar*. *Sin su apoyo, nuestro equipo de ventas no tendrá éxito*, is Spanish for, *Without your support, our sales force will not be successful*. Be mindful that *sostener* also means support, but this is primarily in a non-business context. If someone is frail and they need help standing up, then you can support them, or *sujetar* or *sostener*, by physically holding them up. If your child is out of school and unemployed, it might be necessary to *sostener* their living expenses for the time being. In business situations, on the other hand, most kinds of *support* are adequately expressed in Spanish by *apoyar*.

Supposed to be / *Se Supone Que*

The dangers of translating a phrase word-for-word are never ending, indeed. While in English the phrase "supposed to be" is correct ("I'm supposed to be directing the effort on this project."), in Spanish the phrase "estoy supuesto" is incorrect. Yes, *supuesto* is a word, but it refers to a supposition, as in a hypothesis. The proper way of expressing the idea of being supposed to be doing something is through the expression *se supone que*. The proper translation would begin with "Se supone que debo estar dirigiendo el esfuerzo en este proyecto." Bear in mind there are other ways of expressing this sentiment, such as using *deber*, to say that you should be heading the project (*Debería estar dirigiendo el esfuerzo en este proyecto.*) or you could be more direct and take ownership of the initiative altogether by using *tener* (*Tengo que dirigir el esfuerzo en este proyecto.*). But when you are supposed to do anything, you are never to use *estoy supuesto*, and always translate "supposed to be" as "se supone que."

Survey / *Encuesta*

This is one of the simple words that is often the cause of much confusion. How many times have I heard someone try to get away with the unfortunate *anglicismo* of *surveyo* or *surveyando*? More than I would like to remember. Yet, this is one of those words you have to commit to memory. *A survey*, in Spanish, is *una encuesta*. This refers to a survey or an opinion poll. (It needs to be pointed out that *encuesta* is also used by law enforcement to describe a police inquiry.) In most general business usages, however, *encuesta* is the right word to use—and please refrain from making up words by adding the letter "o" at the end of an English-language word! OK-o?

T

Take advantage of / *Aprovechar*

If we keep taking advantage of business opportunities, we might be on to something, one director tells another. *Taking advantage of* an opportunity or a competitive advantage is one thing, but *taking advantage of* a consumer or a colleague is another. In business English to *take advantage of* an opportunity or a competitive advantage is expressed by a single word in Spanish: *aprovechar*. Learn it. Then learn to use it as a word in business Spanish that can be used for many English-language expressions. *Taking advantage of* is very close to *making the most of* or *putting to good use*. These three common expressions used colloquially in the course of business can be translated into business Spanish by using the word *aprovechar*. *Taking advantage of the opportunity to impress management* is *aprovechar de la oportunidad para impresionar la administración*. *Making the most of the task* is *aprovechando al máximo de la tarea*. *Putting to good use fully* is *aprovechar completamente*. On occasion you will hear native Spanish speakers use the phrase *sacar provecho*, which also means *aprovechar*. A manager might tell his staff that "Hay que sacar provecho de la oportunidad de dar una presentación," meaning "We must take advantage of the opportunity to give a presentation." With this in mind, taking advantage of opportunities has a sinister side in Spanish. The world is full of opportunists, and Latinos are at risk. Recall the time when that modern-day cacique of U.S. Latinos, Raúl Yzaguirre, who ran the National Council of La Raza, commented on the rise in hate crimes against Hispanics by saying, "It seems that open season has been declared on our community. Private citizens and law enforcement officials feel they can harass or attack Hispanic Americans with almost complete impunity." This was in 1999, and it was his way of noting with alarm the number of opportunists that were taking advantage of the hostility many non-Hispanics feel towards Latinos in the U.S. In this current decade, and in light of the situation for Latinos in California, it would be remiss not to warn Latinos that there are those out there in public office that target Latinos, who have track records of using the law as a weapon against Latinos, and who the Latino community cannot trust. Kamala Harris, California Attorney General, while District Attorney in San Francisco, empowered rogue prosecutors to target Latinos and Hispanic organizations, protect anti-Latino bigots, and used her office to undermine the civil rights of Hispanics. These are my opinions, but in the same way that I have an obligation to offer advice on improving your business Spanish, it is my moral obligation to warn California Latinos of the enemies to the community who are in positions of authority and who harbor biases against Hispanics. I'm simply *aprovechando* of this entry to do just that.

Take it to the Next Level / *Llevar al Próximo Nivel*

Don't tell me I have to carry this burden up another flight of stairs? Oh, that's not what you meant. Well, what precisely do you mean by the expression, *take it to the next level*? If you are trying to say that the project at hand is ready to move forward to the next phase, bringing it closer to being fully realized, and you have to say it in Spanish, then the expression is *llevar al próximo nivel*. Remember, this is a straightforward proposition: *level* is *nivel* and *next* is *próximo*. Those words settled, the expression is easy to compose, one of those rare cases when English and Spanish coincide beautifully.

Take Ownership / *Asumir Responsabilidad*

"Taking ownership" is one of those phrases that enters language, and you know it's going to be a short-lived phenomenon simply because it is insipid. Then again, what do I know? The only things that I've taken ownership of are *paper clips*, just because one never knows when there will be a *stapler* crisis. Taking ownership is *tout le mode* in the 2010s. It is only natural that you should be prepared to translate it into Spanish should the unfortunate need arises. The phrase is *asumir responsabilidad*, which literally means *to assume responsibility*. Learn it, because if you don't the tendency will be to translate the first word, *take*, into *tomar*, and then you will be at a loss. *Take* what? *Tomar posesion*—take possession. That sounds very much like repossessing something. That won't do, unless you're driving a tow truck and are looking for cars that are being repossessed. No, that definitely won't do, will it? When it comes to "ownership," what we really mean is "responsibility." If it's a question of taking responsibility, you really are assuming the responsibility for something: *asumir responsabilidad*.

Team Player / *Cumplido*

In the American workplace, sports analogies are often used as a metaphor for business. Do we have a winning strategy? Is she a team player? How do you handicap the competition? "There's a reason sports is often used as an analogy for succeeding in business. It's the same road map," Herb Greenberg, founder of Caliper, told Leigh Buchanan of the *Harvard Business Review* in 2005. Managers want every member of their staff to be a committed team player. But in business Spanish there is far less emphasis on sports as metaphors or analogies in the course of conducting business. In the U.S., sports are serious business, while in the Spanish-speaking world, sports are serious leisure. Whereas Americans study sports to see what they can glean for the workplace, in the Hispanic world sports is a way to forget about life for a while. So how does one translate "team player" into business Spanish? The word is *cumplido*, by which you mean that the person in question meets the expectations of *work*, *dedication* and *loyalty*. If you want to be more precise simply use it in connection with the team—equipo. *Es muy complido con el equipo.* He fulfills his obligations to the team. What you're saying, in essence, is, *He's a team player on whom you can count.*

Test / *Examen* or *Prueba*

If you must know, *test* has been incorporated into the Spanish language by the Spanish Royal Academy, with a caveat: it is recognized as acceptable but not recommended. With this in mind, when speaking business Spanish, remember that the two words for *test* that are recommended are *examen* and *prueba*. In business there are many kinds of tests, and the expressions that are more commonly used in business English have their equivalents in business Spanish. If something is bought on a test basis, such as office equipment, it is *de prueba* (meaning, pending approval). If something (or someone) is put to the test by fire, in business Spanish, that's a *prueba de fuego*. A piece of equipment that is subject to an endurance test is said to be subject to *una prueba de resistencia*. If a candidate is required to take an aptitude test, he or she is subject to a *prueba de aptitud*. If you are asked to put your skills to the test, then your skills are asked to be *puestas a prueba*. The use of *examen*, however, is more prevalent. If you pass a test, then congratulations are in order because you *aprobaste un examen*. If you failed that test, then sorry to hear that you *reprobaste un examen*. Either way, you were required to take a test (*hacer un examen*). If you have to administer the test to a candidate, it is said that you are the one who *pones un examen al candidato*.

What kind of test was it? A driving test is *un examen de conductor*. A written test is *un examen escrito*. This is different from an oral test, which is *un examen oral*. A final exam is *un examen final*. More companies require a medical check-up, or exam, which is *un examen médico* (or *un chequeo médico*). On occasion employees are asked to reflect upon bigger picture, and to examine their place in the firm, which is translated as *someterse a examen*. If you take a good look at yourself, in Spanish this is expressed as *hacerse un examen de conciencia*. And if you are confident that you can *ace a test*, then in Spanish it's *clavar un examen*. *Examen* or *prueba*, it's always a *test*. That's life.

This Monday / *Hoy Lunes*

If it is Monday morning, and there is a meeting scheduled at 3 p.m., would you say, "This Monday we're scheduled to meet at 3 p.m."? Of course not. You would say, "Today we're scheduled to meet at 3 p.m." On occasion, however, someone might use "this Monday," and there might be a bit of confusion. Is it today, or next week? In business English the expression "this Monday" refers to the immediate future: the *following* Monday. To avoid misunderstandings, it's not uncommon to hear someone say, "This coming Monday …" That makes it exactly clear that it is not today, but Monday next week. The reason this is important is that, if you're like so many Latinos in the U.S., you tend to translate "this Monday" as "este lunes." In business Spanish, however, that doesn't work, since it makes no sense linguistically. The correct formulation is to say "hoy lunes"—today Monday—or "el próximo lunes" — "this coming Monday." In Spanish if it is an event that takes place on that specific day of the week, it is correct to say, *hoy lunes, mañana martes, pasado mañana* miercoles, el próximo jueves, el próximo viernes, ayer domingo or anteayer sábado. Any of these are acceptable, but never, ever use *este lunes*, since you will confuse the Spanish-dominant listener.

Throw in the Towel / *Dar por Vencido*

Without question, there comes a time when a project or initiative isn't going well and out of frustration someone says they are going to throw in the towel. This speaks both to a sense of frustration and of defeat. How would you convey this in Spanish? Oh, I don't have to tell you that I've heard "tirar la toalla," as if literally throwing a towel in English conveyed the same sentiment in Spanish, do I? It does not. To throw a towel in Spanish is not a metaphor. It means just that: tossing a towel of some sort somewhere. Is the towel being thrown in the hamper? If you're speaking in Spanish, that is probably the case. The correct expression to convey frustration or defeat in Spanish, on the other hand, is *dar por vencido*, meaning *to be defeated*. I certainly hope it happens infrequently in your career, but when it does, the proper phrase is *dar por vencido*.

Ticket / *Boleto* or *Entrada*

Once again I am the bearer of bad news: *ticket* does not exist in Spanish. The correct words are either *boleto* or *entrada*. Be aware that if you are referring to a ticket for transportation, whether it's for air travel, trains and so forth, the words to use are *billete* or *pasaje*. Other kinds of tickets, such as a traffic ticket, are called *infracciones*. If it's a fine for breaking a rule, that ticket is an *infracción*. Otherwise, in business Spanish a *ticket* is either *un boleto* or *una entrada*.

Time / *Hora*

It's *time* for this, and it's *time* for that. It's *time* to sit down and work on that report. It's *time* to go to the conference room for the conference call. It's *time* to head to the airport. It's *time* to go over the PowerPoint presentation. It's always *time* for something or other in business English. Not so in Spanish! It's never time for anything ... but it's *time* for the appointed *hour*, which has arrived! Remember that in Spanish *time—tiempo—* refers to the weather; or a specific period of time, such as a season or a harvest; or a defined period of time with specific dates, such an epoch, a political period, a social movement; or the specific dates of an armed conflict. As a result, in business Spanish, *time* is *hora*. *It's time for the conference to begin* is translated as *Es hora para que comienze la conferencia*. In business, if it's *time* for something, then the word to use is *hora*.

Time Period or Installment or Terms / *Plazo*

What is the time period for this contract? How many installments are left on the equipment lease? What are the payment terms for the company car? So many different words ... *Time periods ... installments ... terms*. In Spanish the one concise word for all these terms is *plazo*. Before we get to *plazo*, however, a short digression is in order to a more familiar word, *plaza*. Everyone knows that *plaza* is the main square of any town. It means *place* and this place is either physical (*plaza mayor* is the main square), or places in a specific area (*plazas limitadas en el estacionamiento* are limited spaces in the parking lot), or a position of employment (*plaza de dentista* refers to a vacancy for a dentist). "Place" being so generic, it could mean just about anything from *a plaza de toros* (a bullring) to *a plaza de artesanos* (a handicraft market) to *a plaza de comercio* (a shopping center). What about *plazo*? In business Spanish the word *plazo* wears many hats. It means a period of time. *A corto plazo, a medio plazo,* and *a largo plazo* mean, respectively, short term, medium term and long term. *En el plazo de una semana* means within a week (*semana* means *week*). If someone speaks of *un plazo de entrega*, they are referring to delivery time. If someone points out that *mañana termina el plazo de inscripción*, they are letting you know that the deadline for registration ends tomorrow. In each of these cases *plazo* refers to a specific period of time. It also means installments. *Un plazo mensual* refers to a monthly installment payment. One can buy on installment (*comprar a plazo*) and one can pay in installments (*pagar a plazos*). In a more general business sense, *plazo* refers to the terms of a transaction. When one asks what the terms are, they can do so in Spanish by saying, "¿Cuáles son los plazos?" The notion is that in a business context *plazo* conveys the idea of something that has a time restraint to it, whether it is the lease on a car, or the time when a payment is due, or how a consumer can make a purchase on an installment plan. It's a word that you will often encounter when conducting business in Spanish. Learn it now.

Timeframe (*See,* Time Period)

To Whom It May Concern / *A Quien Corresponda*

If there were an SAT test for Latinos who claim to speak Spanish, then this would be the #1 phrase on the test! It's such a common and easily understood expression, but it continues to trip up Latinos every single day. "To whom it may concern" is a standard salutation when making an inquiry, and the sender does not know the name of the person who is the recipient. In business Spanish the correct translation is: *A quien corresponda*. The expression sums up the request that the matter at hand be delivered to the appropriate person responsible. If you have to repeat this phrase a hundred times in order to remember it, then that's what you will have to do. It is, without question, one of the crucial expressions in business Spanish.

Too Much / *Demasiado*

Demasiado is one of those words that make Spanish so intriguing ... at least according to the folks who make Kahlúa. On a more serious note, however, it's a bit disconcerting to have to disclose that many eyebrows have been raised by Hispanics when a Latino blurts out "too *mucho*," without realizing that this is more than *Spanglish*—it's nonsensical. It's normal to stutter, or misspeak or use the wrong word once in a while, especially for Hispanics who are surrounded by English every day by virtue of living in the Hispanic diaspora in the United States. That's no reason, however, to be careless, and in fact it's important to be more conscientious of these kinds of linguistic lapses. To think that others won't notice, and form a negative opinion of you professionally, when "too *mucho*" comes out of your mouth is ... *demasiado* ... to ask.

(To) Touch / *Conmover*

It's a myth that business has to be dispassionate. On the contrary: the most rewarding forms of employment are the ones that touch people's lives. This is true whether you work in the medical field, education or are a firefighter who saves lives. There is a great deal of satisfaction among restauranteurs and caterers who provide memorable meals for special events; and airline employees who know they are reuniting families, or taking people to destinations they have dreamed all their lives about visiting. At the University Club in New York, I knew a bartender who found joy in making the perfect martini. In San Francisco there was an older gentleman who prided himself on his exquisite skill at rebuilding shoes. There are countless examples of people in business who touch the lives of others. So what's the word in Spanish to describe this? Careful! If you say "tocar," then you are mistaken. In Spanish, *tocar* means to touch alright, but it means to touch physically. In the discussion above, we are speaking about touching emotionally, and the word for that is *conmover*, which means to find something moving or touching in an emotional way. It's possible to say that you are touched by a colleague's passion. (*Me conmueve la pasión que tiene.*) It's also possible to describe how you were touched by thoughtfulness that went into making sure everything was perfect at the reception hall for your parents' anniversary celebration. (*Me conmovió todo en la recepción.*) It's perfectly fine to be touched in the course of business, just make sure that you use the word *conmover*, and not *tocar*. After all, you want to make sure you convey the idea that you were emotionally moved, and not suggest that your person was inappropriately fondled.

Tracking / *Rastrear*

Traquear sounds like the noise castanets make when some frenzied flamenco dancer is engaged in performance. That doesn't make it a word. Yes, I know you are going to say that *traquear* is as much a word as is *clicquear*. I'm going to reply with something equally stupid: Flamenco dancing might be the only profession where it is reasonable to use amphetamines as a job enhancement. No, I'm afraid that in business Spanish, the word for *tracking*, as in *tracking number*, is *rastrear*, as in *número de rastreo*. If it helps, remember that *rastrear* also means *to rake*, and that's precisely what you are doing: You are "raking" through information to find a specific fact. Indeed, this is probably the only use in business that you will see for *rastrear*: identifying the tracking number on a package, shipment or item that was sent by expedited courier services. That is, of course, unless you shipped a box of castanets and failed to pack them properly, in which case they are rattling around as they are scanned every step of the way. If that's the case, they'll be easy to track.

Training / *Capacitación*

This is one of those cases when a word does double-duty in English, but not in Spanish. Remain vigilant! Training is indeed *entrenar*. But unless you are referring to physical training—sports and at the gym—you probably mean professional learning. In this case the proper word to use is *capacitación*. In the business world, when we speak of training, whether it is being trained on a new computer system, or going to a workshop for a seminar on the new regulatory requirements of this or that, you are really referring to continuing education of one sort or another. *Capacitación* refers to an intellectual process necessary to become informed, educated and acquire knowledge. This process of learning is also called *adiestramiento*, so be aware should you come across this word, although in Mexico and Spain the more common word is *capacitar* and *capacitación*. Hey, if you think about it, that's what this book is all about: *capacitando al lector para que tenga éxito en su carrera*—training the reader for success in his or her career!

Try / *Tratar* or *Probar*

What are we *trying* to accomplish in this quarter? Did anyone *try* the soup before it was served at today's luncheon? In business English *try* has two distinct meanings: To attempt or to test (taste). There are two different words in Spanish. *To try* to do something is *tartar*, and many Latinos have no problem using that word. But the second word, *probar*, which means *to test* and *to taste*, is elusive. Be mindful that whether you are referring to trying out the new video game or the new recipe for soup, it is *probar*. *Tratar* almost always means to attempt, but if it's about *testing* something or *tasting* it, it's *probar*.

Turning the Page / *Seguir Adelante* or *Punto y Aparte*

In most business situations when one is advised "to turn the page," it usually means to get over it, and get on with it. The past is the past, and whatever page is being turned, it belongs to the past. How do you convey this idea in business Spanish? Ah, yes, on occasion one hears a literal translation—*voltar la página*—and then one cringes in horror. I'm afraid that in business Spanish using such an *anglicismo* won't fare well. This idea is more adequately expressed with the phrase *seguir adelante*—to move forward. Turning the page, after all, is expressing the need to move forward. Another expression used to convey this notion is *punto y aparte*, literally, *period and apart*. Where does the expression *punto y aparte* originate? It's a carry-over from the time before there were personal computers in the workplace.

In those days, there used to be a class of employees whose job it was to write business correspondence, reproduce texts and transcribe dictation. If you look at re-runs of *Perry Mason* or the current series *Mad Men*, you see that women were employed as secretaries whose duties included dictation. In the Spanish-speaking world, a (male) executive would be dictating a letter, a memo or some other document to a (female) secretary. At times he would wander off topic—much like this entry—and then he would say, *punto y aparte*. This would indicate that that run-on sentence was over—*period*—and a new paragraph was about to begin—*apart*. It would be the secretary's job to reorganize his last rambling digression into a coherent sentence, and then continue on with a new paragraph, or topic. That expression is still used to mean put a *period* on that episode and it's time to move on to a *different topic*. Whether it's time to *seguir adelante*, or it's *punto y aparte* on that subject, the point is the same: Turn the page and get on with it!

Undermine / *Minar* or *Socavar*

How do you handle unpleasant people that you are bound to encounter in the course of your career? Let us face it: the world is full of assholes. Oh, yes, I use that word because Robert Sutton, a professor of management science and engineering at Stanford University in California, used that word in the title of his bestselling book, *The No Asshole Rule: Building a*

Civilized Workplace and Surviving One That Isn't. It's not my intention to promote his book, but the point I'm making is that you will undoubtedly encounter people who will work to undermine you, your position and your career. It happens to everyone at some point. How do you describe that frustration? How do you explain that someone is simply working against you, and undermining you? There are two words in Spanish you can use: *minar* or *socavar*. *Minar*, which means to weaken the foundation of something by burrowing beneath it, is suggestive of mining and aptly describes someone who is working to weaken the foundation of your position. *Socavar*, on the other hand, conveys the idea of weakening or damaging something through indirect or duplicitous means. It will probably be easier to remember *minar*, since it resembles undermine, but *socavar* is the more elegant way of describing how that asshole did everything possible to sabotage you and undermine your project.

Unsubscribe / *Darse de Baja*

Yes, technology does have its drawbacks, and these include unsolicited e-mails, and being on the receiving end of many, many promotional material via e-mail. But how do you unsubscribe to an unwanted e-mail list? These are the perplexing challenges of the world in which we live. Spanish is catching up to meet the needs of the new technologies that shape the way we conduct business. The correct phrase is *darse de baja*. This works when notifying a sender that you want to be removed from future mailings. The phrase nicely mirrors the one for registering online: *darse de alta*.

Update / *Actualizar*

If you were to update your files, how would you express that? If you had updated the report, how would you convey that? In Spanish, to update is *actualizar*, meaning to bring up to date. An update, on the other hand, is an *actualización*. The verb is *actualizar*. Please update the report is *Por favor actualiza el informe*. The noun is *actualización*. *La actualización esta mejor* means *The update is better*. If, however, you are referring to updating someone, what you are doing is briefing someone to make them current. In this case, you should express this by saying that you are going to *poner al gerente corriente de los antecedentes* or *poner al gerente al día de los antecedentes* (you are going to update the manager). (See, Antecedent / *Antecedente*.) The notion is that you are making the manager current on the matter by giving him (or her) the most recent information available. In every other business usage, it's either *actualizar* or *actualización*.

Use Precaution / *Tomar Precaución*

"Please use caution when opening overhead bins, as items may have shifted during the flight." How many times have you heard that? Use caution? How about abuse caution? Is that possible? Will it result in an addiction, as it occurs when you abuse alcohol? (Let us think about this one over a shot of mezcal. I digress.) In English *caution* is something that can *used*. Not so in Spanish! *Caution*, or rather, precaution, is something to be *taken*. The correct business Spanish translation is *tomar precaución*. Whether it's opening overhead bins, crossing the street, or running up the stairs because you are late for the meeting and can't wait for the elevator, it is always wise to *tomar precaución*. As an interesting aside, in English, while *caution* is *used*, *precaution* is *taken*. The Centers for Disease Control in Atlanta, for instance, always advises the public to *take precautions* every winter when the flu season arrives. They might as well be speaking Spanish! And maybe one day they will!

Waiting for / *Esperando a*

What are you waiting for? It could be anything. You could be waiting for your flight to start boarding, or you could be waiting for everyone to arrive at the conference room. If you had to relay this information to someone in Spanish, what would say? "Estoy *esperando por* el avión," or "Estoy *esperando por* los participantes"? You could, but if you did, then you'd be mistaken. Be mindful that "waiting for" in Spanish becomes "esperando a." Yes, what you are doing is "*esperando a* abordar el avión," or "*esperando a* que lleguen los participantes" expected to attend the meeting.

We'll Be in Touch / *Estamos en Contacto*

Being in touch is a form of following up on something. In business English, the expression conveys the notion that more information or further discussions are forthcoming. The person saying that he or she will be in touch makes the commitment of getting back to the other person. It's a mistake to use "tocar" in any sense whatsoever in translating the idea of being in touch. Why? Because in Spanish *tocar* is used exclusively to mean to touch physically something or someone. The correct expression is to be *in contact* with the person.

We'll be in touch is properly expressed in Spanish as *Estamos en contacto*.

When All is Said and Done (*See,* At the End of the Day)

Work Hard / *Trabajar con Empeño*

If it's time to roll up your sleeves and get down to business, then it's time to work hard. If you had to say this in Spanish, I'm afraid that *trabajar duro* won't cut it. The correct business Spanish translation is *trabajar con empeño*. The word *empeño* denotes great determination and engagement, an earnest desire and firm perserverance. If you are determined to do something, the Spanish-language phrase to use is *tener empeño para hacer algo*. If you are engaged with great determination and eagerness, then it can be said that you are working *con empeño*. A great effort to achieve something can be described as to *poner empeño para lograr algo*. The reverse, of course, is true. There are phrases in business English that convey toughness that are expressed colloquially. The two most common expressions that one encounters are the descriptions of someone who is either a tough cookie (*un tipo duro* or *una tipa dura*) or who is a hard nut to crack (*un hueso duro de roer*). Then again, for Latinos in the U.S. the fact of the matter is that you have to work extra hard, and even then recognition is elusive. Consider Carl Quintanilla, the anchor and reporter on CNBC, who has been one of the Hispanic pioneers in business reporting on cable television. Once, when I made an inquiry about the address of their new offices, a person from CNBC referred me to "Jose Quintilla." Work hard, and on occasion, they still don't get your name right! It's enough to drive one to a bar where everybody knows your name—a bar in Boston called *Cheers*. But before you head down for Happy Hour (*la Hora Feliz*, by the way), makes sure you have *trabajado con empeño*.

Worldwide Web / *Red Mundial*

What can be said about this calamity that has befallen humanity? Oh, I am just kidding. Everyone knows the world is better off now that we are all theoretically connected to the Internet via the worldwide web. There's no need to translate "Internet," since, like other inventions of generations past—"television" and "radio"—the word is derived from Latin, which forms the basis of much of the vocabulary of both English and Spanish. Words that are derived from English, on the other hand, do need to be translated. "Worldwide" in Spanish is "mundial." (Remember that *global*, meaning that which pertains to the globe on which we live, is the same in English and Spanish.) But what of *web*? Why was the word *web*, as in *spider web*, chosen to denote a global network of computers linked through various interfaces to each other? Probably because the consensus emerged that it was easier to remember "www" than it would be "wwn"—as in "worldwide network." Geeks being the way they are, they gave the world those three letters, an easy acronym to remember. In Spanish, however, the proper translation for worldwide web is *red mundial*. (Remember, Latino, *red* in Spanish means *network* and *net*—as in the nets that fishermen use.) Also keep in mind that *red* is feminine, meaning that in Spanish, it's correct to speak of *la red mundial*. If you don't believe me, just Google it!

Wrap Up / *Poner Punto Final a*

If we are at the letter "W" we are close to wrapping things up. *¡Qué bueno!* I'm confident you're happy about that. I haven't settled on how to wrap up the discussion when the time comes. "Wrap up" in English has two distinct meanings. The first is literal: to wrap things up in something. If you're wrapping up a present for someone (bookstores will gladly gift wrap this book, by the way), then the word in Spanish is *envolver*. It's also possible to describe someone as being "wrapped up" in whatever they're doing—and if it involves a teenager you are probably correct in assuming that she or he is wrapped up with their cell phone or video game, or playing some video game on a cell phone. One can also speak about being wrapped up—as toddlers are wont to look when cold weather arrives. In this sense, wrap up is used to mean to dress warmly; the Spanish word is *abrigarse*. It is the other sense, the business usage, that interests us, however. To wrap up a meeting is to bring it to its conclusion. In Spanish, the expression is *poner punto final a* ... whatever it is you are wrapping up. *Poner punto final a* is an expression that literally means to place the final period at the end of something. This is derived from the old practice of having meetings transcribed, and the speaker would indicate to the secretary that this was the final point at the end of the final sentence, meaning the discussion being recorded was now concluded. "Let us wrap things up" can be translated in Spanish as "Vamos a poner el punto final a esto." "Wrapping up the meeting," becomes "Poniendo punto final a la reunión." Be mindful that there are other times when "wrap up" is used in colloquialisms. If you can't wrap your head around something, in Spanish you can say that "no entiendo algo." If your boss is impatient and interrupts you by saying it's time to wrap it up, what she or he is saying is that it is time to stop. You can say translate your boss's impatience by saying "Es hora de terminar." For the most part, however, in standard business usage, wrap up is *poner punto final a* ... this entry.

Yield (or Return) / *Rendimiento*

If you find yourself behind the wheel of a motor vehicle, you are required to *yield* to pedestrians. But if you are conducting business, well, Latino, that's a different kind of *yield*. What's the *yield* on this investment? What's *gross yield*? What's the *capital yield*? In all these cases, the word for *yield* is *rendimiento*. A *rendimiento* is the *yield* on an investment or a business. It is also a measure of productivity of an employee or the abundance of a harvest. The *yield* on the money market account is 2.45% interest. The *productivity* of their division increased 3% over last year. The *harvest* was down 4% because of inclement weather. In each of these cases the words "yield," "productivity" and "harvest" are used to denote the *return* on the investment or asset. In each of these cases, the word *rendimiento* is in order. Be mindful that when it comes to using "yield" in financial phrases—gross yield and capital yield—the proper Spanish-language translations, respectively, are: *rendimiento bruto* and *rendimiento de capital*.

Part II
—Legal and Law

Law and Legal

Words, Phrases and Terms

English	Spanish
A	
abandonment	abandono, deserción
abbreviation	abreviación
abduction	secuestro
ability	capacidad
ability to pay	capacidad para pagar
abolish	abolir
abortion	aborto inducido
absent parents	padres ausentes
abuse of authority or power	abuso de poder
accessory	accesorio, cómplice
accessory after the fact	encubridor
accessory before the fact	cómplice instigador
accident	accidente
accomplice	cómplice
according to law	conforme a la ley

account balance	saldo de una cuenta
account number	número de cuenta
accountant	contador
accredited school	escuela acreditada
accrued benefits	beneficios acumulados
accusation	acusación
accuse	acusar
accused – defendant	acusado
acknowledge	reconocer
acquit	absolver
acquittal	absolución
ad litem	ad litem, para el proceso
addendum	addenda, adiciones, añadiduras
adjourn	levantar (la sesión)
adjudged, ordered and decreed	adjudicar
adjudication	adjudicación, fallo
adjustment	ajuste
adjustment of status	cambio de condición, ajuste de estatus
administrative law judge	juez de ley administrativo, juez de derecho administrativo
admissible	admisible
admission – confession	admission de culpabilidad, confesión
alias	alias, nombre supuesto

admonish	admonición, advertencia, el aviso
adopted child	hijo adoptivo
adoption	adopción
adult education	educación para adultos
adult protective services	servicios de protección de adultos
adultery	adulterio
adulthood	edad adulta
advance filing	reclamación por adelantado
advance medical directive	instrucciones médicas anticipadas o adelantadas
advance notice	intimación por adelantado
advance payment	pago adelantado
adverse claim	reclamación adversa
adverse party or opposing party	parte adversa
advertisement	anuncio, aviso
advice	consejo
advise	aconsejar
advisement of rights	informar a alguien sobre sus derechos
affidavit	affidavit, declaración jurada
affidavit of prejudice	declaración de prejucio
affidavit of support	declaración jurada de manutención (o sustento)

affirmative action	programa diseñado para remediar práticas discriminatorias
affirmative defense	defensa afirmativa
age	edad
aged, blind or disabled	anciano, ciego, o discapacitado
agent	agente, representante
aggravated assault	agresión agravada
aggravating circumstances	circunstancias agravantes
aggressor	agresor
agreement	acuerdo, convenio
agricultural labor	trabajo agrícola
aid	asistir, ayudar, auxiliar
aid and abet	instigar y ayudar a cometer un delito
alcoholic	alcohólico
alibi	coartada
alien	extranjero
alien lawfully admitted	extranjero legalmente admitido
application fee	cargo de solicitud
alien registration card	tarjeta de registro de extranjero, tarjeta de residencia
alien smuggler	coyote
alien status	estado legal de extranjero

alimony	pensión alimenticia del cónyuge divorciado
allegation	alegación, alegato
allege	alegar
allotment	asignación, repartición, porción
altercation	disputa
alternative dispute resolution	procedimientos para resolver disputas sin litigio
ambassador	embajador
ambulance	ambulancia
amend	enmendar
amended birth certificate	acta de nacimiento enmendada
amendment	enmienda
amnesty	amnestía
amortization	amortización
amount of money	importe de dinero
amount owed	el saldo debido
amputation	amputación
anger management class	programa para enseñar como controlar el enojo
annotation	anotación, comentario
annual income	ingreso anual
annual leave	licencia anual
annual percentage rate (APR)	la tasa anual de porcentaje
annuitant	pensionista

annuity	pensión vitalicia, anualidad
annulment	anulación
anonymous	anónimo
answer – to a charge	contestación de la demanda, respuesta
appeal – noun	apelación
appeal – verb	apelar
appeal bond	fianza de apelación
appeal rights	derechos de apelar
appeals council	consejero de apelaciones
appearance	comparencencia, presencia
appellant	apelante
applicant	solicitante
application	solicitud
application form	formulario de solicitud
apply	solicitar, pedir
appoint a representative	nombrar un agente
appointment – for a meeting	una cita
appointment – to a position	designación, nombramiento
appointment date	fecha de entrevista
appraisal – valuation	valoración
apprentice	aprendiz
approval	aprobación, consentimiento

approximate	aproximado
aptitude test	examen de capacidades
arbitrary	arbitraria
arbitrary arrest	arbitrariamente detenido
arbitration	arbitraje
arbitration clause	cláusula arbitral
area code	código de area telefónica, zona telefónica
argument – dispute	disputa
argument – legal argument	argumento, razonamiento
armed robbery	robo a mano armada
arraign	leer la acusación
arraignment	acusación formal, instrucción de cargos, lectura de acusación
arrears – behind in payments	pagos atrasados, en mora
arrest – noun	arresto
arrest – verb	arrestar
arrest warrant	órden de arresto, mandamiento de arresto
arson	incendio intencional, delito de incendio
article	artículo
assault	agresión, asalto
assault and battery	asalto con agresión, agresión y maltrato
assault warrant	una orden de arresto por agresión

assault with a deadly weapon	acometimiento a mano armada, asalto a mano armada
assets	bienes activos
assign	nombrar, designar
assignee	beneficiario, cesionario
assignor	cedente, transferidor
assistance	asistencia, ayuda
assistant	asistente, ayudante, apoyante
assistant manager	gerente asistente
assisted living facility	establecimiento de convivencia asistida
association	asociación, alianza, organización
asylum – refuge	asilo
asylum hearing	audiencia de asilo
at will employment	empleo a voluntad
attached document	documento adjunto
attachment of property	embargo de propiedad
attainment of age	cumplimiento de edad
attention deficit disorder (ADD)	trastorno de deficiencia de la atención
attest	certificar
attorney	abogado, licenciado
attorney-client privilege	privilegio de comunicaciones entre abogado y cliente

attorney fees	honorarios del abogado
attorney general	procurador general, fiscal general
attorney of record	abogado que consta
attorney-in-fact	apoderado
auction	subasta
audit	auditoría
auditor	auditor
authenticate	autenticar
authority	autoridad
authorization	autorización
authorize	autorizar
authorized agent	agente autorizado
authorized representative	representante autorizado
automatic deduction	deducción automática
automatic enrollment	inscripción automática
automatic entitlement	derecho automático a ciertas prestaciones
automatic increase	aumento automático
automatic recomputation	recomputación automático
automatic teller machine (ATM)	cajero automático
automobile insurance	seguro de automóvil
autopsy	autopsia
availability of funds	disponibilidad de fondos
average	promedio
average yearly earning	salario annual promedio

award certificate	certificado de adjudicación, certificado de beneficio

B

baby sitter	niñera
bachelor's degree	egresado
back pay	pago retroactivo
back taxes	impuestos atrasados
background	antecedente, historia
bad check	cheque sin fondos
bad debt	deuda incobrable, deuda que no se puede cobrar
bad faith	mala fe
bail	fianza
bail bondsman	fiador
bail forfeiture	confiscación de fianza
bailiff	guarda de sala
balloon payment	pago final mayor
bank	banco
bank account	cuenta bancaria, cuenta de banco
bank statement	estado de cuenta, informe bancario
bankruptcy	bancarrota, quiebra
bankruptcy court	tribunal de quiebra

bankruptcy discharge	rehabilitación en quiebra
bankruptcy discharge hearing	una audiencia de descarga de bancarrota
bankruptcy petition	petición de quiebra
baptismal certificate	certificado de bautismo, registro bautismal
bar association	colegio de abogados
battery	agresión física
beat – hit	golpear
become effective	entrar en vigor
behavior	comportamiento
bench – judge's position	corte, tribunal, cuerpo de jueces
bench warrant	orden de arresto
beneficiary	beneficiario
benefit amount	cantidad de beneficio
benefit estimate	cálculo de beneficio
benefit increase	aumento de beneficio
benefit payments	pagos de beneficios
benefit period	período de beneficios
bequest	legado
best evidence	pruega directa
best interest of the child	mayor beneficio del menor
beyond a reasonable doubt	fuera de toda duda razonable
bias	prejuicio

bill – for goods or work	factura, cuenta
bill – for legislation	propuesta de legislación
bill of complaint	escrito de agravios, escrito de demanda
bill of particulars	relación detallada de la materia de la demanda or contrademanda
billing statement	factura
binding agreement	convenio obligante
biographic information	información biográfica
birth certificate	acta de nacimiento, certificado de nacimiento
birth control	prevención de embarazo, anticonceptivos
bite	mordida
black market	mercado negro
blacklist	discriminar contra miembros de una lista
blackmail – noun	chantaje
blackmail – verb	chantajear, extorsionar
block – on claim form	encasillado en un formulario
blood transfusion	transfusión de sangre
board of directors	junta de directores
board of trustees	junta de fidicomisarios
boarding house	casa de huéspedes, pensión
bona-fide	auténtico

bond – custody release	fianza
bond – financial certificate	bono
bond reduction	reducción de fianza
bonus	sobresueldo o bono
bonus received at Christmas	aguinaldo
bookkeeper	tenedor de libros, contador
border – international	frontera
border patrol	patrulla fronteriza
borrower	presatario
braces – dental	ganchos dentales
branch office	sucursal
brandishing a weapon	amenezar a alguien con un arma
brawl	pelea
breach of contract	incumplimiento de pacto
break – from work	recreo
break up with someone	cortar relaciones con alguien
breakdown – of machine or car	malfunción
breaking and entering	escalamiento, allanamiento de morada
breathalyzer	alcoholímetro
breathlessness	falta de respiración
bribe – noun	soborno, cohecho
bribe – verb	sobornar, cohechar
bribery	cohecho

brief – case summary	informe
brochure	folleto
broken bone	hueso fracturado, hueso quebrado, hueso roto
bronchitis	bronquitis
bruise	magulladura, contusion, moretón
budget	presupuesto
bully – noun	el matón, el valentón
burden of proof	carga de la prueba
bureaucracy	burocracia
burglary	robo
burn – an injury	quemadura
burial – funeral	sepultar, enterrar
business – enterprise	negocio
business card	tarjeta de negocios
business hours	horas de trabajo, horas laborables, horas de oficina
business school	escuela de comercio, colegio de negocio

C

calendar year	año calendario
cancellation	cancelación
cancelled check	cheque cancelado
cancer	cáncer

cane	bastón
capias	orden de detención, orden de arresto
capital punishment	pena capital, pena de muerte
car title	título de automóvil
cardiac arrest	ataque de corazón, fallo cardíaco
caretaker	cuidador, protector
carrier – Part B	agencia de seguros de Medicare Parte B
case	caso, causa
case dismissed	causa desechada, caso desechado
case law	precedentes, jurisprudencia
case number	úmer del caso
casefile	expediente
casefile – closed	archivo
case-load	número de casos para resolver
cash	dinero en efectivo
cash a check	cobrar un cheque
cash wages	sueldo, salario, pago en efectivo
cast – plaster	enyesado
catastrophic coverage	protección contra catástrofe
catastrophic illness	enfermedad catastrófica

cause of action	derecho de acción
caveat	advertencia
caveat emptor	caveat emptor, que tenga cuidado el comprador, a riesgo del comprador
cease and desist order	orden para cesar alguna actividad
census	censo, empadronamiento
cerebral palsy	parálisis cerebral
certificate	certificado, la constancia
certificate of deposit	certificado de depósito
certified	certificado
certified check	cheque certificado
certified copy	copia certificada
certified mail	correo certificado
certifying of payments	certificación de pagos
cessation of benefits	terminación de prestaciones
cessation of disability	terminación de incapacidad
chain of command	cadena de mando
chain of custody	cadena de custodia
challenge – noun	reto
challenge – verb	recusar, objetar, retar
challenge for cause	recusación jusificada
chambers	despacho del juez

change in living arrangements	cambio de tipo de alojamiento
change of payee	cambio de representante
change of residence	cambio de residencia
change of venue	traslado de lugar de un juicio
character – nature or disposition	carácter
charge – accusation	denuncia, el cargo
charge – accuse	acusar
charging document	la demanda
charitable organization	organización sin fines de lucro, organización caritativa, associación de beneficienia
charter	carta, contrato de fletamento
cheat	engañar, estafar
check – money	cheque
check – to check	comprobar, verificar
check list	lista de comprobación
check stub	talón de cheque
checking account	cuenta corriente
chemotherapy	quimoterapia
child abuse	abuso de menores
child advocacy	defensa al menor
child care	cuidado infantil
child care expenses	gastos de cuidado de menores

child care services	servicios de guardería
child custody	custodia de menores
child in need of services	menor en necesidad de servicios
child in need of supervision	menor en necesidad de supervisión
child labor	empleo de menores
child molestation	abuso sexual de menores
child protective services (CPS)	servicios de protección de menores
child support	sostenimiento de menores, mantenimiento de los hijos
child support order	orden de manutención para hijos
child support guidelines	pautas para la manutención de los hijos
childhood	niñez
childhood disability benefits	beneficios de incapacidad en la niñez
chiropractor	quiropráctica
choke – verb	estrangular
circuit court	tribunal de circuito
circumstances	circunstancias
circumstantial evidence	evidencia circunstancial, prueba circunstancial
citation – summons	citación para presuntarse en la corte
citation – quote of legal authority	citación de autoridad legal

citizen	ciudadano
citizenship	cuidadanía
civil action	acción civil
civil case	caso civil
civil code	código civil
civil disobedience	desobediencia civil
civil law	ley civil
civil rights	derechos civiles
civil status	estado civil
civil suit	litigio civil
claim – legal request	reclamación, demanda
claim for Medicare payment	reclamación de pago de Medicare
claim number	número de reclamación
claimant	demandante, reclamante
class action suit	acción de clase
classified advertisements	avisos clasificados
clause – in a legal document	clásula
clergyman	clérigo
clerk of the court	secretario del tribunal, escribiente de la corte
client	cliente
client evaluation	evaluación de cliente
clinical record	archivo médico
closing argument	argumento final de un abogado
closing statement	declaración del cierre

coalition	coalición, federación
co-defendant	codemandado
codicil –supplement to will	codicilo, adición o cambio a un testamento
coercion	coerción
cohabitation	cohabitación
collateral	seguridad colateral
colleague	colega
collection account	cuenta de cobro
collection agency	agencia de cobros
collective bargaining	negociación colectiva
college degree	egresado
collision	colisión
confirm	confirmar
color – of skin	color
color of law	apariencia legal, semejanza de derechos
combination of impairments	combinación de impedimentos
comity of nations	cortesía entre cortes de una jurisdicción con las de otra jurisdicción
commission – authority	encargo
commission – money	recargo
commit – perpetrate an offense	cometer
commit suicide	suicidio, suicidarse

commitment to institution	internación en una institución
committee or commission	comisión, junta
common good	para el bienestar general, bien común
common-law marriage	matrimonio de ley común
community based organization	organización comunitaria
community outreach	comunidad de rescate
community property	bienes comunales
community service	trabajo comunitario
commutation of a sentence	reducción de sentencia
comp time	tiempo libre en compensación por horas extras trabajadas
company	compañia, empresa
compensation – for loss or injury	compensación, indemnización
complainant	querellante, demandante
complaint – legal	complaint demanda
complete an application	llenar una solicitud
comply	conformarse
comply with	cumplir con
compound interest	interés compuesto
compromise – noun	compromiso, arreglo
compromise – verb	comprometer
concealed weapon	arma encubierta
concealment	encubrimiento

concerning	concerniente a
concordance of evidence	concordancia de pruebas, armonía de pruebas
concur	concurrir
concurrent authoritiy	autoridad concurrente
concurrent sentence	sentencia concurrente
concussion – type of head injury	pérdida de conocimiento por golpe
conference	conferencia
confess	confesar
confession	confesión
confidence game	embaucamiento
confidentiality	confidencialidad
confinement	encerramiento
confiscate	confiscar
conflict of interest	conflicto de intereses
conflict resolution	resolución de conflictos
congressman	congresista, representatne al congreso
conscientious objector	objector de conciencia
conscription – draft	reclutamiento, conscripción
consecutive interpretation	interpretación consecutiva
consecutive sentence	sentencia consecutiva
consent	consentimiento, acuerdo
consent order	orden por consentimiento

consent to judgment	consentimiento a juicio
conservator	depositario jurídico
conspiracy	conspiración, complot
constitution	constitución
constitutional amendment	enmienda constitucional
constitutional right	derecho constitucional
constructive discharge – from employment	despido forzado
constructive payment	pago implícito
consular officer – foreign service	oficial consular
consulate	consulado
consult	consultar
consultation fee	honorario de consulta
consulting physician	médico consultor
consumer	consumidor
consumer law	ley de consumo
contempt for human rights	desprecio a los derechos humanos
contempt of court	desacato al tribunal
contest – to dispute	oponerse, disputar
contested hearing	audiencia contestada
continuance	continuación, aplazamiento
continuance of eligibility	continuación de elegibilidad
continuing disability	incapacidad continua
contraceptive	preservativo

contract	contrato, convenio
contractor	contratista
contradict	contradecir
contribution	contribución
contributory negligence	negligencia contribuyente, imprudenica concurrente
convalescence	convalencencia
convict – noun	convicto, presidiario
convict – verb	condenar, declarar culpable
conviction	convicción, condena
coordinate	coordinar
co-owner	co-propietario, condueño
copy – noun	copia, ejemplar
copyright	derechos de autor, propiedad intelectual
coroner	médico forense, médico pesquisador
creditor	acreedor
corporal punishment	castigo físico, pena corporal
corporation	corporación, person jurídica
correspondence course	curso de correspondencia
corroborate	corroborar
corroborating evidence	prueba corroborante
corruption	corrupción

co-signer – for a loan	co-deudor
co-sponsor	copatrocinador
cost of living	costo de vida
costs	costos
counsel – lawyer	abogado
counsel – verb	aconsejar, avisar
counsel of record	abogado que consta
counseling services	servicios de consejo
counselor	consejero
count – numbered	charge el cargo
countable resources	recursos computables
counter claim	contrademanda
counterfeiting	falsificación
country of origin	país de origen
court	tribunal, juzgado, corte
court appointed attorney	abogado asignado por el tribunal
court clerk	secretario del tribunal
court costs	costos judiciales
court interpreter	interprete de la corte, interprete del tribunal
court order	orden judicial
court reporter	relator del tribunal, taquígrafo del tribunal, escribiente del tribunal
court-martial	tribunal militar
courtroom	sala del tribunal

coverage – insurance coverage	cobertura
co-worker	compañero de trabajo, colega
credibility	credibilidad
credit bureau	agencia de reporte y clasificación de crédito
credit card	tarjeta de crédito
credit card fraud	fraude por tarjetas de crédito
credit counseling service	servicio de asesoría sobre crédito
credit rating	calificación de credito
credit repair	reparación de crédito
credit report	informe de crédito
credit reporting agency	agencia de informes de crédito
credit union	cooperative de crédito
creditor's bill of equity	lista de bienes del deudor
cremation	cremación
crime	crimen, delito
criminal	criminal, delincuente
criminal case	caso penal, caso criminal
criminal charge	cargo criminal
criminal law	leyes criminales
criminal record	archivos criminals, antecedents criminales
crippled	lisiado, tullido

crisis counseling	consejería en momentos de crisis
criteria	criterios
cross-examination	contrainterrogatorio
current market value	valor actual en el mercado
currently insured	actualmente asegurado
custodial care	cuidado custodial
custodial parent	padre con custodia
custody – child custody	custodia de un menor
custody – of suspect or convict	custodiade un sospechoso o condenado
custody order – child cusdody	orden de custodia
customer service	servicios al cliente
customs – traditions	costumbres, tradiciones
customs officer	oficial de aduana

D

daily maintenance	manutención diaria, mantenimiento diario
damage	daño
damages – compensation	compensar por daños y perjuicios
danger	peligro, riesgo
date of birth	fecha de nacimiento
daughter-in-law	hija política, nuera
day laborer	trabajador por día, jornalero

daycare	guardería infantil
de novo trial	proceso de novo
deadline	límite de tiempo, fecha de vencimiento
deadlock	empate
deaf	sordo
death certificate	certificado de defunción, acta de defunción
death penalty	pena de muerte, pena capital
debate	debatir, discutir
debt	deuda
debt collection	cobranza de deudas
debt consolidation	consolidadción de deudas
debt repayment	amortización de deudas
debtor	deudor
deceased	difunto, muerto, fallecido
deceive	engañar, embaucar
declaration	declaración
declaration of paternity	declaración de paternidad
declare under oath	declarar bajo juramento
decree	decreto
decree of divorce	sentencia de divorcio
deductible	deducible
deduction – from paycheck	deducción
deed – title to property	escritura de propiedad, título de propiedad

deed of trust	escritura de fideicomiso
deem	atribuir
defamation	difamación, calumnia
default	incumplimiento
default judgement	fallo por falta de comparecencia, fallo por incumplimiento
defect –imperfection	defecto
defendant	acusado, demandado
defense – defense attorney	defensa
defense – evidence	pruebas para la defensa
defense attorney or counsel	abogado defensor
deferment	aplazamiento
deferred compensation	compensación aplazada
defined benefit plan	plan de beneficio definido
defraud	defraudar, estafar
degrading treatment	trato degradente y humillante
delay	demorar, aplazar
deliberation	deliberación, consulta entre los miembros del jurado
delinquent – past due	atrasado
delinquent – person	delincuente
delinquent taxes	impuestos morosos
dementia	demencia
demonstration – political	manifestación

demurrer	objeción
denial	denegación
denial notice	aviso de denegación
denied	negado
dental care	cuidado dental
dentist	dentista
deny – a request	negar, denegar
deny – deprive	denegar
department of social services	departamento de servicios sociales
dependent	dependiente, familiar a su cargo
deponent	declarante, deponente
deportation	deportación
deportation proceedings	tramite de deportación
deposit	depósito
deposition	declaración, deposición
depreciation	depreciación, amortización, desvalorización
depression – emotional	depresión
desertion – of family	abandono
desertion from military	abandono militar
detention	detención
detention – after school	retención escolar
deterioration	deterioro, desmejora

determined period of time	período de tiempo determinado
detinue warrant	demanda por rentención ilegal de propiedades
developmental	de desarrollo
diabetic	diabético
diagnosis	diagnóstico
diagnostic test	prueba diagnóstica, exámen diagnóstico
dialect – of language	dialecto
diploma	diploma
diplomat	diplomático
direct deposit	depósito directo
direct evidence	pruebas directas
direct examination	interrogatoria directo
disability	incapacidad, impedimento, invalidez
disability denial notice	aviso de denegación de incapacidad
disability evaluation specialist	especialista en evaluación de incapacidad
disability insurance	seguro de incapacidad
disability pension	pension por discapacidad
disabled person	persona incapacitada
disabled veteran	veterano de guerra incapacitado
disallow	denegar
disaster	desastre, calamidad

disbarment	suspension o revocación de la licencia de un abogado
discharge – from a hospital	dar de alta del hospital
discharge – from employment	el descargo del trabajo, desipdo
discharge – from military service	licenciado del servicio militar
discharge hearing – bankruptcy	audiencia de descargo
disclaimer	clause renuncia, denegación de una responsabilidad
disclosure of information	revelación de información
discount – of price	descuento
discovery	revelación
discrepancy	discrepancia
discrimination	discriminación
dismiss – a case	desestimar
dismiss – an employee	despedir
dismiss charges	desestimar, desechar
dismissal with prejudice	desestimar con pérdida de derecho a nuevo juicio
dismissal without prejudice	desestimar sin pérdida de derecho a nuevo juicio
disorderly conduct	desorden público
disposition	acuerdo, arreglo
disqualify	descalificar
dissolution	disolución

district attorney	fiscal, procurador general
district court	tribunal de distrito
district manager	gerente de distrito
disturbing the peace	perturbación de la paz pública
diversion – alternative program	desviación – procedmiento de rehabilitación
diversity	diversidad, variedad
dividends	dividendos
divorce	divorcio
divorce decree	decreto de divorcio absoluto
divorce from "bed and board"	divorcio de "techo y sustento"
divorce from the "bond of matrimony"	divorcio de la "unión del matrimonio"
divulge	divulgar
docket	orden del día, lista de causas
doctor or physician	doctor, médico
document	documento
domestic violence	violencia doméstica
domestic worker	persona empleada en servicio doméstico
domicile	domicilio
donation	donación

door-to-door sales	venta puerta a puerta
double jeopardy	doble exposición por el mismo delito
down payment	pago inicial
Down's syndrome	síndrome de Down
driver's license	licencia de manejar, permiso de conducer, licencia de conducir
driving while intoxicated (DWI)	conduciendo borracho o intoxicado
drop-out from school	abandonar la escuela
drug addict	drogadicto, narcómano
drug addiction	adicción a drogas
drug test	prueba de drogas
drunk driving	conduciendo borracho o intoxicado
due date	fecha de vencimiento
due diligence	diligencia debida
due process of law	debido procedimiento de ley, debido proceso legal
duly sworn	debidamente juramentado
dunning	acreedor importune
dunning notice	aviso de importuner a un deudor
duplicate claim	reclamación duplicada
durable power of attorney	poder legal durable
duration	duración

duress	coacción, compulsion

E

earned income	ingresos por trabajo
earnings	ganancias
earnings record	registro de ganancias
earnings test	límite de ganancias, prueba de ganancias
easement	derecho incorpóreao distinto de la propiedad del suelo
economic hardship	dificultades económicos
edit	repasar, preparar para la publicación
effective date	fecha efectiva, fecha vigente
elder law	leyes para ancianos
elderly person	anciano
election	elección, nombramiento
elector – in elections	compromisario
electronic benefits transfer (EBT)	transferencia electrónica de beneficios
eligibility	elegibilidad
eligible	elegible
eligible individual	individuo elegible
eliminate	eliminar, suprimir
emancipation	emancipación

embassy	embajada
embezzlement	desfalco, malversación
emergency	emergencia
emergency medical assistance	asistencia médica de urgencia
emergency protective order	orden de protección de emergencia
emergency relief	socorro de emergencia
emergency room	sala de emergencia
emolument	emolumento
emotional abuse	abuso emocional
emotional disability	trastorno emocional
emotional distress	angustia emocional
empanel a jury	elección del jurado
employee	empleado
employee relations	relaciones de empleados
employer	patron, empleador
employment agency	agencia de empleo
employment application	solicitud de trabajo
employment authorization	autorización de trabajo
employment certification	certificado de trabajo
employment contract	contrato de trabajo
employment law	ley de empleo
empower	capacitar
enclosure – attachment	contenido, adjunto
endorsement	endoso, aprobación

end-stage renal disease	enfermedad renal en etapa final
enforce	hacer cumplir, ejecutar
enforcement of law	hacer cumplir la ley
engagement – to marry	compromiso de matrimonio
enroll – register	inscribirse, darse de alta
enrollment period	período de inscripción
enter a plea	declararse
enter into force	entrar en vigor
entitled	autorizado, tener derecho a
entrapment	acción de inducir engañosamente, acción de entrampar
epilepsy	epilepsia
equal pay for equal work	salario igual por trabajo igual
equal protection of law	protección igual ante la ley
equality	igualdad, eqidad
equitable	equitativo
equitable distribution	distribución equitativa
equity value	valor líquido
error	error, equivocación
establish	establecer, fundar
estate tax	impuesto sobre herencia
estimate	estimación, evaluación

estimated value	valor estimado
estrangement	extrañamiento, alejamiento
ethnicity	etnia
evade– taxes or customs	evader, evitar
evaluation	evaluación
evict	desalojar, desahuciar
eviction	desalojo, desahucia, evicción
eviction order	orden de desalojo
evidence	prueba, evidencia
ex-convict	ex presidiario
ex parte	ex parte, de una parte
ex post facto law	ley ex post facto
exact	exacto, preciso
exception	excepción
exchange rate	tipo de cambio, tasa de cambio
exclusive possession	posesión exclusiva
execute – contract or agreement	ejecutar un contrato o un acuerdo
execution – of a person	ejecutar a una persona
execution of a will	testamento firmado y en conformidad con las normas establicidas
executive director	director ejecutivo
executor – of a will	albacea, administrador de sus bienes

exempt	exento
exemption	exención
exhaust – use up	agotar, gastar
exhibit – courtroom display	documento u objecto de prueba
exile	desterrar
exonerate	exonerar
expedite	apresurar, despachar
expel	expulsar
expenses	gastos, costos, desembolsos
expert	experto, pericial
expert witness	testigo perito
expedited	removal
expiration date	fecha de vencimiento
exploitation – of people	explotación
expunge	borrar
extended care tratamiento	prolongado, extendido
extended coverage	protección prolongada, extendida
extension	extensión, prórroga
extenuating circumstances	circunstancias atenuantes
extortion	extorsión
extra curricular activities	actividades extra curriculares
extradition	extradición
extreme hardship	dificultades extremas

eyewitness	testigo ocular

F

face-to-face interview	entrevista en persona
fact	hecho, acontecimiento
failure to appear	incumplimiento de comparacer
failure to comply	incumplimiento
fair market value	valor normal en el mercado
fairness or impartiality	imparcialidad
false accusation	acusación falsa
false arrest	arresto ilegal
false document	documento falso, documento falsifacado
false information	información falsa
false imprisonment	encarcelamiento ilegal, detención ilegal
false statement	declaración falsa
family abuse	abuso familiar
family law	ley familiar
family planning	planificación familiar
family register records	archivos familiares
farm workers	trabajadores agrícolas
father-in-law	suegro
fatigue	fatiga, cansancio

favoritism	favoritismo
federal poverty level	nivel federal de pobreza
fees	honorarios
felony	delito mayor, delito grave, felonía
fence – stolen property	traficante de objetos robados
fiancé	prometido
fiancée	prometida
fiduciary	fiduciario
file – casefile	expediente
file – closed casefile	archivo
file – verb to file in file cabinet	archivar
file a motion	presentar una solicitud, presentar una moción
file a tax return	radicar una declaración de impuestos
file an application	radicar una solicitud
file charges	presentar una acusación, presentar cargos penales
file for civil action	entablar una acción civil
filing date	fecha de radicación
filing fees	cuotas de presentación de papeles en la corte
fill out a form	llenar un formulario
final judgment	sentencia final, sentencia definitiva

finance charge	cargos financieros, costo por financiamiento
financial assistance	asistencia financiera
financial hardship	privación económica
financial status	condición financiera
financial support	ayuda financiera
financing	financiamiento
find guilty	hallar culpable
finding – legal	resultado de una investigación, determinación
fine	multa
fingerprints	huellas digitales
fire – from a job or position	despedir
fire department	servicio de bomberos
fire insurance	seguro contra incendio
firearm	arma de fuego
fiscal year	año fiscal
fixed income	ingreso fijo
fixed interest rate	tasa fija
flextime	horario flexible
follow-up	recordatorio, seguimiento
food stamps	estampillas para alimentos
forced labor	trabajo forzado
foreclosure	remate hipotecario, juicio hipotecario

foreman – of work crew	capataz
forfeiture	pérdida, confiscación, caducidad
forger	falsificador, falsario
forgery	falsificación
form – paperwork	formulario
form letter	carta modelo
forma pauperis	declaración jurada de condición indigente
foster care	cuidado tutelar, cuidado de crianza
foster child	hijo de crianza
foster home	hogar provisional
fracture or break of bone	fractura de hueso
frame – to make appear guilty	estratagema para incriminar a una persona inocente
fraud	fraude, estafa
fraud and abuse hotline	línea directa de fraude y abuso
freedom	libertad
fringe benefit	prestación suplementaria
frisk	registrar a la persona
frivolous suit	juicio sin fundamento
full faith and credit	entera fe y crédito
full-time	tiempo completo
full-time employment	empleo a tiempo completo

full-time nursing care	cuidado de enfermería de tiempo completo
full-time student	estudiante de tiempo completo
fully insured	totalmente asegurado
funeral	entierro, funeral
funeral home	funeraria

G

gag order	prohibición de hablar del caso
gambling	apostar, jugando por dinero
gang	pandilla
garnish	embargar, retener los ingresos
garnishment	retención de sueldo
gender	género
general district court	tribunal general de distrito
general durable power of attorney	poder general duradero
general enrollment period	período de inscripción general
general power of attorney	poder general
general relief – assistance	subsidio general, prestación social general

give notice	dar aviso
glossary	glosario
good cause	razón justificada
good faith	buena fe
good moral character	caracter de buena moral
government	gobierno
governor	gobernador
grace period	período de gracia
graduate school	universidad de grado
grand jury	gran jurado
grand larceny or theft	hurto mayor, robo grande
grant	beca, subvención
green card	tarjeta verde
grievance	una queja
grievance procedure	procedmiento de agravio, procedmiento de queja
gross income	ingreso bruto
gross negligence	negligencia grave
ground – cause or reason	motivo, fundamento
grounds for divorce	motivos de divorcio, causa de divorcio
group insurance	seguro colectivo
guarantee	garantía
guardian	tutor nombrado por la ley
guardianship	apoderado legal, tenencia
guess – verb	advinar, suponer

guidelines	guía, normas
guilty	cupable
gun	pistola, arma de fuego

H

habeas corpus	habeas corpus
habitual criminal or offender	delincuente habitual
half brother	medio hermano
half sister	media hermana
halfway house	institución que ayuda a personas a reintegrarse a la sociedad
handcuffs– manacles	esposas, manilas de hierro
handicap	discapacidad, impedimento
handicapped individual	persona discapacidada
harass – usually sexual in nature	acoso sexual
harass – general harassment	hostigar
harassment	acosamiento, hostigamiento
hardship	dificultad, apuro
hardship excepton	excepción de privación
head of household	jefe de familia
health and safety code	código de sanidad y seguridad
health care declaration	una declaración sobre el cuidado de la salud

health care provider	proveedor de atención a la salud
health maintenance org. (HMO)	organización para el mantenimiento de la salud
hearing	audiencia
hearing aid	audífono, prótesis auditiva
hearing officer	oficial de audiencia
hearsay	testimonio de oídas
heart attack	ataque cardíaco, ataque al corazón
hereinafter	más adelante, a continuación
heretofore	hasta ahora
high blood pressure	alta presión sanguínea, alta presión de la sangre
high school	escuela secundaria, preparatoria
hire	emplear, contratar, dar empleo
hit and run	chocar y huir
hobbies	pasatiempos
holiday	día festivo
home health aid	ayuda médica en el hogar
homeless	desamparados, desahuciados, sin hogar
homestead deed	excepción aplicable a reclamos contra propiedad en tramites de bancarrota

homestead		
	bankruptcy exemption	excepción de propiedad en tramite de bancarrota
homework		tarea
homicide		homicidio
homosexual		homsexual
honorarium		honorarios
hospice care		cuidado de hospicio
hospital		hospital, clínica
hospital stay		estancia, estadía en el hospital
hostage		rehén
hotline		línea de emergency
hourly earnings or pay		pago por hora
hours worked		horas trabajadas
household chores		quehaceres domésticos, aseo
household expenses		gastos de la casa
household worker		trabajadora doméstica, criada, servicio doméstico
housing assistance		la asistencia para la vivienda
housing law		ley de vivienda
human immunodeficiency virus		virus de inmuodeficiencia humana (VIH)
human resources department		departamento de recursos humanos
human rights		derechos humanos

human trafficking	trata de personas
humiliation	humillacíon
hung jury	jurado en desacuerdo, sin veredicto
husband	esposo, marido
hypertension	hipertensión, alta presión de sangre
hysterectomy	histerectomía

I

income tax return	declaración de impuestos
identification card ID	tarjeta de identificación
identity theft	robo de identidad
illegal	ilegal
illegal search and seizure	búsqueda y captura ilegal
illegitimate child	hijo ilegítimo
illiterate	analfabeto
illness	enfermedad
immaterial	inmaterial, no esencial
immediate danger	peligro inmediato
immigrant	inmigrante
immigrant visa	visa de immigrante
immigration judge	juez de inmigración
immigration law	leyes de inmigración
immigration officer	oficial de inmigración

immigration records	expedientes de inmigración
immoral	inmoral
immunity	inmunidad, exención
immunization	inmunización
impairment	incapacidad específica, impedimento
impartial jury	jurado imparcial
impeachment	procedimientos de residencia
impeachment of a witness	desacreditación de un testigo
implied contract	contrato implícito
impound	confiscar, embargar, acorralar
imprisonment	encarcelación, reclusion
improper touching	tocar de manera inapropiada
impugn	impugnar
in a maner prescribed by law	de la manera prescrita por ley
in advance	por adelantado
in good faith	buena fe
in loco parentis	adulto que actue como padre legal
in persona jurisdiction	jurisdicción con respecto a la persona
in rem jurisdiction	jurisdicción sobre un objeto o una propiedad

inadmissible	inadmisible
incapacitated person	incapacitado, incapacitada
incarcerate	encarcelar
income	ingresos
income tax	impuesto sobre el ingreso
incompetent	incompetente
inconvenient	inconveniente
incorrect information	información incorrecta
incriminate	incriminar, inculpar
incur	incurrir
indebtedness	endeudamiento
indecent exposure	exhibición impúdica
indemnity	indemnidad, reparacón
independent contractor	contratista independiente
indictment	acusación por gran jurado, procesamiento
indigent	indigente
ind. retirement account (IRA)	cuenta de retiro individual
ineligible	inelegible
inform	informar, comunicar
informant	informante, informador
informed consent	consentimiento informado
infraction	infracción, violación
infringe upon a person's rights	coartarse
inheritance	herencia

inhuman treatment	tratos crueles, inhumanos o degradantes
injunction	prohibición judicial
injury	lesión
inmate	recluso
innocent	inocente, inofensivo
innocent until proven guilty	presución de inocencia
insanity	locura, demencia
insolvency	insolvencia
inspection	inspección
installment paying or plan	pagar a plazos
insubordination	rebeldía
insult	insulto, ultraje
insurance	seguro
insurance adjuster	ajustador de seguros
insurance policy	póliza de seguro
insurance premium	prima o premio de seguro
intake officer	oficial de recepción
intake specialist	especialista de recepción y elegiblidad
intent	intención
intentional program violation	violación intencional del programa
intercourse – sexual	relaciones sexuales
interest – on a loan	interés sobre un préstamo
interest rate	tasa de interés

interim report	informe provisional
interlocutory appeal	apelación interlocutoria
interlocutory order	decreto interlocutorio
international law	derecho internacional
interpret	interpretar
interpreter	interprete
interrogation	interrogación
interrogatories	interrogatorios
interview	entrevista
intestate – die without a will	intestado, intestada
intestate succession	sucesión intestada
intimidation	intimidación
intoxicated	intoxidado, ebrio
invalid – disabled person	persona incapacitada
investigation	investigación
investment	inversion
investment account	cuenta de inversiones
involuntary manslaughter	homicidio involuntario
involuntary servitude	servidumbre involuntaria
irrelevant	irrelevante, no pertinente
irrevocable	irrevocable, inalterable
is subject to	está sujeto a
item	detalle
itemize	detallar
itemized deductions	deducciones detalladas

J

Juvenile & Family Court	tribunal de menores y relaciones familiares
jail	prisión, cárcel
job	empleo, ocupación
job description	descripción de trabajo
job interview	entrevista de trabajo
job offer	oferta de trabajo
job performance evaluation	evaluación de trabajo
job seeker	persona que busca trabajo
job training	capacitación o entrenamiento o adiestramiento de empleo
job-related injury	lesion relacionada al trabajo
joinder – combines several cases	acumulación de cargos
joint account	cuenta conjunta
joint custody – of children	custodia conjunta
joint debt	deuda conjunta, deuda mancomunada
joint liability	responsabilidad mancomunada
joint ownership	copropiedad, posesión conjunta
joint property	propiedad en conjunto
joint return – income tax return	declaración conjunta
joint sponsor	patrocinador conjunta

joint venture	empresa en conjunto
judge	el juez
judge's discretion	decisión del juez
judgment	juicio, fallo, sentencia
judgment proof	exento de juicio
jump bail	huir después de depositar fianza
junior high school	escuela media
jurisdiction	jurisdicción
jurisprudence	jurisprudencia, teoría del derecho
juror – or jurist	miembro del jurado
jury	el jurado
jury duty	servicio de jurado, juraduría
jury trial	juicio por jurado
justice	justicia
justice of the peace	juez de paz
juvenile court	tribunal de menores
juvenile delinquency	delincuencia de menores, delincuencia juvenil

K

kidnap	secuestrar, raptar
kidnapping	secuestro, rapto
kidney transplant	transplante del riñon

knife	el cuchillo, la navaja, la cuchilla
knock down	tumbar, derribar
knock out	dejar sin sentido, hacer perder el sentido

L

labor	labor, trabajo
labor certification	certificado de labor
labor contract	contrato colectivo laboral
labor dispute	conflicto laboral, conflicto colectivo
labor law	derecho labor, ley laboral
labor relations	relaciones laborales
labor union	gremio laboral, sindicato obrero
laborer	trabajador, obrero, persona que labora
landlord	arrendador, propietario, dueño de propiedad
landlord-tenant law	ley de vivienda, ley de propietario e inquilino
language	idioma, lengua
language access coordinator	coordinador de acceso a idiomas
larceny	latrocinio, ratería, hurto
last name – surname	apellido

last will and testament	testamento, última voluntad
late charge	cargo adicional por pago atrasado
late payment	pago tardío
law	ley, derecho
law school	facultad de derecho, escuela de leyes
law student	estudiante de derecho
lawful admission	admisión legal, entrada legal
lawful permanent resident	residente legal permanente
lawsuit	demanda, pleito, proceso
lawyer	abogado, licenciado
lawyer fees	honorarios de abogado
lawyer referral service	servicio de referencia para abogados
lay-off – of workers	despedir (a un trabajador) temporalmente, cesantía temporal
leading question	pregunta que insinúa la repuesta
lease – noun	contrato de arrendamiento, contrato de locación
lease – verb	alquilar, rentar
leave – authorized time off	permiso, autorización, licencia

leave without pay	licencia sin goce de sueldo
lecturer	lector
legal	legal, jurídico
legal advice	consejo legal
legal aid	asesoramiento jurídico gratuito
legal argument	argumento legal
legal assistant	asistente legal
legal documents	documentos legales
legal guardian	tutor legal, guardián legal
legal research	investigación legal
legal separation	separación legal
legitimate child	hijo legítimo
lender	prestamista
leniency	misericordiosamente
lesbian	lesbiana
letter of denial	carta de denegacíon
letterhead paper	membrete, encabezado
levy on property	embargo de bienes
lewd conduct	comportamiento obsceno
liability	responsabilidad, obligación
liability insurance	seguro de responsibilidad (por daños a terceros)
liaison	vinculación, unión
libel	difamación

license	licencia, permiso
lie – noun	mentira
lie – verb	mentir
lie detector	detector de mentiras
lien	gravámen, derecho de retención
life expectancy	promedio de vida
life imprisonment	cadena perpetua
life insurance	seguro de vida
life prolonging procedures	procedimientos para prolongar la vida
light work	trabajo ligero, trabajo liviano
limit	límite, restricción
line of credit	línea de crédito
litigation	litigación, litigio
living arrangement	arreglo de alojamiento
living expenses	gastos de subsistencia
living wage	sueldo suficiente para sobrevivir
living will – health care	declaración o testamento para vivos, testamento en vida
loan	préstamo
loan agreement or contract	contrato de préstamo
local agency	agencia local
lock	cerradura
lockout – in labor dispute	huelga patronal

lockout – of a house	prohibir la entrada a la casa a un residente
loitering	vagar, dilatar
long arm statues	estatutos que se extiendan jurisdicción personal sobre personas en otros estados
long-term care	atenciones a largo plazo
loss	pérdida
loss of major functions	pérdida de funciones básicas o principales
low-income	de ingresos limitados, de bajos ingresos
lump-sum payment	pago global, monto único
lure	atraer con engaño

M

magistrate	el magistrado
maiden name	apellido de soltera
mail fraud	fraude postal
mailing address	dirección postal
maintain records	mantener los archivos o registros, llevar registros
malice	malicia
malicious	malicioso, maligno
malicious intent	intención maliciosa

malicious prosecution	acción penal sin fundamento, denuncia maliciosa
malnutrition	desnutrición
malpractice	negligencia profesional
managed care program	programa de cuidado administrado
management – of a company	administración
manager	gerente
mandatory sentence	sentencia obligatoria
manner prescribed by law	una forma prescrita por la ley
manslaughter	homicidio sin premeditación
manual labor	trabajo manual
marital property	bienes del matrimonio
marital status	estado civil
market value	valor en el mercado
marriage	matrimonio
marriage certificate	certificado de matrimonio
marriage fraud	fraude marital
minority group	grupo de minoridad
master's degree	licenciado
material evidence	prueba material
material fact	hecho pertinente
maternal abuduction	secuestro maternal
maternity leave	licencia por maternidad

maturity date	fecha de vencimiento
means-tested public benefits	prestaciones públicos que dependen de los recursos
mediation	mediación
mediator	mediador, intercesor
medical assistance	asistencia médica
medical bills	cuentas médicas
medical coverage	cobertura médica
medical examination	chequeo médico, examen médico
medical expenses	gastos médicos
medical power of attorney	poder médico, poder legal médico
medical record	historial médico
medical tests	chequeos médicos, exámenes médicos
medicine	medicina, medicamento
meet requirements	reunir los requisitos, reunir las condiciones
meeting of creditors	junta de acreedores
meeting or conference	reunión, conferencia
mental anguish	angustia mental
mental competence	competencia mental
mental cruelty	crueldad mental
mental health	salud mental
mental illness	enfermedad mental
mental impairment	impedimento mental

mental incompetence	incompetencia mental
mental retardation	retraso mental, retardación mental
merchant	comerciante, vendedor
merits of the case	justificación legal para un caso, argumento legal
metal detector	detector de metales
midwife	comadrona, partera
migrant worker	trabajodor migratorio
military law	derecho militar
military service	servicio militar
minimum wage	sueldo mínimo, salario mínimo, pago mínimo
minister – Protestant clergyman	ministro protestante
minor – not yet adult	menor
miscarriage	aborto natural, abort esponatáneo, malparto
misconduct	mala conducta, comportamiento ilícito
misdemeanor	delito menor, contravención
misrepresentation	declaración falsa, declaración errónea
missing person	persona desaparecida, pesona extravíada
mistrial	juicio nulo
misunderstanding	mal entendimiento
misuse of benefits	mal uso de beneficios

mitigating circumstances	circunstancias atenuantes o mitigantes
modification	modificación, enmienda
money order	giro
monthly benefit	beneficio mensual
monthly earnings test	prueba de ingresos mensuales
monthly income	ingresos mensuales
monthly payment	pago mensual
month-to-month lease	contrato de mes a mes
mood	estado de ánimo, humor
moot court	tribunal ficticio
moral obligation	obligación moral
moral turpitude	torpeza moral
mortgage – noun	hipoteca
mortgage – verb	hipotecar
mother-in-law	suegra
motion	petición
motion denied	petición rechazada, moción rechazada
motion for a new trial	petición para un nuevo juicio
motion for continuance	peticitión para aplazamiento del procedimiento
motion for judgment	demanda civil
motion granted	petición otorgada

motion to compel discovery	moción para obligar revelación
motion to discover	moción de revelación de pruebas
motion to dismiss	moción para desechar
motion to reopen	acción de reapertura de un caso
motive	motivo
motor vechicle	vehículo de motor
move – change residences	mudar, trasladar
mug shot	foto de detenido
multicultural	multicultural
murder – noun	asesinato
murder – verb	asesinar
mute	mudo
mutual consent	consentimiento mutuo

N

name change	cambio de nombre o apellido
narcotics	narcóticos
nation	nación, país
national origin	origen nacional
nationality	nacionalidad
native language	lengua materna
natural disaster	desastre natural

naturalization	naturalización
naturalization certificate	certificado de naturalización, acta de naturalización
nearest living relative	el pariente más cercano que esté vivo
neglect	negligencia, descuido
negligence	negligencia, descuido
negotiation	negociación
nervous breakdown	ataque nervioso, ataque de nervios
net income	ingreso neto
net loss	pérdida neta
net profit	ganancia neta
next of kin	parientes más cercanos
nickname	apodo
night shift	trabajo nocturno
no fault divorce	divorcio sin causa
nolle prosequi	nolle prosequi
nominal value	valor nominal
non-citizens	extranjeros
non-compliance	incumplimiento
non-covered work	trabajo que no está cubierto por el Seguro Social
non-custodial parent	padre sin la custodia
non-immigrant	no-inmigrante

non-payment of rent	el no pagar la renta
non-profit organization	organización sin fines lucro
non-receipt	no recibido
non-renewable	no renovable
nonsuite – nonsuit a case	abandonar una acción judicial
nonsupport	falta de sostenimiento
non-work day	día no laborable, día inhabil
normal wear and tear	desgaste normal
not guilty	no culpable
notarize	otorgar ante notario, autenticar por un notario público
notary public	notario, escribano, corredor público
notice	el aviso, la notificación
notice of appeal	notificación de apelación
notice of non-coverage	aviso de protección negada
notice of planned action	aviso de acción proyectada
nuisance	perjuicio, daño, acto perjudicial
null and void	nulo y sin valor, nulo y de ningún efecto
nurse	enfermera
nursing care	cuidado de enfermería

nursing home – for the elderly	hogar de ancianos, casa de cuidado de ancianos
nutrition programs	programas de nutrición

O

oath	juramento
object – verb	objectar, oponerse, tener inconveniente
objection	objeción, oposición
objection overruled	objeción no admitida
objection sustained	objeción admitida
obstruct	obstruir, estorbar
occupation – job	ocupación, profesión
occupational hazard	riesgo de trabajo, riesgo profesional
off the record	extraoficial
offender	ofensor, delincuente, infractor
offense	ofensa, delito
office	oficina
offset	ajuste, descuento, reducción
old age	edad avanzada, vejez
on point	en punto
ongoing benefits	beneficios regulares
onset of disability	fecha de comienzo de la incapacidad

on-the-job training	formación práctica en el empleo
opening statement	declaración inaugural, delcaración de apertura
opinion	opinión jurídica
opposing party	parte contraria
oppression	opresión
optional state supplement	suplemento opcional del estado
oral agreement	contrato oral, contrato verbal
order	la orden, el decreto
order to show cause	orden de comparecer para explicar incumplimiento judicial
ordinance – municipal law	ordenanza – ley municipal
organization	organización
origin	origen
original document	un documento original
orphan	huérfano
orphanage	orfelinato
orthopedic	ortopédico
out-of-court settlement	acuerdo o arreglo extrajudicial
outpatient	paciente externo, paciente ambulatorio
outreach programs	programas de alcance comunitario
outstanding balance	el remanente de deuda

outstanding debt or loan	préstamo pendiente
overdraw an account	sobregirar una cuenta
overpayment	sobrepago, pago en exceso
overpayment recovery	recuperación de sobrepago
overpayment refund	reembolso de sobrepago
overrule	denegar, desestimar, declarar sin lugar
overtime hours	sobre tiempo
overtime pay	pago por sobre tiempo
overtime wage	salario por horas extras
own expense	gastos propios
own recognizance	en libertad bajo promesa de comparecer
owner	dueño, propietario

P

pacemaker	marcapasos cardíaco, aparato cardiocinético
package of benefits	conjunto de beneficios
paternity	paternidad
paid in full	pagado en su totalidad, liquidado
paid leave or vacation	licencia pagada
pain	dolor

pain and suffering	dolor y sufrimiento
palpitations	palpitaciones
pamphlet	folleto, panfleto
panderer – pimp	alcahuete
paperwork	tramites, papeleo
paralegal	asistente legal
paralysis	parálisis
pardon	indulto, la amnistía, la remission de pena
parent company	compañia matriz
parental rights	derechos de los padres
parenting classes	classes de padres
parole	libertad vigilada, libertad condicional
parole board	junta de perdones
part time	tiempo parcial
part time nursing care	servicio de enfermería de tiempo parcial
partial adjudication	adjudicación parcial
partial disability	discapacidad parcial
partial payment	pago parcial
participation	participación
partnership	sociedad o compañía colectiva, asociación
passport	pasaporte
past due child support	manutención de hijos adeudada

patent	patente
paternity test	examen para determinar paternidad
pathology	patología
patient	paciente
pay as you go basis	pagar según se recibe
pay by installment	pagar a plazos
pay in cash	pagar en efectivo
pay increase	aumento salarial
pay or quit notice	aviso de pago o de irse (renunciar o dimisión)
pay scale	escala salarial
pay stub	recibo de pago, talón de pago
payable	pagadero
payee	tutor del beneficiario
payment	pago, renumeración
payment in full	pago total
payment in kind	pago en especie
payment plan	plan de pagos
payroll	nómina, planilla de sueldos
payroll deduction order	orden de descuentos directos a su salario
peace bond	fianza de paz
pediatric physician	pediatra
peer pressure	presión de los compañeros

peer review organization	organización de revisión de normas profesionales
penal code	código penal
penal servitude	reclusión con trabajos forzados
penalty	sanciones, pena, penalidad, castigo
penalty clause	cláusula penal
penalty deductions	deducciones por multa o penalidad
pendente lite	pendent lite, mientras el juicio continúa
pending	pendiente, en trámite
penitentiary	penitenciaría
pension	pensión
peremptory challenge	recusación sin causa
performance appraisal	informe de trabajo
period of benefits	período de beneficios
perjury	perjurio, testimonio falso
permanent address	residencia permanente
permanent resident	residente permanente
permit – authorization	permiso, licencia
persecution	persecución
persistent vegetative state	condición de vegetativa persistente
personal check	cheque personal
personal expenses	gastos personales

personal ID number (PIN)	número de identificación personal (NIP)
personal income tax	impuestos sobre ingresos personales
personal injury	lesión personal, lesión corporal
personal property	bienes muebles
personal recognizance	reconocimiento personal
personality	personalidad
personnel department	departamento de personal
petition – noun	petición
petition – verb	peticionar, pedir
petitioner	demandante
petty larceny or theft	pequeño hurto, ratería
pharmacist	farmacéutico, boticario
physical custody	custodia física
physical impairment	incapacidad física
physical therapy	fisioterapia
physician	médico
pickpocket	carterista
picture ID	identificación con fotografia
piece rate	pago por pieza, pago a destajo
pill – medicine	pastilla
pimp	el alcahuete, el chulo
pinch	pellizcar

place of birth	lugar de nacimento
plaintiff	demandante, querellant, quejoso
plea – noun	alegato, defensa, declaración
plea – to enter a plea	declarar
plea bargain n	negociación para una declaración de culpabilidad arreglada
plea of nolo contendere	alegación en la cual no se contesta a la acusación
plead	declarse
plead guilty	declararse culpable
plead not guilty	declararse no culpable, declarase inocente
pleadings	alegatos
please be advised	por favor tome en cuenta
plot	complot
police department	la policía
police officer	oficial de policía
policy – guiding principles	política, normas
policy – such as insurance policy	contrato, póliza
policy number	número de póliza
polygraph	aparato para detectar mentiras, polígrafo
political asylum	aslio político
political opinion	opinión política
political party	partido político

poll the jury	preguntar a los jurados individualmente su conformidad con el veredicto
polyandry	poliandria
pooled income	ingreso combinado
poor debtor exemption	exención de propiedades en un tramite de bancarrota
pornographic	pornográfico
pornography	pornografía
port of entry	puerto de entrada
position – at work	pocisión, colocación
possession of drugs	posesion de drogas
post traumatic stress disorder (PTSD)	syndrome post traumático
postal money order	giro postal
post-dated check	cheque posfechado
posters	carteles, afiches
posthumous	póstumo
postponement	aplazamiento
poverty level	nivel de pobreza
power of attorney (POA)	poder legal, poder notarial, poder
praecipe	orden judicial
prayer for relief	petitorio
preamble	preámbulo
precedent	precedente, antecedente

predatory lending – usury	préstamo con tasas de interés ilegal, usura, agiotaje
preemptory challenge	reto preventivo
preferential	preferencial
pregnancy	embarazo
pregnant	embarazada, encinta
prejudice	prejuicio, parcialidad
preliminary hearing	audiencia preliminaria
preliminary investigation	investigation preliminar
preliminary protective order	orden preliminar de protección
premeditated	premeditado
premeditation	premeditación
prenatal care	atencion prenatal
prepay or pay in advance	prepagar, pagar por adelantado
prepayment	pago adelantado
preponderance of evidence	proponderancia de pruebas
prescription	receta, prescripción
pre-sentence report	informe anterior a la sentencia
president – of a country or nation	presidente
president elect	presidente electo
presumption	presunción, conjetura
presumption of innocence	presunción de inocencia
presumptive disability	incapacidad presunta

pretext	pretexto
pre-trial confinement	prison preventiva, encarcelado antes de la sentencia
pretrial release	liberación antes del juicio
priest – Catholic clergyman	sacerdote, cura, padre
priest – Buddhist	sarcedote budista
prima facie evidence	prueba adecuada a primera vista
priority	prioridad
priority date – immigration law	fecha de prioridad
prison	prisión, cárcel, penitenciaría, penal presidio
prison sentence	condena de prisión
prisoner	prisonero
prisoner of war (POW)	prisonero de guerra
private insurance	seguro privado
private insurer	asegurador privado
private school	escula privada
privatization	privatización
privilege	privilegio
pro bono	pro bono, servicios proporcionados gratuitamente
pro bono coordinator	coordinador del programa pro bono
pro bono program	programa pro bono

pro bono program assistant	asistente del programa pro bono
pro bono program paralegal	asistente legal del programa pro bono
pro se	pro se, por uno mismo
probable cause	motivo fundado
probate	validación de testamento
probate estate	el caudal verificable
probate proceedings	juicio testamentario
probation	libertad condicional
probation department	departamento de probación
probation officer	oficial de probación, consejero de libertad condicional
probationary period	período probatorio
procedural law	derecho procesal
proceeding	procedimiento, trámite
proclamation	proclamación
production	producción
profit	utilidad, ganancia
program violation	violación al programa
progressive illness	enfermedad progresiva
prohibit	prohibir
promise	promesa, compromiso
promissory note	pagaré, vale
promotion	promoción, ascenso

proof	prueba, comprobación, comprobante
property	propiedad, bienes
property damage	daño de propiedad
property insurance	seguro de vivienda
property settlement agreement	acuerdo de separación y distribución de la propiedad
property tax	predial, impuesto de propiedad, impuesto sobre bienes
property valuation	tasación de la propiedad
prorate	prorratear
prosecute	someter a proceso
prosecution	enjuiciamiento, prosecución
prosecutor	fiscal, abogado del estado
prospective payment	pago eventual, pago potencial
prostate cancer	cáncer de la próstata
prostitute	prostituta
prostitution	prostitución
protective order	orden de protección
prove	verificar, comprobar
provider of services	proveedor de servicios
provision – of article	estipulación
provision of law	estipulación legal
provocation	provocación

proxy	poder, apoderado, mandatario
proxy statement	declaración para accionistas antes de que voten mediante poder
psychiatrist	psiquiatra
psychologist	psicólogo
public assistance	asistencia pública
public benefits	beneficios públicos
public charge	carga pública
public defender	abogado defensor público
public good	bienestar público
public health	salud pública
public housing	vivienda pública
public office	cargo público
public record	registro civil
public school	escuela pública
public trial	juicio público
publication – court proceedings	publicación
punch – hit or strike	puñetazo
punishment	pena, castigo
punitive damages	indemnización punitiva
purported	implicado
pursuant to	de acuerdo con, en conformidad a, según
putative father	padre putativo
pyramid selling	venta en pirámide

Q

qualifications	calificaciónes
qualify – to be qualified for	calificada
quarters of coverage	cuartos de protección
quash	anular, rescindir, dejar sin efecto
quid pro quo	quid pro quo
quitclaim deed	transferencia de propiedad mediante la cual se renuncia a todo derecho
quitclaim	quitación, finiquito, renuncia a un título
quota	cuota

R

rabbi – Jewish clergyman	rabino
race	raza
racial discrimination	discriminación racial
radiation therapy	radioterapia, terapia de radiación
raise children	criar niños
rap sheet	hoja de antecedents penales, historia delictivo
rape	violar sexualmente

rape in concert	violación conjunta, violación grupal
ratification	ratificación
real estate	bienes raíces, bienes inmuebles
real estate agent	agente de bienes raíces
reasonable accommodation	acomodación razonable
reasonable doubt	duda razonable
rebuttal	refutación
recant	retractar, revocar
receipt	recibo
recidivist	reincidente, delincuente o criminal habitual
recipient	recipiente, beneficiario
reckless driving	manejar un vehiculo con abandono
recommendation	recomendación, surgerencia
reconciliation	reconciliación
reconsideration	reconsideración
re-contact	contactar de nuevo
record – noun	registro, los antecedents
record – verb	registrar, inscribir, anotar
recourse	recurso
recover – recoup	recobrar
recover -regain health	recuperar
recur	recurrir, repetirse

red tape	trámites burocráticos, papeleo
red-handed	in fraganti
	en falgrante
redress of grievances	reparación de agravios
reduce	reducir
reduction in force (RIF)	reducción de empleados obligatorio
re-entitlement	readquirir derecho, recalificar
reentry permit	permiso de reingreso
reference – on job application	referencia
referral	referencia, derivación
refinancing	refinanciamiento
reform – verb	reformar, corregir
reforms	reformas
refugee	refugiado
refund	reembolsar, restituir dinero
refund form	formulario de reembolso
refute	refutar, impugnar
regain	recuperar
register – to sign up	inscribir, matricularse
registered mail	correo certificado, correo registrado
registration	egistro, inscripción
regret	remordimiento
regular services	servicios regulares

regulation	reglamento
rehabilitation	rehabilitación
reimburse	reembolsar
reinstate	restablecer, reponer, reinstalar, reincorporar
related by marriage	emparentado
relationship	relación, parentesco
relatives	parientes
release – from liability	finiquito, relevo de responsabilidad
release of information	divulgar
religion	religión
relinquishment	abandono, renuncia
relocate – move	mudarse
remand – case	devolver un caso a una corte inferior
remarks	comentarios
remarriage	casarse por segundas nupcias
remedy	remedio, recurso
removal proceedings	tramites de deportación, procedimientos de deportación
renew – a contract	renovar
renounce	renunciar, repudiar
rent – noun	la renta, el arriento, arrendamiento
rent – verb	alquilar, arrendar, rentar

rental income	ingreso de rentas
repay	devolver
repeal – of a law	derogar
repeat a grade	repitir de grado
report – noun	informe, el reporte
report – verb	informar sobre, hacer un reportaje de
report card	libreta de calificacciones
report of work activity	informe de actividad de trabajo
repossession	reclamación de bienes, reposición
representation agreement	acuerdo de representación legal
representative – congressperson	representante
representative payee	representante del beneficiario
reprieve la suspension	suspensión temporal de un castigo
reprimand	reprender
reprisal	represalia
reputation	reputación
request not timely filed	petición fuera de tiempo
required to participate	requerido para participar
requirement	requisito
rescind	rescindir
reservation of rights	reservación de derechos

residence	residencia
resident alien	extranjero residente
resignation – from a job	resignación, dimisión
resolution	resolución, decisión
resources	bienes, recursos
respite care	relevo de descanso al cuidador
respondeat	superior
respondent	demandado
responsibility – duty	responsabilidad, obligación
rest the case	terminar la presentación de pruebas
restitution	restitución, restablecimiento
restoration of rights	restoración de derechos
restraining order	orden de entredicho
restricted function	función restringida
restricted license	licencia con restricciones
restriction	restricción, limitación
résumé–cirriculum vitae	curriculum vitae
resumption of payment	reanudación de pagos
retainer – agreement	acuerdo de representación legal
retainer fee	contrato para los servicios de un abogado
retaliation	tomar represalias
retire	jubilarse, retirarse

retirement	jubilación, retiro
retirement benefits	beneficios de la jubiliación
retirement insurance	seguro de retiro, seguro de jubilación
retroactive	retroactivo
revaluation of assets	revaluación de bienes
reversal	revocación, echarse atrás
reverse discrimination	discriminación inversa
review – verb	revisar
revocable trust	fideicomiso revocable
revocation	revocación
revoke	revocar
rider – additional document	clásula adicional
rifle – firearm	rifle
right of recission	derecho de recisión
right to vote	derecho al voto
rights	derecho
riot	motín, tumulto
robbery	robo
role model	ejemplo positivo
room and board	alojamiento y comida, cuarto y comida
roommate – or housemate	compañero de cuarto, compaño de vivienda
rule	regla, el precepto, la decision

rule out	descartar, desechar, excluir, no admitir
rule to show cause	una orden para mostrar razones por incumplimiento
rules and regulations	reglas y regulaciones
rules of evidence	reglamento de pruebas admisibles
ruling	el fallo, la decision, la resolución

S

safe deposit box	caja de deposito de seguridad, caja fuerte
salary	salario, sueldo
sales	contract salario
savings account	cuenta de ahorros
savings and loan association	asociación de prestamos y ahorros
savings bond	bono de ahorros
scam	estafa
scar	cicatriz
schedule – time	horario
school attendance	asistencia escolar
school board	junta escolar
school counselor	consejero escolar
scratch – verb	rasguñar, arañar

scrutiny	escrutinio
seal – to affix a seal	sellar
search & seizure	registro e incautación, hallanamiento y confiscación
search warrant	orden de hallanamiento, orden de cateo
seasonal unemployment	desempleo estacional, desempleo de temporada
seasonal work	trabajo estacional
second consecutive month	segundo mes consecutivo
second mortgage	segunda hipoteca
second opinion	segunda opinión
secured debt	deuda garantizada
securities	valores, títulos
security deposit	deposito de seguridad
seizure – convulsion	convulsión
seizure – confiscation	confiscación
self-defense	defensa propia
self-dialysis	autodiálisis
self-employment	trabajo por cuenta propia
self-employment income	ingresos de trabajo por cuenta propia
self-esteem	amor propio o amor a sí mismo
self-help eviction	desalojo de autoayuda
self-incrimination auto	incriminación o culparse a sí mismo

semester	semestre
semi-skilled worker	trabajador mediocre
senator –congressperson	senador
senile	senil
senior citizen	ciudadano de edad avanzada o de la tercera edad
seniority prioridad	antigüedad laboral, precedencia laboral, consideraciones basadas en tiempo empleado
sentence – noun	condena, la sentencia condenatoria
sentence – verb	sentenciar, condenar
separation	separación
separation agreement	acuerdo de separación matrimonial
service by publication	notificación mediante publicaciones
service contract	contracto de servicios
service of legal process	entrega de documentos judiciales
servitude	servidumbre
setting policy	poliza con vencimiento
settle out of court	arreglar extrajudicialmente
settlement	arreglo, ajuste, liquidación
severance pay	cesantía, indemnización por despido

severe condition	condición grave, condición severa
severe impairment	incapacidad severa
sex – gender	sexo
sexual abuse	abuso sexual
sexual assault	acometimiento sexual
sexual harassment	acoso sexual, hostigamiento sexual
sexual intercourse	relaciones sexuales, el coito
sexual orientation	orientatación sexual
sexual relations	relaciones sexuales
sexually transmitted diseases (STD)	enfermedades transmitidas sexualmente
shares of stocks	acciones
shelter	albergue, casa de refugio
sheriff	alguacil
shift – daily work period	horario de trabajo, horas de trabajo
shipping charge	cargo de envio
shoplifting	ratería en las tiendas, hurto en las tiendas
shove – push	empujón
sick leave	ausencia por enfermedad
sickness	enfermedad
sight	vision

signature	firma
simultaneous interpretation	interpretación simultánia
single – not married	soltero
sister-in-law	cuñada
skilled nurse	enfermera especializada
skilled nursing facility	institución de enfermería especializada
skilled worker	trabajador experimentado
skip school	ausencias injustificadas de la escuela
slander	difamación oral, calumnia
slap – hit with open hand	palmada, bofetada
slavery	esclavitud
smuggler of aliens	contrabandador de extranjeros, cayote
social case history	historia social del caso
social justice	justicia social
social security card	tarjeta de seguro social
social security contributions	contribuciones al seguro social
social security number	número de seguro social
social services	servicios sociales
social work	trabajo social
social worker	trabajador(a) social, consejero
socioeconomic status	nivel socio económico
sodomy	sodomía

sole custody	custodia exclusiva
solemnly swear	jurar a decir la verdad
solitary confinement	confinamiento solitario
solvency	solvencia
son-in-law	yerno
special education	educación especial
specialist	especialista
speech therapy	terapia del habla
speeding – traffic infraction	infracción por exceso de velocidad
sponsor – verb	patrocinar
spousal support	manutención del cónyuge, pension alimenticia
spouse	cónyuge
springing power of attorney	poder condicional
squatter	intruso
stab	apuñalar
stalking	acoso
standard language (legalities)	cláusulas usuales
standard of living	nivel de vida
state – to declare	declarar
state agency	agencia estatal, agencia del estado
state attorney general	fiscal general del estado
state laws	leyes estales
state of mind	estado de ánimo

state supplement	suplemento estatal, suplemento del estado
statement	declaración
statement of earning	declaración de ganancias
statistics	estadística
status	estado
status hearing	audiencia para determinar el estado del caso
statute	estatuto, ley escrita, reglamento
statute of limitation	ley de prescripción, estatuto de limitaciones
statutory	estatutario
statutory law	derecho estatutario, ley escrita
statutory rape	relaciones sexuales con una joven menor de la edad del consentimiento ilegal
stay	la suspensión, la prórroga
stay of deportation	demorra por deportación
steal – rob	hurtar, robar
stepbrother	hermanastro
stepchild	hijastro, hijastra
stepdaughter	hijastra
stepfather	padrastro
stepmother	madrastra
stepsister	hermanastra

stepson	hijastro
stereotype	estereotipo
sterilization – prevent pregnancy	esterilación
stillbirth	parto de un niño muerto
stimulants	estimulantes
stipulate	estipular
stipulation – or provision	estipulación
stock dividends	dividendos de acciones
stocks	acciones
stop payment on a check	detener el pago de un cheque
strike – of workers	declarase en huelga, estar en huelga
strip search	registro al desundo
stroke – cerebral	derrame cerebral
subcontract – noun	subcontrato
subcontract – verb	subcontratar
subcontractor	subcontratista
sublease – verb	subarrendar
submit – present evidence	presentar pruebas
subordinate	subordinado
subpoena	citación, citación legal
subpoena a witness	citar a un testigo
subpoena duces tecum	citación para comparecer y exhibir documentos
subsequent claim	reclamación subsiguiente

subsidiary	subsidiario
subsidy	subsidio
substance abuse	abuso de sustancias o drogas
substance abuse treatment	tratamiento para el abuso de intoxicantes
substantial gainful activity (SGA)	trabajo sustancial y lucrativo
subtenant	subinquilino, subarrendatario
sue	demandar, poner pleito
suffrage – right to vote	sufragio
suicide	suicidio
suit	demanda judicial
summary deportation	deportación sumario
summons	citación de una persona, orden de comparecer
suspect – verb	sospechar
suspect – person under suspicion	sospechoso
superior court	tribunal superior
supervised visitation	visitas supervisadas
supervisor	supervisor
supplementary income	ingreso suplementario
support group	grupo de apoyo
support order	orden de manutención
supporting documents	documentos de ayuda
suppression of evidence	supresión de prueba

supreme court	tribunal supremo
surcharge	recargo
surgeon	cirujano
surname	apellido
surrender	ceder
surveillance	vigilancia
surviving spouse	cónyuge sobreviviente
survivor	sobreviviente
suspended imposition of sentence	imposición de sentencia suspendida
suspended sentence	sentencia suspendida
suspicion	sospecho
swear	jurar
swindle	estafa
swindler	estafador
sworn statement	declaración jurada
syndicate	sindicato

T

tablet – medicine	pastillas
take-home pay – net pay	pago neta, salario neto
tamper with	adulterar
tape recorder	grabadora
tax	impuesto

tax assessment	valuación impositiva
tax collection	recaudación de impuestos
tax credit	crédito impositivo, crédito fiscal
tax declaration	declarción de impuestos
tax deduction	deducción impositiva, deducción fiscal
tax evasion	evasion de impuestos
tax exemption	exención impositiva
tax lien	gravámen por impuestos no pagados
tax refund	reintegro de impuestos
tatax return	declaración de impuestos
taxes	impuestos
taxpayer ID number (TIN)	número de identificación del contribuyente
telemarketers	telemercadores
telephone interview	entrevista telefónica
temp agency	agencia de trabajadores temporarios
temporary	provisional, temporal
temporary employment	empleo temporal
temporary protected status (TPS)	estado de protección temporal
temporary restraining order	orden inhibitoria temporal
temporary visitation v	isitación temporal
tenant	inquilino, arrendatorio
term insurance	seguro por un término fijo

terminal condition	situación incurable, condición médica incurable
terminally ill	enfermo terminal, enfermo mortal
termination notice	aviso de terminación
termination of parental rights	terminación de derechos de padres
testify	testificar, atestiguar, dar testimonio, atestar
testimony	testimonio
theft	hurto, robo
thereafter	en adelante, después de
thereby	en consecuencia, por medio de, con lo cual
therein	adentro, en eso
thereinafter	posteriormento, después
thereof	de eso, de esto
third parties	terceros
third party liability	responsabilidad de una tercera persona
threat	amenaza
timely	a tiempo, puntual
title – to property	título
tolerance – of human differences	la tolerancia
toll free	sin cargo, gratuito
tort	agravio
torture	toturas

total income	ingreso total
totality of circumstance	totalidad de las circunstancias
tow truck	camión remolcador o camion de remolque, carro grúa
trade or vocational school	escuela de obreros, escuela de vocación
trade union	sindicato, unión obrera
traffic accident	accidente de tránsito
traffic citation	citación de trafico
traffic court	juzgado de tránsito
trainee	aprendiz
training	entrenamiento, adiestramiento
transcript	transcripción
transitional insured status	transitoriamente asegurado
translation	traducción
translator	traductor
transliteration	transliteración
travel expenses	gastos de viaje
treason	traición
trespassing	entrar sin autorización en una propiedad, allanamiento
trial	juicio, causa, proceso
trial by jury	jucio por jurado

trial work period	período probatorio de trabajo
trimester	trimestre
truancy	faltar a clase sin permiso
trumped up charge	cargo fraudulentamente concebido
trust account	cuenta de fideicomiso
trust fund	fideicomiso, fondos fiduciarios
trustee	fideicomisario
trustee – in bankruptcy	síndico concursal
tuition	matrícula
tumors	tumores
tyrant	tírano

U

unauthorized	sin autorización
uncollectable	incobrable
uncollectable account	cuenta incobrable
unconscionable	desmedido, falto de escrúpulo
unconscious	inconsciente
unconstitutional	inconstitucional
uncontested divorce	divorcio sin oposición, divorcio de mutuo acuerdo
undeliverable	imposible de entregar

undeniable	inegable
under age	menor de edad
under color of law	bajo color de la ley
under oath	bajo juramento
undercover	secreto
underpayment	pago insuficiente
undersigned	suscrito
undocumented alien	indocumentado
undue hardship	dificultades innecesarias, dificultades abusivas
unearned income	ingreso no derivado del trabajo
unemployed person	desempleado
unemployment	desempleo
unemployment compensation	compensación por desempleo
unemployment insurance	seguro por desempleo
unemployment rate	tasa de desempleo
unenforceable	que no se puede hacer cumplier, inexigible
unfair	injusto
unfair labor practices	práctica laboral desleal
unforeseen circumstances	circunstancias imprevistos
unfounded	improcedente, sin lugar
uninsured	no asegurado
union – labor	sindicato, unión
university	universidad

unjust	injusto
unlawful	ilegal
unlawful assembly	reunión ilícito
unlawful detainer	demanda de desalojo, demanda de desahucio
unless otherwise agreed	salvo que se acuerde lo contrario
unless otherwise stated	salvo que declarar lo contrario
unpaid balance	saldo no pagada
unreasonable	irrazonable
unreported income	ingresos sin informar
unsecured loan	préstamo sin garantía
unsigned	sin firma
unskilled labor	trabajo elemental
unwarranted	sin justificación, injustificado
update	actualizar, poner al día
uphold	sosetener
usary	usura
utilities	servicios públicos
utility turn-off	interrupción de servicos públicos

V

vacancy – position	vacante, plaza
vacation pay	pago de vacaciones

vaccination	vacuna
vagrancy	vagancia, vagabundaje
valid	válido
valid contract	contrato válido
validity	validez
value	valor
vandalism	vandalismo
vehicle inspection	inspección vehicular
venue	jurisdicción, competencia
verbatim	al pie de la letra, palabra por palabra
verdict	fallo, veredicto
verification	verificación
veteran – military	veterano, veterano de guerra
vice president – of a country	vicepresidente
vice president – of a company	vicepresidente de una compañía o empresa
victim	víctima
victim impact statement	una declaración sobre las repercusiones a la víctima
vindicate	vindicar
violation	violación
violence	violencia
visa	visa
visitation rights	derechos de visitación
vital statistics	estadísticas vitales

vocational rehabilitation	rehabilitación vocacional
vocational training	entrenimiento vocacional
void	nulo, inválido
voidable contract	contrato anuable
voluntary	voluntario
voluntary departure	salida o dimisión voluntaria
voluntary manslaughter	homicidio impremeditado cometido voluntariamente
volunteer	voluntario
vote	voto, votación
voter registration	registro de elector
vouch for	hablar en favor de alguien

W

wage	salario
wage cut	reducción de salario, recorte de salario
wage earner	trabajador asalariado
wage increase	alza salarial
wage statement	informe de sueldo
wages	salario, sueldo, pago, jornal
waiver	renuncia
waiver of rights	renuncia de derechos
walkout	huelga laboral

want ad	aviso clasificado de trabajo
warden	guardián
warning	aviso, advertencia
warrant	mandamiento, autorización judicial
warrant in debt	auto de dueda, citación de deuda
warrant of arrest	orden de arresto
warranty	garantía
weapon	arma
wear and tear	desgaste natural
weight of the evidence	preponderancia de la prueba
welfare	asistencia pública
welfare reform	reformas al sistema de bienestar público
wheelchair	silla de ruedas, sillón de ruedas
whereabouts unknown	paradero desconocido
whereas	por cuanto, en tanto que
whereupon	después de lo cual, sobre que
wholesale	venta al por mayor, mayoreo
whom it may concern	a quien corresponda, a quien concierna
widow	viuda
widow's pension	pension para una viuda

widower	viudo
widower's pension	pension para un viudo
wife	esposa, mujer
will	testamento
willful	intencional, premeditado
with prejudice	sin la oportunidad de iniciar una nueva acción
withdrawal money	retiro de fondos
withhold	retener cierta cantidad, descontar
without fault	sin culpa
without notice	sin notificación
without prejudice	sin perjuicio, sin menoscabo
witness – noun	el testigo
witness stand	sitio de declaración de testigos
witness subpoena	orden para que un testigo comparezca
witness tampering	manipulación de un testigo
work – noun	trabajo
work activity	actividad de trabajo
work authorization or permit	autorización de trabajo
work history	historia de trabajo, antecedentes laborales
work on a commission basis	trabajar bajo una comisión
work permit	permiso de trabajo

work related accident	accidente de trabajo
work requirement	requisito de empleo
worker	trabajador
working hours	horas laborables
workmen's compensation	seguro de accidents y enfermedades de trabajo
workmen's compensation offset	descuento por compensación de trabajadores
workplace	lugar de trabajo
writ	orden judicial
writ of habeas corpus	el auto de habeas corpus
writ of possession	mandato de posesión
write off	eliminar, amortizar completamente
written agreement	convenio escrito
written consent	consento escrito
written evidence	constancia por escrito, evidencia por escrito
wrongful discharge from job	despido injusto, despido injustificado

X

xenophobia	xenofobia
x-rays	rayos X

Y

your honor – to address a judge	su señoria
your request	su pedido

Z

zip code	zona postal, código postal

Disclaimer:

The preceding compilation of words, phrases and terms are more commonly used in the legal and law professions in the U.S. While every good faith effort has been made for accuracy, no warranties are made by either the author or publisher. The Spanish-language translations are provided for educational and entertainment purposes and do not constitute legal advice or translation services. Any errors, corrections or omissions will be corrected in future editions of this book.

Part III
—More than Words

Rewarding Patience

At the beginning of this book, I made the commitment of rewarding you with two gifts. The first one is to embolden you by pointing out that speaking a minority language is always a challenge, and Spanish in the United States is (still) a minority language. The other is to provide an exquisite retort to anyone who is fluent in Spanish and has made you feel inadequate because your Spanish has been lacking.

One theme of this book is that many of the linguistic shortcomings that Latinos demonstrate when speaking business Spanish derive from the fact that by living in an English-language-dominant country, they lose the nuances of speaking Spanish. If it's a consolation, consider that learning another language is always a difficult task. The challenges Latinos face when speaking business Spanish also applies to non-Hispanics who attempt to use Spanish in the United States.

Gift #1

Consider the *New York Times*. If there are institutions in the United States that are qualified to edit something properly, the *New York Times* must be included among them. Somehow, the simple task of placing accents on Spanish-language names correctly continues to elude that publication. I'm not sure why they are doing this in the first place. Perhaps the editors are trying to be culturally sensitive (politically correct) by attempting to place accents on Spanish-language names. Their incompetence at it, however, strikes me as either patronizing (caring enough to feign sensitivity without actually following through entirely) or mocking (deliberately ridiculing Latinos and the ascendance of Hispanics in the U.S.). Consider a simple five-word sentence published April 26, 2011, in an article titled "The Chef's Table at Brooklyn Fare," written by Sam Sifton. This article begins with the following sentence: "'PARDON me,' said César Ramirez." In Spanish, both "Cesar" and "Ramirez" have accents, yet only one name has an accent in this report. The sentence could be written: *"PARDON me," said César Ramírez.* It could also be written: *"PARDON me," said Cesar Ramirez.* But it cannot be written properly the way it was published. This isn't an isolated incident, of course. In another article, written by Andrew Rice, titled "Life on the Line," published on July 28, 2011, the same thing occurs. Accents are added whimsically to some names, such as Pepé, but omitted from others (Chavez). On occasion I have brought this to the attention of the newspaper's editors. Andrew Rice was kind enough to reply, via e-mail, "Well, it's a bit embarrassing. Maybe my editor can talk to the copy desk about hiring someone who speaks Spanish to be an accent policeman." Latinos, don't hold your breath.

What strikes me as poignant is that Carolyn Curiel, who sat on the editorial board of the *New York Times*, is the granddaughter of a Mexican who came to the U.S. illegally. Her grandfather's name was Jesús Ortiz. What I find terribly sad is the consistency in that newspaper's inability to spell Spanish correctly. In fact, I can assure you that just about any edition of the *New York Times* that has an article with Spanish-language names will have mistakes. (I do not mean to pick on the *New York Times*, especially since the *New Yorker* magazine is consistently inconsistent as well. Consider this unfortunate sentence: "A woman named María Sanchez had brought food for her extended family of twenty, and she offered him a tostada." This was written by Connie Bruck in a profile of Los Angeles Mayor Antonio

Villaraigosa, on May 21, 2007. If an accent is placed on "María," why not on "Sánchez"?)

Neither the *New York Times* nor the *New Yorker* is capable of doing the simple task of placing accents on Spanish names correctly. They should not be doing it at all, unless the person in question specifically instructs the writer how his or her name is to be written. I doubt, however, people request to have their names published incorrectly.

It makes one wonder whatever happened to the childhood instruction "Be thy labor great or small, do it well or not at all." Trust me when I say with confidence that making a wager on this point is an easy way of winning a bet.

Do you now understand how embarrassing it is when a simple thing such as putting accents on names is done so poorly?

All this talk of the *New York Times* and the *New Yorker*, by the way, gives us a reason to speak about another word: *illiterate* in Spanish is *analfabeto*.

This aside, the consolation is that if even the *New York Times* is unable to get Spanish names right most of the time, be gentle with yourself as you work to improve your command of business Spanish.

Gift #2

The other morsel I offer you is one of a retort to anyone from Spain or Latin America who has made you feel inferior or inadequate because your Spanish was incorrect, or your accent Anglicized. It has to do with the linguistic challenges one faces when surrounded by a foreign language. With the Internet being what it is—the breathtaking speed with which it has become a fixture in the lives of people around the world—the Spanish language has been playing catch-up. For many in the Spanish-speaking world, words such as

"Internet," "e-mail," "website," and "online" have entered their consciousness almost instantly. Some have been readily translated: *Internet, correo electrónico*, and *en linea*. But what about "website"? It turns out that in a lazy, sloppy, but ubiquitous linguistic shortcut, throughout the Spanish-speaking world "website" has been translated into "sitio web." *Visit our website* has become *Visite nuestro sitio web*.

Sitio web here, *sitio web* there, *sitio web* everywhere!

It's all wrong. *Web* in Spanish is *telaraña*, literally, and *red* figuratively (as in *web* meaning a *network*, an abbreviation for *worldwide web*). Furthermore, *sitio* is Spanish for *site*, but it has to be a *physical* site, not a *metaphysical* one in *cyberspace*. This means that the correct Spanish-language phrase for *website* is the awkward *Página Electrónica en la Red Mundial*. Yes, it's a mouthful, but so is *máquina de escribir* for *typewriter*, and no one has had a heart attack using *máquina de escribir* for the past two centuries.

Here, then, Latino, is your opportunity for dishing out some payback. In an e-mail to anyone who has affected superiority or embarrassed you because of your command, or lack thereof, of proper Spanish, feel free to end your communication by reminding them that more information is available at your company website. *Para mayor informes, visite nuestra Página Electrónica en la Red Mundial (sitio web)*.

What a delicious sentence! Not only are you using Spanish as King Juan Carlos of Spain would do so, but you are reminding the recicipient that he or she may not be familiar with proper language usage, and as a courtesy you are, in parenthesis, using the slang with which he or she is probably familiar.

Sitio web. Isn't that funny? Anyone who speaks like that deserves some comeuppance, or as one would say in Spanish, *tendrá su merecido*.

Beyond Language

There's more to success than command of business Spanish. There is how you see yourself, and how others see you. To that end, what follows is a general discussion of related topics, beginning with "Hispanic diaspora." I've used this phrase throughout this book without defining it. Let us do that now and then get on with addressing other issues that are pivotal to your career success, from how to dress for success to confidence in your speaking-Spanish-with-an-accent.

The Hispanic Diaspora in the United States

The world is full of displaced people, or peoples who are minorities because their cultural, ethnic, religious, or racial identities stand in contrast with the mainstream in the nations in which they live. Oftentimes these peoples are described as living in diasporas. Since the creation of the state of Israel, for instance, the Jewish diaspora now has a homeland, which means that, within the worldview of the Jewish people, Jews who are not in Israel remain in the diaspora. The Chinese, who have a long tradition of being merchants around the world and establishing trading colonies, have a name for the Chinese who live outside China: huáqiáo. Mainland Chinese express concerns about these colonies and have developed outreach programs to help maintain the linguistic and cultural identity of the Chinese diaspora around the world. Among the French, Paris is so concerned with addressing the needs of French expatriates living overseas that French expats vote for a representative to the French parliament who speaks for their concerns and looks out for their interests.

In rough figures, one in 25 of all Hispanics in the world lives in the Hispanic diaspora in the United States. These are persons who identify culturally, ethnically, linguistically, or socially as Hispanic or Latino but happen to live in the United States. The most direct way of understanding the predicament of the Hispanic diaspora is this: If a Hispanic, Latino, or Latin person wakes up in a country in which the constitution is not written in Spanish or a related Iberian language, then he or she is living in a diaspora, which is a form of cultural estrangement.

To understand this idea, it is necessary to consider how U.S. Latinos are seen by Hispanics around the world. Many Israeli Jews, for instance, consider every other Jew in the world who is not in Israel to be *homeless*. It matters not that Steven Spielberg looks over the Pacific from his estate in Malibu, or that Henry Kissinger admires his Nobel Peace Prize before laying down his weary head on his pillow in his home in New York. Although both men may consider themselves to be perfectly happy, Israelis consider Spielberg and Kissinger homeless Jews, worthy of pity. What's more, many Jewish religious leaders believe that Jews outside Israel have the obligation to make Aliyah (a visit to Israel) as their religious duty. Similarly, Hispanic societies believe it is the duty and the moral imperative of U.S. Hispanics to be fluent in Spanish and to reject certain cultural values of the greater Anglo-Saxon Protestant mainstream society of the United States.

Latinos' perceived estrangement from the community of Hispanic nations is exacerbated by the knowledge that significant portions of U.S. territory were once New Spain. There is a lingering sense of loss at what is interpreted as a humiliation: The border crossed a segment of the greater Hispanic nation, severing U.S. Hispanics from the Hispanic peoples to which they rightfully belong. The concern, particularly among Hispanic intellectuals outside the United States, centers on the alienation of Latinos. This describes the obstacles that U.S. Latinos encounter in their careers from their inability to speak Spanish, lack of knowledge of Hispanic history, fluency in Hispanic culture, and the inability to function effortlessly in both societies.

As such, when Latinos dismiss the word "Hispanic," it is a source of anguish for Hispanic society: It underscores how uninformed this community of the Hispanic family has become and the disadvantage in which they find themselves.

What does this mean? For one thing, don't be surprised if the "Latinos" in your organization have never heard of "Día de la Hispanidad," which is a measure of both their ignorance of the global Hispanic community and their relative alienation from the mainstream of Hispanic culture. Several repercussions of this kind of social and cultural isolation and alienation are well documented by the U.S. government: Latinos lag by virtually every measure, from educational attainment level to higher risk for diabetes, from household income to greater likelihood of being the victim of violent crime.

To these documented social facts that speak to the state of the lives of U.S. Hispanics, there is another component: How Hispanics are viewed by non-Hispanic Americans. How other groups in the societies in which Hispanics live view Hispanics is an important factor in Latinos' emotional well-being and also impacts the civility they enjoy in the communities in which they live. In Germany, for instance, second- and third-generation Germans of Turkish ancestry remain alienated from the mainstream of German life—and by choice. Turkish-Germans (who are Muslim) look at their fellow German countrymen who are Christian and of Teutonic (Caucasian) ancestry with contempt. To the Turkish-Germans, their fellow countrymen are people who pollute their bodies with alcohol and pork and who lack enough sense to accept Muhammad as the true prophet.

In a similar vein, non-Hispanic Americans view Hispanics and Latinos with suspicion: Who are these short brown-skinned interlopers who have arrived in the country, refuse to learn English or assimilate into the mainstream of American life, and now make demands on non-Hispanics to the point where it is impossible to dial any toll-free number and not be affronted by the "Oprima 2 para español" message that is as grating as nails screeching down a blackboard?

These are the realities that members of diasporas live, and why throughout this book there has been emphasis placed on the linguistic challenge Latinos encounter by virtue of living in the United States, surrounded by English speakers. That said, bottom line, if only one out of 25 Hispanics in the world lives in the Hispanic diaspora, which makes U.S. Latinos a very small minority among the world's Hispanics. Indeed, Hispanics the world over, deep down, consider Latinos in the U.S. to live in a kind of homelessness, much the same way that Israelis consider Jews who do not live in Israel to be homeless.

The great Cuban liberator José Martí first articulated this sad commentary on the existence of Hispanics in the U.S. in 1895: "I have lived in the monster and I know its insides; and my sling is the sling of David." Agree or disagree with this sentiment, it makes no difference, since this is how the vast majority of the world's Hispanics see U.S. Latinos: Davids against a Goliath, living in a state of homelessness.

The Four Recommendations for Success
An Editorial & Social Commentary

Tu no puedes comprar las nubes,
Tu no puedes comprar los colores
Tu no puedes comprar mi alegría,
Tu no puedes comprar mis dolores.
Vamos caminando, aquí estamos de pie.

— Calle 13

The inherent cultural estrangement of the Hispanic diaspora, however, does not mean you cannot succeed in the United States. Here are the four things that require your attention: How you speak, how you dress, how well you take care of your health, and how mindful you are of the bigotry around you.

Accents

Everyone speaks Spanish with an accent simply because Spanish is spoken in so many places in the world that no single pronunciation dominates. The closest thing to a "neutral" Spanish diction is what has emerged over the past two decades as a result of television and the news anchors reporting from Mexico City and Atlanta for audiences throughout the world. Univision (Mexico City) and *CNN en Español* (Atlanta) are at the forefront of nurturing a uniform "broadcast" standard Spanish pronunciation, much the same way that, in the 1950s, a Midwestern accent came to dominate broadcast English in the United States, primarily thanks to Walter Cronkite and the two television networks, CBS and NBC.

One thing to bear in mind is that it's always possible to compensate for an accent by using language correctly. The purpose of this book is to give you the confidence that, if your pronounciation is not flawless, at least your command of language will be. Then again, there is something to be said for practicing your spoken Spanish. Trust me, no one wants to speak Spanish the way Univision's Jorge Ramos speaks English!

Dress

If you are going to speak Spanish for career success, you also have to dress for success. Clothing should reflect a conservative yet contemporary flair. You cannot dress as if you will hit a nightclub immediately after work. Although I am not encouraging you to shop at any specific store or wear any specific label, it is advisable for every professional Latina to take a look at Talbot's or Anne Klein—their websites are Talbots.com and AnneKlein.com—simply because these merchants best reflect the aesthetics of the White Anglo Saxon Protestant female in a contemporary way that is perfectly suited for business. You don't have to shop at their stores, but you should use them as the inspiration for your business attire.

For the Latino male, the question of clothes is easier to handle. Simply visit Brooks Brothers. Whether you choose to purchase from them is up to you, but this is the clothier that sets the standard for professional attire in the workplace. Their website is BrooksBrothers.com. Use it as a guide for style and tailoring. In recent years, this clothier has updated its offerings of casual wear, so it also offers insights into the kind of clothing that can be informal and professional at the same time. Stay away from wearing cologne or facial hair.

Many Hispanics see the dress of the American professional as dowdy, almost as if corporate America were channeling an updated version of the austere dress of the Puritans. They are, but so be it. This is how it is done in the U.S., and this is how you have to dress if you want to advance your career and make it up through the ranks of a professional organization.

Mind Your Health

For reasons that are not well understood, Latinos are at higher risk for certain chronic diseases than non-Hispanics. There is speculation that the unconscious stress associated with living in the Hispanic diaspora in the U.S. contributes to increased vulnerability. Perhaps the communal traumata Latinos experience through the vilification of and hostility towards Hispanics by non-Hispanic Americans in the U.S. are factors. No one knows. What is not in dispute, however, is that Hispanics are at higher risk for:

Diabetes: "For Latinos, acculturation was related to increased education, and more acculturated Latinos were less likely to have experiential models of the disease [diabetes]," Catherine Chesla et al. wrote in "Differences in Personal Models among Latinos and European Americans."[1] This means that Hispanics, Latinos and Latins with lower educational attainment—and the accompanying incomes—are at greater risk for diabetes. The estimated costs to American business is a staggering $174 billion a year in health care costs, and the problem is so acute there is an organization dedicated to helping employers develop strategies to deal with diabetes in the workplace: diabetesatwork.org. The costs for non-Hispanic employees are higher, reflecting both a higher incidence of diabetes and the fact that Latinos, more so than Hispanics or Latins, acquire diabetes at an earlier age.

Obesity: The American population is experiencing an epidemic of obesity and related health issues associated with being overweight. Hispanics, Latinos, and Latins, in fact, are among the segments of the population that are at higher risk for obesity. It is believed that the stress related to acculturation contributes to the coping mechanisms within the Hispanic diaspora that lead to higher rates of obesity. "Among Latinos, acculturation has been associated with obesity risk, suboptimal dietary choices including lack of breast-feeding, low intake of fruits and vegetables, a higher consumption of fats and artificial drinks containing high levels of refined sugar, smoking, and alcohol consumption," Rafael Pérez-Escamilla and Predrag Putnik reported in the *Journal of Nutrition*.[2] These findings are confirmed by other studies.[3] This chronic condition affects the overall health costs of every organization, and as Hispanics, Latinos, and Latins increase their presence in the American workforce, preventing obesity among employees becomes a more urgent management task.

Alzheimer's: Although a genetic predisposition is not suspected, for the Hispanic diaspora there is a higher incidence of Alzheimer's. Several "factors, many linked to low income or cultural dislocation, may put Hispanics at greater risk for dementia, including higher rates of diabetes, obesity, cardiovascular disease, stroke and possibly hypertension," Pam Belluck reported in the *New York Times*. "Less education may make Hispanic immigrants more vulnerable to those medical conditions and to dementia because scientists say education may increase the brain's plasticity or ability to compensate for symptoms. And some researchers cite as risk factors stress from financial hardship or cultural adjustment."[4] In this report, public health officials are studying factors that may be responsible for the higher incidence among Hispanics: "We are concerned that the Latino population may have the highest amount of risk factors and prevalence, in comparison to the other cultures,"

María Carrillo, director of medical and scientific relations at the Alzheimer's Association, explains. Is there subconscious stress of living in the Hispanic diaspora that increases the risk factors associated with degenerative cognitive conditions?[5] That appears to be the case.

Beware the Bigots

To live in the Hispanic diaspora, for most Latinos, is to live with apprehension and, at times, in fear. Even if you have been here for more generations than most Americans, as is often the case for Hispanics in New Mexico, for instance, the fact remains that the anti-immigrant sentiment that is prevalent in the U.S. casts a cloud over every Hispanic, simply because no one can know with certainty your citizenship or immigration status by looking at you. Earlier in this discussion, I made light of Raúl Yzaguirre, who ran the National Council of La Raza, when he declared that "open season" had been declared on Latinos. In my mind, when I hear "open season" the first thing I think of is Bugs Bunny and Elmer Fudd.

The point Yzaguirre made, however, was that Latinos are vulnerable and at risk. But as I remind you to be beware of the bigots out there, I have to pose the following question to you: Which is worse, individual bigots or institutionalized racism?

Consider the commendable job the FBI does in compiling statistics on hate crimes against Hispanics and in prosecuting hate crimes. A few years ago, it was headline news when misguided youth on Long Island, New York, set out to "hunt" Latin immigrants, for no other reason than, in their minds, Hispanics were probably in this country illegally and could be attacked with impunity. "To them, it was a sport," Thomas J. Spota, Suffolk County's district attorney, told reporters during a news conference after the defendants were arraigned. "We know for sure that there are more victims out there."

Few other victims, probably because they were Latin American immigrants who had entered the U.S. unlawfully, or had outstayed their tourist or student visas, and were afraid, stepped forward to avail themselves to law enforcement. If Latins live in the shadows, their disenfranchisement is exacerbated, and the natural stress that comes with living in the Hispanic diaspora in the U.S. becomes greater.

What about institutional racism and its impact on Latinos? In my opinion, the greater threat to Latinos is not hate crimes by individuals but institutionalized racism that disenfranchises the entire Hispanic community and empowers bigots to act with impunity. Let me offer an example of why, I believe the State Bar of California harbors an anti-Latino bias and encourages racism against Latinos in California. A few years ago, there was an organization that was criticized by Hispanic and Latino activists and community leaders, including this writer. Two of that group's leaders, Lester Olmstead-Rose and Greg Merrill, outraged that they would be criticized by an insignificant and powerless minority, made it clear that "Latinos" had "no right" to criticize them—and worse still, to complain about them to San Francisco city government officials. (Their organization received public funding.) Olmstead-Rose and Merrill complained to members of their board, which included partners from Heller Ehrman and McCutchen Doyle, two powerful law firms. The result was a lawsuit against the Hispanic and Latino critics that, in essence, sought to intimidate them into surrendering their rights to free speech, to petition the government with a grievance, and to assemble peacefully to organize their activities.

When I pointed out these concerns to Jeff Sheehy, who at that time worked at San Francisco's District

Attorney's office, he characterized the lawsuit as a malicious attempt to intimidate Latinos in San Francisco and "to punish" them for exercising their rights. "The community won't stand for this outrage," he said. It didn't. In a series of meetings, it was clear that San Francisco mayor Willie Brown was infuriated. Lester Olmstead-Rose and Greg Merrill were forced to resign; both board members whose law firms filed the laswsuit also resigned; and Heller Ehrman and McCutchen Doyle terminated their pro bono work on behalf of this organization. (Heller Ehrman went bankrupt after Lehman Brothers went under during the Great Recession of 2008, and McCutchen Doyle had been absorbed by Bingham in a merger a few years before.) The point of this episode, however, is that despite numerous complaints to the State Bar of California to take action as well, it refused.

In my opinion, the failure of the State Bar of California to disbar the attorneys who were involved in this outrageous case is proof that the State Bar of California allows individuals to use the privilege to practice law as a weapon to attack the civil rights of Latinos in California. In my opinion, this is institutional racism, which constitutes a greater danger to Hispanics and Latinos than do some misguided young bigots armed with baseball bats.

Latinos, watch out, since it is clear that institutional racism and bigotry are a continuing threat to your success.

A Final Word

If it be now, 'tis not to come; if it be not to come, it will be now; if it be not now, yet it will come. Readiness is all.

—William Shakespeare

Read this book again. Learn these words. Memorize these phrases. Dress for success. Take care of your health. Watch over your shoulder for the bigots who lurk out there. Embrace your Hispanic culture. Cherish the gift you have been given in the Spanish language. Rejoice in the power of bilingualism. Be thankful to live in the United States. Seize the opportunities that this country and life have given you. Create opportunities by taking the initiative. Be a mentor to Hispanic youth. Love your family. Believe in yourself.

Do these things, and you will be successful.

Websites

The following websites should be of interest to readers:

Academia Norteamericana de la Lengua Española (North American Academy of the Spanish Language)
www.anle.us

Anne Klein
www.anneklein.com

Brooks Brothers
www.brooksbrothers.com

Hispanic Economics
www.hispaniceconomics.com

Ki' Xocolatl
www.ki-xocolatl.com

Real Academia Española (Royal Spanish Academy)
www.rae.es

Talbot's
www.talbots.com

Notes

1 *See* "Differences in Personal Models Among Latinos and European Americans," by Catherine Chesla, Marilyn Skaff, Robert Bartz, Joseph Mullan and Lawrence Fisher, in *Diabetes Care*, Volume 23, Number 12, December 2000.

2 "The Role of Acculturation in Nutrition, Lifestyle, and Incidence of Type 2 Diabetes among Latinos," by Rafael Pérez-Escamilla and Predrag Putnik, *Journal of Nutrition*, April 2007.
See http://jn.nutrition.org/cgi/content/full/137/4/860

3 *See* "Physical Activity Patterns Among Latinos in the United States: Putting the Pieces Together," by Sandra A. Ham, MS, Michelle M. Yore, MPH, Judy Kruger, PhD, Gregory W. Heath, DHSc, MPH, Refilwe Moeti, MA, Centers for Disease Control, Volume 4, Number 4, October 2007. Available at:
http://www.cdc.gov/pcd/issues/2007/oct/06_0187.htm?s_cid=pcd44a92_x

4 *See* "More Alzheimer's Risk for Hispanics, Studies Find," by Pam Belluck, *New York Times*, October 20, 2008.

5 *See* "More Alzheimer's Risk for Hispanics, Studies Find," by Pam Belluck, *New York Times*, October 20, 2008.

About the Author

Louis E. V. Nevaer, an economist and journalist, is the director of Hispanic Economics, Inc. Recognized as one of the nation's leading authorities on Hispanics in the U.S., he is the author of the acclaimed book, *Managing Hispanic and Latino Employees*. He also co-authored *HR and the New Hispanic Workforce*, an authoritative guide for Human Resources professionals to the challenges of Hispanic ascendance in the American workplace.

He is a member of the National Association of Hispanic Journalists and PEN, an organization that champions the rights of writers. In addition, he is an in-demand speaker and consultant on the implications of the growing influence of Hispanics in the United States to Fortune 100 companies, governmental entities and non-governmental organizations (NGOs).

His next book, co-authored with Rose Guilbault, *The Latina's Guide to Success in the Workplace*, will be published in July 2012.

He divides his time between New York City; Saugerties, NY; and Mérida, Mexico.

www.ingramcontent.com/pod-product-compliance
Lightning Source LLC
Chambersburg PA
CBHW071652160426
43195CB00012B/1441